The United States of Repression

Adam Steevens

ISBN: 1545056382
ISBN-13: 978-1545056387

CONTENTS

ADAM STEEVENS

The Ethnostate

‡‡‡

Chapter 1

"YOU START OUT IN 1954 BY SAYING, "NIGGER, NIGGER, NIGGER." BY 1968 YOU CAN'T SAY "NIGGER"—THAT HURTS YOU, BACKFIRES. SO YOU SAY STUFF LIKE, UH, FORCED BUSING, STATES' RIGHTS, AND ALL THAT STUFF, AND YOU'RE GETTING SO ABSTRACT. NOW, YOU'RE TALKING ABOUT CUTTING TAXES, AND ALL THESE THINGS YOU'RE TALKING ABOUT ARE TOTALLY ECONOMIC THINGS AND A BYPRODUCT OF THEM IS, BLACKS GET HURT WORSE THAN WHITES.... "WE WANT TO CUT THIS," IS MUCH MORE ABSTRACT THAN EVEN THE BUSING THING, UH, AND A HELL OF A LOT MORE ABSTRACT THAN "NIGGER, NIGGER." -LEE ATWATER

═══

"BLACKS CAN'T RUN IT. NOWHERE, AND THEY WON'T BE ABLE TO FOR A HUNDRED YEARS, AND MAYBE NOT FOR A THOUSAND...DO YOU KNOW, MAYBE ONE BLACK COUNTRY THAT'S WELL RUN?" -RICHARD NIXON

═══

In the bleary winter months of 2016, a group of men, armed to the teeth invaded and occupied a tract of federally owned property. This provocation, one could fairly assume, could not go unchallenged. What manner of vengeful military retribution must be coming? The United States is infamous, dubious, even, for the heavy-handed retribution it has dished out to rebellious movements, no matter how small. They are the broilers of Waco, the arsonists of Atlanta, and they do not take armed challenges to their power lying down. Surely, these occupiers are in store for a beating, and no matter how well armed, their resources and proficiencies must pale in comparison to the prowess and expertise of American law enforcement.

The incident I am referring to, of course, is the armed invasion of the Malheur National Wildlife Refuge by a militia group sympathetic to the dopey Clive Bundy clan. No such response would be forthcoming. What ensued was a forty-one day standoff, in which American authorities *negotiated peacefully* with twenty-six gunman. In a society in which African-American teenagers are frequently shot dead in an instant for even the slightest offenses, how can so many white men, armed with rifles, annex federal property *with military force* and escape in one piece? The answer to this question is simple: America was built to preserve and protect the first-class citizenship offered only to white men.

Under the façade of partisanship and scandal, American politics have been able to conceal a sordid truth – nearly half of its citizens are compiling their efforts and resources in the interest of building and maintaining an

Ethnostate. President Trump rode this quiet undercurrent into power, as his campaign promises were replete with overtly racist language. Mr. Trump promised to build a wall on the southern border with Mexico (wisely enraging the third largest trading partner of the United States.) Mr. Trump promised to shut the door on all Muslim immigration, which was a threat he nearly carried out with an Executive Order not two weeks into his young Presidency that barred entry from seven Muslim-majority nations. The construction and maintenance of a white-male society, in fact, can be appropriately used as a lens to view the entirety of American history. The ebb and flow of partisanship has lulled millions of Americans to sleep. In a matter of just a few months, the United States has been plunged backwards, chained to the craven outbursts of a egomaniacal demagogue. What faces our nation, now, is a battle for the ownership of its very soul. Who will survive? Will rampant greed and fear triumph over liberty and compassion? Will America, in spite of her former beauty, now turn away those yearning masses, hungry for freedom? Will the famed destroyer of walls now sell its soul and begin constructing them? Americans are deeply divided, and things that were once considered basic political decorum (like not threatening to jail your political opponents if elected, or only accepting the results of a democratic election if you won, for instance) have been trampled eagerly underfoot by a dangerous political cabal willing to risk humanity's continued existence to win a single election.

White, male, Republican Americans most frequently define themselves through their violent opposition to the growing influence of alternative ethnicities and sexual preferences. This demographic of bigoted whites are not content to simply live in the increasingly isolated existence that their walled-off values often create; they are menacingly interested in excluding others, with the overt goal of diminishing the social and economic advancement of minorities and women. Admittedly, the attempt to divide the racial anxieties of the right wing in general from the gendered ones in the conservative male white consciousness is challenging. These resentments draw from the same well of anger and insecurity. That said, one of the first alarm bells that should capture our attention is the worship of the "Anglosphere," and the latent appeals to white purity:

> "The conservative British historian Andrew Roberts, author of the important new book *A History of the English-Speaking Peoples Since 1900*...Robert's book, though, exhibits some of the potential problems that can befall a defense of the Anglosphere. One shows up in its title. You will notice that Arthur Conan Coyle referred to the English-speaking 'races.' On the model of Winston Churchill's famous book of almost the same name, Roberts prefers the term 'peoples.' But this is to make a distinction without much difference. No such thing as

6

an Australian or Canadian 'race' exists, so one either means to describe people of originally Anglo-Saxon 'stock' (as we used to say) or one doesn't. It hasn't been very long since Lionell Trilling was denied tenure on the grounds, frankly stated, that a Jew could not understand English literature…determined to shoehorn everything into one grand theory, Roberts flirts with tautology. For example, he mentions the opening of the Hoover Dam at Boulder City and comments: 'The English-speaking peoples had long excelled at creating the wonders of the modern industrial world: the Great Eastern, the Brooklyn Bridge, the Sydney Bridge, the American, Canadian and Australian transcontinental railroads, the Panama Canal among them.' A theory that tries to explain everything explains nothing: We can all think of countries that have accomplished industrial and engineering marvels."[1]

The point, as often made by those with closeted white supremacist sympathies, is that those with Scandinavian or Norwegian heritage, for example, have every right to celebrate that heritage as any African-American, and that loathsome enemy of political correctness makes this sane practice completely impossible. The whine is a banal one, and their unique WASPY-ness is completely predicated upon an absence of any other ethnic presences, rather than the amplification of their own. At the core, it is *always* an argument for addition by subtraction, and a notoriously sloppy one at that. This lens of the Ethnostate is a useful utility for viewing both the conflicts buried within American history and those confrontations unfolding at present. Critically, the racial overtones of U.S history are frequently diluted or overlooked altogether.

> "Although we were not enthusiastic warriors, there was a true hatred of the enemy. We were convinced that the "Japs" were subhuman; and our atrocities against them pretty much matched theirs against us. I was in the Pacific Theater of Operations, where the war was not only imperial but racial: the white race was fighting the yellow race, and the crown would go to us as we were the earth's supreme race, or so we had been taught. One of the ugliest aspects of that war was the racial stereotyping on both sides." [2]

Vidal's analysis – based here off his own military service during this era – leaves out atrocious racism of the internment camps created for Japanese-Americans. Once the Second World War drew to a bloody close, domestic turmoil was lying in wait in the United States. Women became accustomed to the economic liberation the conflict had provided them, and suddenly found themselves being hemmed back into the traditional roles of housekeeping and childrearing. Blacks and other minorities, while fighting honorably alongside their white counterparts, returned home to two different universes. The white man would enjoy decades of prosperity, while the black man would subjected to decades of horrific police brutality, and would have to fight a war of attrition for every minor advance in civil rights that continues to this day.

> "The story of how George W. Bush and Dick Cheney ended up running the country goes back half a century, to the years when the *National Review*, edited by a young William F. Buckley, was defending the right of the south to prevent blacks from voting – "the White community is so entitled because, it is, for the time being, the advanced race" – and praising Generalissimo Francisco Franco, who overthrew a democratically elected in the name of church and prosperity, as "an authentic national hero." The small movement then known as the "new conservatism" was, in large part, a backlash against the decision of Dwight Eisenhower and other Republican leaders to make their peace with FDR's legacy." [3]

It cannot be said any other way – American power brokers have always had an adversarial relationship with women and minorities. These outsiders are usurpers to their throne, and their political efforts to conserve the status quo are vicious. It should come as no surprise that right-leaning rhetoric is spiked with paranoia and inane fear – the white men have something to lose from change. High-earners are especially susceptible to these right-leaning sympathies; to them, taxes are theft, those who rely on entitlement systems to eat are work-shy, and the government should be small enough to be crushed under the might of their companies if at any point their interests conflict with one another. It is not enough to say that America was built on the pock-marked back of beaten slaves, one must also admit that the suppression of the poor is itself a profit center for the wealthy white class. Every dollar hoarded and protected against the loathsome taxman is a dollar that can be used to fund their extravagance and conspicuous consumption. The decaying inner-city is of no concern to them. The food insecurity children often face in the inner-city is of no concern to them. The rampant inequality doesn't concern them because they're on top, and when life is this decadent, those at the top can only lose from change. It is usually at this point, if you listen closely, you can hear the high-pitched grumbling from small-minded white men who are convinced both of the aforementioned parties are exaggerating the extent of their wounds, and white 'privilege' is imaginary. This is utterly false, and represents a fundamental (and, often, intentional) misunderstanding of how white imperialism has dominated human history.

"The Western imperialism that began in the late fifteenth century climaxed in the late nineteenth with "the scramble for Africa" and the seizure of new possessions or territorial concessions in East Asia and the new Pacific. The ideology justifying the acquisition of new colonial territories by France, Britain, Germany, and ultimately the United States was transparently racist. Rudyard Kipling summed up this ideology in the poem "The White Man's Burden," which he wrote in 1899, in the wake of the Spanish-American War, to encourage the victorious Americans to establish colonial rule over the Philippines. The duty of the superior race, according to Kipling, was to take responsibility for "new-caught, sullen peoples, half-devil and half-child." His trope artfully combined a Darwinian emphasis on the competitive fitness of the white man with the suggestion of a psuedopaternalistic mission to uplift or improve the natives who were coming under European or American hegemony...Nevertheless, the ideology of imperialism did inspire the architects of segregation in the United States and South Africa." [4]

Indisputably, we can draw a line from the flatly racist origins of Western imperialism to the modern politics of the United States. Notice, too, the same tone of white condescension ('pseudopateralism' as Gregory M. Fredrickson phrases it above) that purports to be able to decide what other races and ethnicities need, and what constitutes discrimination. You will find no shortage of this supervisory snark in the attitudes of the angry white conservatives towards blacks. In the minds of militant white conservatives, blacks loot and steal at any opportunity, they are lazy and refuse to work, they rely on welfare and food stamps to survive, they let their pants sag, they are eager to intermarry with our pure white women, and in general, the blacks are a menace who are most threatened by their own failures in moral fortitude, and if African-Americans even slightly imply that they are being oppressed by systemic racism, they are "race-hustlers" who are inflamed with greed and are solely interested in capitalizing off of white guilt. Living approximately ten minutes away from Ferguson during the Michael Brown riots taught me this lesson remarkably well. That community was a ticking-time-bomb of racial division, and it was ready to explode at any moment. Screaming matches between white and black coworkers on this topic were not uncommon. The atmosphere was toxic, long before Mr. Brown was slain, and will likely not change anytime soon. If the race-relations in the St. Louis area were noxious, then the relationship between the African-American community and the police were downright poisonous.

I worked as a mobile-phone-technician for five years in this area, and I repaired cell phones for a popular telecommunications provider during this time period. The company had a strict insurance policy regarding cracked screens; we were supposed to refuse repair of these devices and force them to pay a steep deductible to replace them. This was wildly unpopular with the clientele, and it usually resulted in the type of angry exchanges that are all too common in the world of retail. One such disagreement arose between a uniformed officer of the Florissant Police Department and a black co-worker. Insults were tossed back and forth, and my co-worker stormed off, retreating to the back of the store. The officer, visibly angry, waited with arms crossed at the door. Ostensibly, the white policeman was intending to stay at this location until my co-worker was to leave for the day. I was, at that time, the "lead" technical consultant and could bypass the insurance requirements at my discretion, so I approached the officer, saw his cracked screen, and offered to replace it, free of charge, if he would forget whatever disagreement he had forged against my co-worker. "You tell *him*," hissed the officer, "if he's got a fuckin' problem with me, I'll take him the *fuck* outside and settle it."

I am not sure I could fully articulate how stunned I was at the officer's hateful screed; it burst my bubble of white ignorance in a single blow. Here was a *uniformed* member of law enforcement threatening to engage in a street-fight with a member of the community he is sworn to serve and protect over *a phone*. Black readers, no doubt, are herein reading nothing new or surprising to them. This is generally how the police treat them; and my white bubble of protection, privilege, and preferential treatment could not comprehend that a police officer could act with such malice. As stated by so many others with far more eloquence; the system works for me because I am white. The law enforcement community and judicial systems reward me for being white. For being pure. American Christianity, via *dominionism*, dips its own toe into the well of racial purity as well, and offers the Ethnostate its tacit support:

> "Dominionism, born out of a theology known as Christian reconstructionism, seeks to politicize faith. It has, like all fascist movements, a belief in magic along with leadership adoration and a strident call for moral and physical supremacy of a master race, in this case, American Christians. It also has, like fascist movements, an ill-defined and shifting set of beliefs, some of which contradict one another…The dominionist movement, like all totalitarian movements, seeks to appropriate not only our religious and patriotic language but also our stories, to deny the validity of stories other than our own, to deny that there are other acceptable ways of living and being. There becomes, in their rhetoric, only one way to be a Christian and only one way to be an American." [5]

This passage, published in 2006, could easily pass as a critique of the

Christian demographic that would gleefully launch President Trump to power a decade later. The right wing campaign to build and defend a white and Christian Ethnostate (with men in the firmest control of power) finds its origin in American Christianity. As a former Christian-minister-in-training, I know this all too well; the American Jesus has been irrevocably white-washed within the religious wing of the Republican Party. Our stereotypical image of Jesus is that of a white man with shoulder-length hair. How a Palestinian carpenter could ever be rendered in this fashion (as he often is, in Kim Jong-Un-styled paintings that adorn the walls of many Christian churches across the nation) is beyond me. It represents a terrifying, and *intentional* distortion of the past; revisionist history maliciously designed to soothe the biting anxieties of a skittish demographic that torpidly believes themselves to be under assault from all angles.

> "The racist and brutal intolerance of the intellectual godfathers of today's Christian Reconstructionism is a chilling reminder of the movement's lust for repression. *The Institutes of Biblical Law* by R. J. Rushdoony, written in 1973, is the most important book for the dominionist movement. Rushdoony calls for a Christian society that is harsh, unforgiving, and violent. His work draws heavily on the calls for a repressive theocratic society laid out by Calvin in *Institutes of the Christian Religion,* first published in 1536 and one of the most important works of the Protestant Reformation. Christians are, Rushdoony argues, the new chosen people of God and are called to do what Adam and Eve failed to do: create a godly, Christian state. The Jews, who neglected to fulfill God's commands in the Hebrew scriptures, have, in this belief system, forfeited their place as God's chosen people and have been replaced by Christians. The death penalty is to be imposed not only for offenses such as rape, kidnapping, and murder, but also for adultery, blasphemy, homosexuality, astrology, incest, striking a parent, incorrigible juvenile delinquency, and, in the case of women 'unchastity before marriage.' The world is to be subdued and ruled by a Christian United States." [6]

The predominant desires of the conservative American right are devastatingly simple: God is the King, the Christians are the salt of the earth, Washington D.C. is the city on a hill, and American society and culture should be permanently inextricable from Judeo-Christian values that are primarily defended by white men. American society was constructed by racism, and when slavery came under siege from abolitionists, the practice was defended with the words of Scripture. Minorities continue to suffer under the systematic repression built into the architecture of the nation itself. To borrow a phrase from Ian Hanley Lopez, this racism is structural:

"Another conception of racism emphasizes structures rather than individuals. Racism under this view is woven into society's fabric; more than the cruel warden, the convict lease system is itself seen to embody racism. The idea of structural racism, also known as institutional racism, entered the American vocabulary in the late Civil Rights era, and a definition from that time drives the meaning home:

> When white terrorists bomb a black church and kill five black children, that is an act of *individual racism,* widely deplored by most segments of the society. But when in that same city – Birmingham, Alabama – five hundred black babies die each year because of the lack of proper food, shelter, and medical facilities, and thousands more are destroyed and maimed physically, emotionally, and intellectually because of conditions of poverty and discrimination in the black community, that is a function of *institutional racism.*

Institutional racism stresses how past mistreatment drives current inequalities. Up through the 1940s, a Southern society built around convict leasing and debt peonage may have trapped half of all African-Americans. Meanwhile the government programs arising in the 1930s and 1940s – efforts that contributed to the great boom in the American middle class – were effectively available to whites only. These racially stratified differences connect across generations to vast disparities today in the average wealth of white and black families. Whereas in 2009 the typical white family had a net worth of $113,149, this outstripped the figure for African-American families by 20-to-1, with the average black family owning assets of only $5,677. Or put this another way: for every dollar held by whites, blacks had a lonely nickel in their pocket." [7]

The American Ethnostate is not merely a racial construct; the submission of women is another load-bearing pillar of the conservative mantra. The Republican Party in the United States has taken under its wing the burgeoning Alt-Right movement that not only openly endorses white nationalism, but rabidly attacks gender equality and feminist progress at every turn. The religious right, of course, routinely denigrates women, and wishes to deny them access to their own reproductive rights. Christian ideology – save for more liberal sects of the emerging church and left-leaning denominations – requires the 'role' of the woman to be primarily tethered to the ancient cycles of birth and childrearing. Say this to a typical American congregation, and you will be chastised instantly. Women will leap to the defense of a system that has held them down for eons. 'Household' is the most frequent buzzword used to defend this ingrained sexism: Christ is the 'head' of the church, and so as the traditional 'family' strives to follow the example of Christ, the man is the 'head' of the 'household.' If you listen closely, you can hear the vertebrae of Christian women cracking as they bend backwards to defend the chains fastened around their ankles. They'll tell you that while the man makes the 'final' decisions, the woman has the greatest amount of influence over the process and is of equal value. A good marriage will have the man compromising and using his power over the woman responsibly, and if he is selfless like Jesus, he will never make a self-interested decision, and will always make equitable judgements. These are all bad lies, and by upholding a centuries-old system of patriarchy, Christian women stick the knives in their own backs.

Even worse, this lamentable system of repression is passed down to their children. Young girls are taught that marriage and family life are to be their highest aspirations, and a genuinely *creepy* cloud of voyeurism descends upon their sexual lives as soon as they reach puberty. Christian pre-teen girls are pressured into 'promise' ceremonies where they pledge their virginity to their future husbands. If you have witnessed these unsettling behaviors in action, it is difficult to truly articulate just how strange they can really be. Fathers hold the promise of sexual abstinence as a possession to be given to the suitor at the time of marriage (oddly enough, the transactional nature of this exchange is the most *accurate* representation of a 'Biblical' marriage I have ever seen.)

This cringe-inducing routine feels icky because it is, simply, borderline incestuous and is a perfect example of sexual repression in action. Women are not given the opportunity to be promiscuous, it is a luxury afforded to men that the fairer sex are not privy to. Growing up in a conservative Christian household with four sisters (two older, two younger) gave me a great deal of insight into this phenomenon. As you might imagine, one hour before church service on a Sunday morning, bathroom time was quite difficult to come by. The girls were usually preening in front of a mirror, applying cosmetics, and fiddling with outfits. Before the family left for church, dad would occasionally perform a visual inspection of the skirts and dresses that my sisters wore to appraise their modesty. If he judged one outfit to be too scandalous, he ordered that lace be added to extend the garment. It didn't seem inappropriate at the time, but like many developmental and formative childhood moments, I realized how wrong it was as I aged. Two aspects are to be gleaned from this baked-in sexism. First, that women, their bodies, and their sexuality are the possessions of the men that sit in *rightful* ownership over them. Second, that this right is given to men from God himself, and the man is to follow the example of God, being the head of the church. The man is to be the God of his family, and his family is to be the obedient flock that he shepherds with grace and dignity. The Ethnostate cannot abide by powerful women who shirk the traditional roles of family. Racist organizations take this edict a few steps further; white women are needed in pure reproductive roles in an urgent fashion to reverse the horrors of race-mixing before the 'white' race becomes extinct. Evangelical leaders are participating in our political systems to impose their beliefs upon the law that governs Christians and non-believers alike with terrifying success:

> "(Timothy) LaHaye has come to the conference with his wife, Beverly, who founded Concerned Women of America, an antifeminist group with 540,000 women 'who were committed to protecting the rights of the family through moral activism.' They were the early pioneers in the Christian Right's attack on the school textbook industry, helping to orchestrate a series of lawsuits against publishers who printed material they found offensive or anti-Christian." [8]

Their intentions are quite clear; they want to remove the option entirely for women to depart from their ancient burdens. If we allow them, they will strip any semblance of gender or racial equality away without so much as a second thought. The rabid and compulsive desire to politically oppress minorities is menacing and pernicious; and American power has historically spared no effort or expense in accomplishing this goal.

> "If you look at the record of who is designated a terrorist, it's shocking. Maybe the most extreme case is Nelson Mandela; who just got off the terrorist list about four years ago. The Reagan Administration, which supported the apartheid regime in South Africa right to the end, condemned the African National Congress as one of "the more notorious terrorist groups" in the world. So Mandela is a terrorist because they say so…Saddam Hussein was taken off the terrorist list in 1982 so the United States could provide him with agricultural and other support that he needed. The whole record is grotesque." [9]

The United States, beyond manipulating the very definition of 'terrorism' when it suited their political goals, operated more brazenly when it could conceal such adversarial action under the cover of darkness:

> "As Shamrock was collecting intelligence on US citizens, another program, COINTELPRO, which was short for Counter Intelligence Program, was being run out of the FBI. COINTELPRO turned up publically due to the investigations by the Church and Pike

committees. The Church committee's final report suggests that COINTELPRO began in 1956 with the goal of subverting domestic dissident groups that challenged the position of the executive in the United States. It finds that COINTELPRO was "a misnomer for domestic covert action" that was aimed at "defending the correctness of US foreign policy," among other status quo policies. COINTELPRO attempted to break up groups as varied as anti-war protesters, the US Communist Party, the Black Panther organization, and the Southern Christian Leadership Conference." [10]

Abortion (a cornerstone of gender equality and a topic covered in greater detail in a later chapter) is a wedge issue between conservatives and liberals because without reproductive rights, women will often be forced into these roles against their wishes.

"We need to talk about abortion in its full human setting: sex and sexuality, love, violence, privilege, class, race, school, and work, men, the scarcity of excellent, respectful reproductive health care, and of realistic, accurate information about sex and reproduction. We need to talk about why there are so many unplanned and unwanted pregnancies – which means we need to talk about birth control, but also so much more than that: about poverty and violence and family trouble, about sexual shyness and shame and ignorance and the lack of power so many women experience in bed and in their relationships with men. Why is it such a big deal to ask a man to wear a condom? Or for a man to do it without being asked?" [11]

Women are not just subjugated in the Christian home – as a result of the cultural impacts of American Christianity – women are oppressed in a multitude of arenas. Why are the sexual needs of women simultaneously enshrined and detested? Why is female virginity treated as *a commodity?* Why is there a gap in power between the sexes at all? Why are the private reproductive choices of American women a political issue at all? There are several fundamental keystones of the conservative movement in the United States. Chiefly among them are the heightened propensity for disgust, predispositions to fear, and a strict adherence to sect conformity.[12] These traits are best exemplified in the Evangelical Christian right wing:

"Despite the fact that it receives very little attention, Christian nationalism (also called dominionism or Christian reconstructionism) is incredibly pervasive in America and is unwittingly supported by many people completely unaware of its goals, harms, and indeed, much of its ideological underpinnings. Adherents to this ideology can be identified by a number of their beliefs, which should ring a bell as natural extensions of common right-wing political messages…Chief among these beliefs are the following convictions:

- The idea that the Bible is the literal word of God, and thus incontrovertible and authoritative in its assertions.
- That the Bible should serve as the sole foundation for every facet of American life – including governance and law.
- That the United States was formed as a Christian nation and must be restored to its original status as what essentially amounts to a theocratic society (something of a neopuritan model.)
- That separation of church and state was not intended by the framers of the Constitution.
- That theology conveys a superiority to conservative Christians, who have dominion – the right to rule – over Americans *vis-à-vis* Genesis 1:28.
- That the United States was once a great country, but that the liberal agenda of secular humanism has steered it in an ungodly direction that it must be corrected.
- Issues such as marriage equality and legalized abortion have become central in mobilizing this movement, though appeals to the three F's of American conservative Christianity – family, flag, and faith – are also routinely engaged with considerable success." [13]

The definition here, while not complete, is certainly comprehensive. These keystones are presented as a way of fairly presenting the conservative world-view in their own terms. Few conservatives would bristle at these bullet points – marriage should be between one man and one woman, abortion is a holocaust, America is a Christian nation, the Ten Commandments are the basis for all morality and law, and humanism creates moral depravity – and in my experience, these are all positions they are quite happy to tell you about themselves. Some Christians deviate from one or more of these staples (openness towards homosexuality is certainly becoming more common, thankfully,) but in general, the true hard-liners have no qualms with these statements. Without reasonable controversy, we have accurately defined much of the basic religious political manifesto. The United States is configured economically and politically in a fashion that represses non-whites and females. This can be said plainly and without much fuss (although many often dispute this basic premise) because the evidence supporting this claim is overwhelming, particularly when it comes to non-white immigrants:

"Additional research tells us that lighter-skinned immigrants, mostly from European nations, earn around 15 percent more than darker-skinned immigrants, even when all the respective qualifications are markers of personal productivity are the same. And according to the most recent annual data from 2009, even when a black person has a college degree, he or she is nearly twice as likely as one of us with a degree to be unemployed, while Latinos and Asian Americans with degrees are 40 percent more likely that we are to be out of work, with the same qualifications. Furthermore, when comparing only persons working in management, business and finance jobs, those of us in such occupations typically earn about 30 percent more in weekly income than our counterparts of color, mounting to nearly $13,000 in additional earnings each year relative to African Americans and Latinos…Overall, the median income for white men who are between twenty-five and thirty-four years old (early in their careers) is one-third higher than the median for black men who are fifty-five to sixty-four years old and already nearing retirement. Research has even found that a white man with a criminal record is more likely to be called back for a job interview than a black man without one, even when their credentials are the same." [14]

There are obvious and undeniable economic advantages to being a white man, and to quarrel with this reality is a fool's errand, although many others often do. How far should a sane person go in the interests of convincing someone else that the sky is blue? When is it *necessary?* When is it counterproductive? Increasingly, I am of the opinion that words matter far more than we often realize, and going on the record matters, too, even for low-hanging fruit. More to the point, these advantages were constructed intentionally and are maintained lovingly by the same white establishment that has fought viciously against every social and civil advance for minorities. It is these same white bodyguards who deny every allegation of prejudice and choose to dig in their heels as the wheels of progress push them backwards. What was the source of this white discomfort with racial integration?

"The crucial turning point in this evolution came after the Civil War, a period of great turbulence in America. In addition to the turbulence we normally associate with the era as a result of the agonies over the reconstitution of the American Republic and over Reconstruction in the South, the American nation underwent a dizzying cultural change in the fifty years that followed the Civil War. The Industrial Revolution truly came to American shores, and with it came urbanization and a progressive ending of agrarian ways of life. New immigrants came in astoundingly high numbers – almost 22 million. Of these, less than 25 percent spoke English as their native tongue, many were not Protestant, and those who were did not belong to churches with historic or theological links to the dominant Puritan ethos of early America. For long-time American families, it was like they were losing their nation to the foreigners." [15]

The torpid and inane fear of losing one's own country to an influx of immigrants is as old as America itself, and did not find its beginnings with the likes of Donald Trump. No, on the contrary, this ethnically-fueled exclusion *is itself* a hallmark of the United States. It is not new, nor is it unique. To a certain extent, I believe this dynamic can also go quite a long way in explaining the political geography routinely found in the United States as well. Metropolitan areas – even in Republican strongholds like Missouri and Texas – are almost entirely filled with Democratic voters, while rural and less-densely populated areas are conservative hotbeds. The conservatives, by and large, left the cities at the first available moment (white flight) and took their (on average) higher-than-black-men wages out of the city and into the suburbs, destroying the tax base as they fled. This is the story that played out in any number of American cities – Detroit, St. Louis, Baltimore [16] – and it left the white suburban class to moan about the crime and poverty in the cities that their abandonment largely created. Once the inner city begins to economically shrivel, the well of white sympathy runs completely dry. Conservative whites store up empathy for fetuses, and reserve only scorn and snide judgement for black babies born into the projects and subsidized housing of the city. We are assured by the conservatives that their aversion of entitlement programs do not conceal a hidden racial element. This claim, like so many others in the conservative manifesto, is patently false:

> "In fact, a comprehensive comparison of various social programs in the United States and Europe found that racial hostility to people of color better explains opposition to high levels of social spending here than any other economic or political variable…Even in the 1980s, when thousands of farmers were losing their land to foreclosures, again in large part because of economic factors beyond their control, we believed in bailing them out. We saw the enemy in those cases as greedy banks, taking advantage of struggling farm families who were the backbone of America, and corporate farmers who were snapping up land and pushing family farms out of business to amass mega-

18

profits. We did not, by and large, blame the small farmers for their station. But when we speak of urban poverty and the conditions of life facing millions of low-income people of color, our rhetoric is quite different as is our level of compassion and forbearance. For them, characterological judgment and condemnation is our first reflex. Whereas white folks are the innocent and deserving poor, black and brown folks are guilty (of something) and undeserving; their condition is believed by most of us to be the fault of their own pathologies and dysfunctions." [17]

Tim Wise is quite right to juxtapose the narrative behind the black and white poor, and what it exposes is a frightening level of pre-judgment and victim-blaming. When the white farmer goes broke, we blame Monsanto and the banks; when the black man in Baltimore goes broke, we tell him to stop being lazy and get a job. The game is rigged against African-Americans, whites have no time to hear their complaints, and when it comes to expending resources to ease their suffering, the purse-strings around the tax dollars get tight. The white establishment made President Obama a chew-toy for thinly-veiled racist attacks. This was a clear warning to a black man who had invaded a space that was, up until that moment, an exclusively white domain.

"Or consider Eric Bolling of Fox Business News, who recently accused the president of hosting "hoodlums in the hizzouse" – using hip-hop slang to characterize the first family's home – all because Obama had met with the leader of Gabon in the White House and had invited rapper Common (whose lyrics are anything *but* gangsterish) to a presidential event a few weeks earlier. This was close on the heels of Bolling's prior remarks that Obama should stop "chugging forties" in Ireland – a reference to forty-ounce bottles of malt liquor stereotypically associated with African-Americans – and come home to check out the devastation wrought by tornadoes in Missouri. Though the president had indeed been photographed having a pint of beer in an Irish pub, it most certainly had not been a "forty," as Bolling had to have known. The use of this imagery was deliberate, a dog whistle to those of us who can't quite deal with the presence of a black man at the top of the nation's political system." [18]

Again, we see the invocation of racist language as a political weapon welded intentionally and with malice. These were, of course, the sort of blows Mr. Obama absorbed from the bigoted right-wing on a regular basis. These vicious and repugnant remarks can only originate from a place of racial hatred, but good luck trying to get a Republican to admit that President

Obama was attacked in this fashion *primarily* because of the color of his skin. They will bristle at this notion, and yammer on and on about wanting a limited government, or fewer federal interventions into healthcare (except, of course, when it comes to federal healthcare interventions *they want*, like a nationwide moratorium on abortion) and snidely side-step the racial problem as if they have managed to fool anyone in the process. Is it any surprise, in retrospect, that a candidate formally endorsed by the Klu Klux Klan took Mr. Obama's place in the White House? Mr. Trump spearheaded the racist blowback with his inane and patently false "birther" movement. Trump is the last gasp; the final blow from an aged and dying generation that still harbors the sectarian mindsets they were born into.

The question of racial equity – of how it could exist in the future, or of how far American society has yet to go to attain it – is a tricky one indeed. We could focus exclusively on the practical hurdles that stand in the way of minorities in the United States; income inequality, disproportionate rates of incarceration, and racially-motivated police brutality are among some of the most glaring problems. We could (as many closeted racists do) focus on the internal struggles of the black community itself and ignore the rest. In my view, these both ignore the root of the problem entirely: the United States was constructed with the repression of minorities fully in mind. These inequities are intentional. They are features of the architecture of the country itself, and, despite what its white bodyguards might claim, they maintain the Ethnostate to preserve their privilege and influence over a society that suppresses women and minorities by default. These systems of control are both political and religious:

> "Whites predominate in both the Conservative and Mainline Protestant churches – 89 percent of Conservatives are white and 92 percent of Mainline Protestants are. Afro-Americans predominate in the traditionally black churches – 95 percent. Jews are 97 percent white. The Latino immigration has diversified the ancestry profile of Catholics, and the pattern of falling away from religion affects each ancestry group and diversifying the "no religion" category." [19]

This is not to say that monotheism (particularly Christianity) is unpopular with African-Americans, but it is simply presented to prove that white conservative Americans have strong desires to create homogenous communities, and are remarkably successful in doing so. The issue of the white Christian's desire to racially isolate themselves is, somewhat, separate from the ingrained racism easily found in the bones of American Christianity itself.

"The white man's Heaven," sings a Black Muslim minister, "is the black man's Hell." One may object—possibly—that this puts the matter somewhat too simply, but the song is true, and it has been true for as long as white men have ruled the world. The Africans put it another way: When the white man came to Africa, the white man had the Bible and the African had the land, but now it is the white man who is being, reluctantly and bloodily, separated from the land, and the African who is still attempting to digest or to vomit up the Bible. The struggle, therefore, that now begins in the world is extremely complex, involving the historical role of Christianity in the realm of power— that is, politics—and in the realm of morals. In the realm of power, Christianity has operated with an unmitigated arrogance and cruelty— necessarily, since a religion ordinarily imposes on those who have discovered the true faith the spiritual duty of liberating the infidels. This particular true faith, moreover, is more deeply concerned about the soul than it is about the body, to which fact the flesh (and the corpses) of countless infidels bears witness. It goes without saying, then, that whoever questions the authority of the true faith also contests the right of the nations that hold this faith to rule over him— contests, in short, their title to his land. The spreading of the Gospel, regardless of the motives or the integrity or the heroism of some of the missionaries, was an absolutely indispensable justification for the planting of the flag. Priests and nuns and schoolteachers helped to protect and sanctify the power that was so ruthlessly being used by people who were indeed seeking a city, but not one in the heavens, and one to be made, very definitely, by captive hands. The Christian church itself—again, as distinguished from some of its ministers— sanctified and rejoiced in the conquests of the flag, and encouraged, if it did not formulate, the belief that conquest, with the resulting relative well-being of the Western populations, was proof of the favor of God." [20]

It is critical to note here the intermingling of interests. Western imperialism was used to achieve the goals of Christianity, and *vice versa*, which goes quite a long way in explaining how the American Ethnostate works. Religion, as an instrument and expression of power, operates where the church cannot. Conservative politics work tirelessly to expand the influence of Christianity in American society. It is a two-thousand-year-old, one-two-punch that continues to shape our country. These ancient pressures are effective because they are fueled by inexhaustible resources; ignorance, arrogance, and fear, among many others. This is part of the reason why they seem so incurable. They prey upon the very vices and numerous shortcomings of humans. It is far easier to be unhealthy than healthy, and it far easier to be foolish than wise. Falsehoods and half-truths are easier to spout than truth.

Also, they are far simpler to *understand,* which increases their popularity. When I claim that the United States is a nation of *repression,* I mean it in both definitions in the word; the country was constructed, primarily, by repressing other ethnicities and genders. The repressive policies of the United States find their motivation and appeal in the psychological self-repression of unwanted desires. Ultimately, we are left trying to explain why nearly sixty-three million American citizens voted for Donald Trump in 2016. In fact, I would go one step further and claim that this number, in and totally of itself, represents a national crisis.

> "So we need to be clear: the connection between race and the Republican Party is not accidental, vestigial, or comical, and it's certainly not trivial. Instead, as we will see, over the last half-century conservatives have used racial pandering to win support from white voters for policies that principally favor the extremely wealthy and wreck the middle class. Running on racial appeals, the right has promised to protect supposedly embattled whites, when in reality it has largely harnessed government to the interests of the very affluent."[21]

So pronounced, is this incessant preference for white men, that Americans elected a hateful reality-television-show host with no political experience instead of an experienced and tenured diplomat in Mrs. Clinton. Not only is this dark-ages thinking harmful to American women and American minorities, but it is actively harmful to the entire nation as a whole. Almost sixty-three million Americans arrived to the polls in November of 2016 and made their choice clear; they wanted a return to a *greater* America, a slogan that made no effort to conceal it longed for a past greatness that, conveniently enough, coincided with non-white and non-male subservience.

> "Two years ago I engaged in a rather lengthy email exchange with someone whose views no doubt mirrored those of millions more. She was upset because of something I had said during a television interview on CNN regarding the Tea Party movement. Being a part of that movement, she took offense to what she perceived to be my position; namely, that the Tea Party was propelled forward by racial hatred of a black president…I had said, however, and do believe that the mantra of taking the country "back" contains an unhealthy degree of racial resentment as part of its "background noise." It isn't racism in the classic sense; rather, it is the rhetoric of white anxiety operationalized in a political movement…The desire to take the country back is not about segregation, she assured me, not about going back to the days of overt racial oppression and Jim Crow. So I decided

to play the game, and asked her quite simply what the Tea Party folks mean when they say they wish to "take their country back?" What *is* that about, if it's not about race? Simple, she said: we mean that we want to go back to a time of lower taxes and smaller government...The Tea Partier insisted to me that she wanted to go back to a time when taxes were lower. Yet she failed to specify when that might be. I wanted to know exactly when in our nation's history did she think we had more or less gotten it right when it came to the proper level of taxation...The answer came back in a matter of minutes: 1957. It was a fascinating answer, because it just so happens that in 1957 the top marginal tax rate in the United States was *ninety-one percent.*" [22]

Mr. Trump's campaign, in his own words, was an attempt to make the nation great again. It was time to rebuild a dilapidated American military (how the U.S. military could ever be portrayed in this light when its annual expenditures exceed the nearest *seven* nations combined is well and truly beyond me,) it was time to end the scourge of illegal immigration, it was time to prevent Muslims from entering the country until we "could figure out what the hell is going on" (if we constructed policy that was contingent upon Donald Trump figuring things out, we might be waiting for quite a long time indeed.) No, these were not practical problems, but attack avenues Mr. Trump used to seduce the anxious white underclasses. He preyed upon their weaknesses, and irritated their fears. Trump exploited their powerful urges for stability, safety, and above all else, outside influence from religions and ethnicities that American whites found scary. Candidate Trump was remarkably skilled at speaking in coded language to this powerful demographic, and crucially, did not shy away from blood. He insulted the honorable military service of Senator John McCain, he maligned the Gold-Star Khan family after they spoke at the Democratic National Convention; even going as far as crudely insulting the appearances of his Republican opponents in the primary races. His base wanted insults, so he gave them insults. His base wanted boasts about financial prowess, so he gave them boasts. His base wanted a departure from dignity, respect, etiquette, and basic decorum. Mr. Trump gave and gave and gave until the whole of the Republican party was dutifully lined up behind him. Our anger should not be directed at Mr. Trump for using such reprehensible methods to attain power, but towards ourselves. There is no Trump presidency without racial hatred. There is no Trump presidency without misogyny. There is no Trump presidency if there was no white fear. Donald Trump could not have become President Trump without our shortcomings, without our concealed hatreds, and the fact that these exist say more about the average American than it does about Mr. Trump.

When Donald Trump first became a serious candidate for the Republican nomination, I viewed it at as a joke. To me, it couldn't have been a less serious bid at power. Surely, no one would believe a massive wall on the Mexican border would slow illegal immigration, I thought. I was unable to take these policy proposals seriously, and mistakenly assumed no one else could, either. If this is evidence of a liberal "bubble" so be it (who would be ashamed to admit that idiotic ideas like Mr. Trump's aren't included in their intellectual armory?) but as the election drew nearer, the support for Mr. Trump was all around me.

A few days before the election, my wife and I took a weekend vacation in Park Hills, Missouri. It is a diminutive municipality just outside of Farmington, adjacent to some of the best parks, trails, and hiking locations in the state. We drove down from our apartment in St. Louis, and I stopped counting Trump yard signs after I got to number thirty-five. Of course, it was no surprise that Missouri was destined to be a Red state, but the stark contrast was biting; an hour drive from the city can transport you to a different world altogether. It is precisely this divide that separates this nation; sixty-two million Americans voted for Trump, and the America they want is more like Park Hills, more like Kansas, more like Texas, and less like cities of culture, art, intelligence, and diversity. Sixty-five million Americans voted for Clinton, and the America they want is more like Paris, Munich, or Amsterdam. The soul of the nation, *right here and right now,* is at stake, and it will be decided on who wins the next decade, politically. Which side are you going to take? This is not, as many suggested after the fact, a conflict that arose because Americans became isolated from one another. Both sides know each other all too well; Republicans aren't shocked when I say that I want them to keep their laws off the bodies of the women in my life, and I'm not surprised when I hear them say (falsely) that America is a Christian nation and that the real problem is that our kids don't pray in school anymore. I know what sort of world the Republicans want to live in. I know all of its intricacies. I know it *viscerally.* I know this because I was born into it, and it is one of the few stories I can tell with some measure of experience and authority.

THE UNITED STATES OF REPRESSION

White Male Anxiety

‡‡‡

CHAPTER 2

"It is fear that makes people so willing to follow brash, strong-looking demagogues with tight jaws and loud voices: those who focus their measured words and their sharpened eyes in the intensity of hate, and so seem the most capable of cleansing the world of the vague, the weak, the uncertain, the evil. Ah, to give oneself over to their direction – what calm, what relief." - Ernest Becker

═══

We have become rather accustomed to the tired tropes of the Republican media universe. Perhaps we're all simply worn out, eager to overlook and ignore the unsightly cauldron of hatred and bigotry being stirred up daily on conservative radio and cable networks. The successes of these entities, in large part, depend on how closely they adhere to Fox's tried-and-true formula; hire bombastic and overly emotional white men to shout into the souls of other angry white men, and contrast their leathery faces with a peroxide-blonde injection of trophy-wife-news-anchors to provide some visual stimulation. The message keeps finding resonance with its intended demographic because many white American men are *permascared*. They exist in a state of perpetual existential terror, and what inflames their fear the most? Women and minorities, who, often, are the targets of their hateful speech or violence.

When did such a powerful sense of alarm and dread seep into the American political structure? Has it been there all along? Why is it inflamed by the most banal and innocuous things? This peculiar structure of their outrage, seemingly stored in limitless reserve, is outwardly puzzling. What difference is it to them, one might wonder, if people of different gender configurations utilize certain bathrooms? What harm might befall them personally? Why wage such a nasty war of attrition with progress? Once we delve into these questions, we are confronted with a brazenly simple truth: American conservatism is primarily comprised of white men, and they are terrified of change, and are wrestling internally with their own overwhelming feelings of inadequacy. Their safe spaces are being steadily chipped away, and their anger-inducing media is one of their last refuges:

"Sociologist Sarah Sobieraj and political scientist Jeffrey Berry call it "outrage media" – talk-radio, blog, and cable news designed "to provoke a visceral response from the audience, usually in the form of anger, fear, or moral righteousness through the use of overgeneralization, sensationalism, misleading or patently inaccurate information, ad hominem attacks, and partial truths about opponents. Sobieraj and Berry trace this development through the technological shifts from radio and TV to cable news, the blogosphere, and talk radio as the news vehicles of choice and to the incredible consolidation of media companies, so that only a handful of companies control virtually all of America's airwaves...But it's also linked to the displacement of white men from every single position of power in the country. Talk radio is the last locker room, juiced not on steroids but on megahertz. It's the circled wagons keeping out the barbarian hordes, who may be just a millimeter away on that dial. It's the Alamo on AM frequency." [1]

White male fear and anger are cultural institutions in the United States. This is especially true in religious circles, and the rising popularity of pundits like Alex Jones come as no surprise. The internet, in many respects, has supplanted talk radio as the primary nest for heated conservative talk. The anger, in and of itself, is amusing to my people; growing up, me and my friends would listen to Michael Savage just to chuckle when he would inevitably yell and scream. We found the anger, totally in and of itself, notable and worthy of our attention. The pundit might not be right about everything, but the audience doesn't expect them to be, and at least they aren't boring. They offer some emotional stimulation, and give their audience something traditional news often doesn't. Beyond the obvious emotional call and response, the complexity drain strikes yet again: infotainment is popular because it doesn't require much work to consume. Angry white men are idolaters of stability, and they worship at the altar of isolationism and homogenization. They loathe the immigrant, the inner-city, and their new female boss, because they are afraid of being challenged. They are petrified by the influx of racial and religious diversity, and see it as a direct attempt to change their way of life. Will the white man's wife be seduced by the charms of an exotic man from an exotic culture? Will the length of his dick pale in comparison to this foreign suitor? This migrant troubadour isn't content with mere wife theft, no, the immigrant wants to take away his job as well, and will do it with a smile on his face, and for ten dollars an hour cheaper.

"Racists, nativists, and anti-Semites all made common cause:

protecting the pure white race from degeneracy required keeping "them" out, away from "our" women, and from competing for "our" jobs. Anti-immigration sentiment from the Know-Nothings of the 1840s to the present day has seen border closings as a win-win: we don't have to deal with "their" ways and accommodate ourselves to their needs for health care or education in their own languages, *and* we can eliminate the additional competition for jobs…Jews were imagined as weak, effete, and bookish nerds, who were so avariciously greedy that they controlled the economy of the entire world. Blacks were lazy, irresponsible, dependent, and also rapacious predatory sexual animals. Feminist women, for that matter, were more masculine than their men. Chinese men were slight, frail, and effeminate, were nonviolent, and wore women's clothing, and, at the same time, they were part of a yellow peril that was maniacally sweeping over California ports. One critic wanted it both ways; the Chinese were, he wrote, "a barbarous race, devoid of energy." [2]

American comedian Doug Stanhope has a terrific joke where he mocks pouty bigots like these for having jobs that can be taught 'by pantomime' to people who don't even speak English. 'How easy is your fuckin' job?' Doug asks, 'If someone can learn it completely with a series of hand-motions alone?' If America is to survive this renewed flirtation with white supremacy, we must look this racial skittishness square in the face. We have to ask why white men and white women are so petrified by people of different ethnic and racial identities, and how can our society outgrow these immaturities? There are two things that white men never like to admit, even in the face of overwhelming evidence: being racist, or being sexist. In my view, this is an ancillary product of the Civil Rights movement that weaponized scorn and shame against overt racists and misogynists. Racism and sexism became, in white consciousness, refined definitions that could fit neatly into 'yes' or 'no' categorizations. There was no problem so long as one could duck the title, and prove (often through tokenism) that any allegations were fabricated. The best moniker for this phenomenon – white defensiveness - was penned by James Baldwin:

> "In 1965, the novelist James Baldwin explored white defensiveness in an essay entitled "White Man's Guilt." Baldwin started by noting how his color seemed to impede human connection with many whites. They saw his color first, and reacting to that, feared an indictment over their own racial position. "And to have to deal with such people can be unutterably exhausting," Baldwin wrote, "for they, with a really dazzling ingenuity, a tireless agility, are perpetually defending themselves against charges, which one, disagreeable mirror

though one may be, has not really, for the moment, made." Baldwin lamented that white defensiveness against possible charges of racism frequently skewed any possible relationship, repeatedly forcing him into exhausting gymnastics meant to reassure whites of their innocence. Just so with contemporary claims of wounded feelings at having been, supposedly, called a "racist." The actual charge of racial malice is almost never made. And yet, racial justice advocates are time after time pushed to provide exoneration from the fictional accusation of personal bigotry. But this is only half the dynamic, and indeed, not the important half. Baldwin wrote that he did not need to level any charges, for the proof of white responsibility for racial oppression was everywhere in society. "The record is there for all to read. It resounds all over the world. It might as well be written in the sky. One wishes that Americans – white Americans – would read, for their own sakes, this record and stop defending themselves against it. Only then will they be enabled to change their lives." [3]

There's a tremendous amount of wisdom in his words here; being "racist" was (and often still is) typically a label reserved only for the worst white offenders. The cultural disease of racism, however, touches most of us in some way, and mostly, we come into contact with exclusionary ideas in manners we do not often notice. As a white man, I have no shame in admitting I have been both racist and sexist, and I am now trying my best not to be in the future. On some levels, this was a result of the "systematic" racism and sexism that powerfully influences our culture. Some of my racism and sexism were volitional, other aspects of it were not.

I was born into an incredibly conservative home, and my family was part of the typical 'white flight' (moving from the city to rural areas) that rejected an integrated neighborhood in favor of the perceived white safety of the suburbs. When I started to edit my first novel, I described a Latino character, for comedic effect, switching from a Spanish-inflected accent to a monotone English accent. I wrote that he returned to a 'normal' inflection – wait – normal? By whose standards? For me, and for my experience, white *was* normal. Abnormality was *non-white*. Now, does this slight ignorance put me in the same neighborhood as a Klansman who tosses a pipe bomb into a black church? Of course not, but both of our experiences *start* from the same position. We are both afflicted, in different degrees, from the same problem. The writer's job, as Gore Vidal liked to say, is to always tell the truth as they see it; I can't pretend to understand or explain what it is like to be the recipient of racial or gender-related prejudice, but I can articulate what it is like to experience the impulses that cause the discrimination. I shouldn't misrepresent myself – I wasn't a member of the Aryan Brotherhood – but I feel well equipped to provide some insight into the existential dread of the racist and sexist white man. For several years, my wife wanted to move into the city of St. Louis, and I bristled at the suggestion. *The crime rates are too high*, I protested. *It wasn't racist not to want your home or car broken into*, I complained. Using these deflections, I managed to delay the inevitable for a little while longer. Once we finally took up residence in the city, some of my internal dialog became impossible to ignore. My heart skipped a beat, during one commute back from work, when I saw a black man at a bus stop with what I thought was a gun. I blinked, and a moment later, I could see it was an umbrella. I am sure, in some way, that the policemen who shoot unarmed black men have similar experiences to mine, especially when the adrenaline clouds their judgement.

Initially, I tried to chalk up this troubling experience as a side-effect of some mild Post-Traumatic Stress Disorder that has hassled me since a gunpoint mugging that occurred a little over a decade ago. The stickup happened at night, and ever since, I am usually paranoid and irritated when outdoors at night, and have a tendency to be curt, even rude, with the panhandling homeless or more talkative drunks. When I drove past that bus stop, I saw a gun in his hand, I tried to convince myself, because I had a traumatic experience with guns that I'm still trying to work through. I have, however, seen plenty of white people with umbrellas, and none of them have frightened me like that. So how do I square that circle? I think its abundantly clear that *white* people are soothing to me, and anything else is a subconscious alarm bell. Sure, I've never screamed racial slurs at anyone, never harassed a woman at work, and never had any thoughts of this nature ever escalate to the level of speech or action. Racism and sexism couldn't *exist* if the thoughts weren't present first. Until white men like me grapple with these cognitive precursors, it won't get better.

"An armed Latino's suspicion that a tall, thin black youth in a hoodie in a gated community at night must be an intruder up to no good closes for me discussion about a post-racial society. Private citizens can now get on a warlike footing with crime, even if the images of the criminal in their heads are racist. Trayvon Martin's moment of instruction – as Henry Lewis Gates Jr. calls the recognition scene when the black youth realizes that he or she is different, and that the white world sees black people as different, no matter how they feel inside – has a history, one that yanks everyone back a step. It would seem that although black people are in the mainstream, black history still isn't, because certain basic things about being black in America – American history – have to be explained again and again. At the end of the Civil War, vast numbers of black men were on the roads looking for work, for sold-off family, for peace. In the late nineteenth century and into the twentieth, black men who could not prove employment or residence in a town that they happened to be passing through were imprisoned and put to work. Vagrancy laws were a form of social control, much like the war on drugs that Michelle Alexander in *The New Jim Crow* (2010) – such an important book – forcefully argues is today's extension of America's overseer-style management of black men. Drug laws have always been aimed at minorities." [4]

Different fields of study have different explanations for racism and sexism. To put it another way, there are no shortages of theories as to *why* humans behave in this fashion. A neurologist might tell you that humans are pattern-seeking by nature, and are driven to classify and categorize everything they come in contact with. An anthropologist might make a case for humans evolving as hunter-gathers who broke off into tribal subsections as a survival mechanism.

"To conceive of racism as a natural and virtually inevitable human response to encounters with strangers or aliens is to take the subject outside of history and into the realm of psychology or sociobiology. But if we continue to think of it as a historical construction associated with the rise of modernity and with specific national or international contexts, we have to conclude that it came to a hideous fruition in the century that has just ended. Its two most persistent and malignant manifestations – the color-coded or white supremacist variety and antisemitism in its naturalistic or secular form – both reached their logical extremes. White supremacy attained its fullest ideological and institutional development in the southern United States between the 1890s and 1950s, and in South Africa between the 1910s and the 1980s, but especially after 1948. Antisemitism of course reached its horrendous climax in Nazi Germany between 1933 and 1945. [5]

Regardless of their origin, sexism and racism have not yet been cured, and humanity still struggles with this troublesome yoke. On this topic, I think the old cliché still rings true – Europeans think a hundred miles is a long distance, and Americans think a hundred years is a long stretch of time. The plantations of the south still stand in many places, scars from an old wound, still haunted by the ghosts of slavery. The place I call home, in fact, was once a popular slave trading post, and an enterprising white man like myself, not two hundred years ago, could be found on Market street in downtown Saint Louis buying humans outright. The history of white supremacy is still all around us, and, at every impasse in American history, most white men of means and wealth stood in opposition to every advance of civil society. I cannot live in this city – Saint Louis – without being struck

31

by the racism that built it, nor can I read even its *recent* history without being overwhelmed by the indignities my neighbors faced in the past, and continue to face today:

> "Even dead black bodies don't escape desecration. Black corpses didn't matter when the Missouri Department of Transportation (MoDot) decided to run Highway 70 through the middle of Washington Park Cemetery in the St. Louis area. Black graves were disrupted again with the building of the MetroLink light rail system in the 1990s. When the graves had to be relocated, I remember families being asked to identify their loved ones' remains from black trash bags as if bones could be scientifically identified by a visual review. It was the height of disrespect." [6]

The thought of having to view the scraped-together bones of my loved ones in a trash bag is enough to knock the wind out of my lungs. How could we let this happen? The answer to the question, to quote W.E.B. DuBois, is reject the premise that the architecture of our nation couldn't fail African-Americans, because it was never designed to defend them. It was designed to defend *me*. It was designed to defend *you*, white reader. White Americans know this innately, instinctually. The source of white fear is not just inadequacy, but guilt: we know, inwardly, that others have been given an unfair deal and we have been given a far better one. Within the scope of this chapter, I will define (in my own view) the primary causes of racism and sexism within bigoted white communities. Chiefly among these factors are perceptions of sexual inadequacy, imaginary threat matrixes, losses of specialization, and institutional worship. But first, we should define, what, exactly, constitutes a racist society from the start:

> "What are the distinguishing features of an overtly racist regime that would distinguish it from the general run of ethnically pluralistic societies in which racial prejudice contributes significantly to social stratification? First, there is an official ideology that is explicitly racist. Those in authority proclaim insistently that the differences between the dominant group and the one that is being subordinated or eliminated are permanent and unbridgeable. Dissent from this ideology is dangerous and is likely to bring legal or extralegal reprisals, for racial egalitarianism is heresy in an overtly racist regime. Second, this sense of radical difference and alienation is most clearly and dramatically expressed in laws forbidding interracial marriage. The ideal is "race purity," and the bans on miscegenation reflect the maintenance or creation of a caste system based on presumed racial differences." [7]

It does not take long to find examples of each of these distinguishing features throughout the long history of the United States. Sexual obsession and fetishization of minorities is one of the many symptoms of subversive racism that existed then, and still exists now. The newest pejorative in the Alt-Right vocabulary is "cuck." Tellingly vulgar and unmistakably sexual, it is an abbreviation of the word "cuckhold," but it strays from the textbook definition (which is simply a person, usually male, who is the cheated-upon party in a romantic relationship) in two ways: there is an added aspect of voyeurism baked in (she cheats on you, and you enjoy watching,) and there is an unambiguous and often overt racial element as well (you enjoy watching a well-endowed black man romantically engaged with your partner.) "Cuck" became shorthand for a SJW (social justice warrior) who is too liberal, permissive, and gets a sexual thrill out of undermining the white majority. The imagery laced within this manner of speech is difficult to unpack comprehensively, but even a cursory glance at this phenomenon reveals, precisely, the overwhelming sexual inadequacy the Alt-Righters feel when confronted with inclusive policies and language. Minorities possess something whites cannot attain – unique ethnic and racial identities – and many white men fall victim to hateful philosophies because they are fearful that they will be unable to compete sexually with men of other races. Of course, this type of hate is not unique, nor is it new. Black men have been grotesquely murdered in the American south for real or imagined sexual advances on white women since the beginning of the nation itself.

Working in the information technology sector has, by necessity, exposed me to the seedy underbelly of the internet. It was this community, alongside wealthy interests, that powered President Trump to victory in the 2016 Presidential Election. On the "politically incorrect" board of 4Chan ("/pol/" as it is known internally) one can find open praise of Adolph Hitler and of the German fascism that systematically murdered six million Jews. It is a white nationalist echo chamber, and it was these right-wing provocateurs that flocked to Twitter to 'mark' Jewish journalists, celebrities, and intellectuals with three parentheses as a sort of digital yellow star. Anti-Semitism isn't their only outlet of white nationalism, of course, they lash out at Muslims and other minorities too (it is, after all, *white* supremacy.) 4Chan's pornographic boards (when not laden with reprehensible revenge porn) tell a vastly different story about minorities and the roles that this demographic often want them to perform in our societies. Permanently available, often across a multitude of boards, are 'cuckhold' threads that heap sexual praise upon 'bulls' (physically intimidating, often black 'alpha males') who have their way with white women. The dichotomy of arousal and disgust is on perfect display with this dynamic; the presence of a stronger, more virile, and more ethnically interesting male specimen contrasted against the fearful, insecure, and *scared* white man who is confronting his greatest and most persistent worry through the safety of sexual fetishization.

"The lynch mobs of the American South often justified their atrocities by alleging the rape or attempted rape of white women by black men. The fear of sexual pollution or violation by the allegedly subhuman race is close to the heart of murderous or genocidal racism wherever and whenever it appears. In the racist imagination, blacks are somewhat more likely than Jews to be viewed as violent sexual predators. The myth of the oversized black penis may be contrasted with the turn-of-the-century antisemetic belief that the large Jewish nose signified a *small* penis, further truncated by circumcision." [8]

There is a sexual aspect to racism, and, in general terms, exclusionary thought is, by its own nature, an attempt to preserve an existing demographic. These ends cannot be achieved without sexual means; the white race *must* resist the influence of minorities. The influx of new ethnicities into the American population via immigration (or even earlier, by the slave trade) inflamed white anxiety and inspired these sexual fears. Of course, there's no shame in a sexual preference or sexual fetish when practiced by consenting adults, but insecure white men flock to these types of erotic expressions to 'reclaim' the trauma implanted by their sexual terror. This is a simple example of cause and effect. White men fear minorities and sexually liberated women, and as a result, they are often drawn to sexual activities that soothe these vexations. This dynamic has existed throughout the entire history of the nation – through slavery, through the Civil War, and through the Civil Rights movements in the 1960s:

"Concurrent narratives of dangerous, lascivious blacks also existed, but the primary racial stereotypes painted blacks as joyfully enslaved. Post-emancipation, these notions faded as more threatening stereotypes quickly gained currency. Almost immediately, blacks came to be seen as wicked, vengeful, lust-filled, and violent – a menacing population prone to terrible crimes that had to be forcefully restrained. Slavery or prisons, the post-bellum South was wont to claim, were needed to control the treacherous nature of blacks. But there's another, more sinister explanation for the rapid rise in black incarceration rates: the material interests of wealthy whites…The Constitutional amendment that banned slavery provided that "neither slavery nor involuntary servitude, *except as a punishment for crime whereof the party shall have been duly convicted,* shall exist within the United States.

Right there in the middle of the Thirteenth Amendment was a gaping hole – one big enough to allow the reestablishment of slavery by another name. Through innumerable stratagems, the South rapidly built a criminal justice system around imprisoning blacks. Fines for major infractions suddenly morphed into jail time. Selective prosecutions of blacks surged. New crimes made their way onto the books. But of course the point was not to fill jail cells; rather, it was to fuel a new form of involuntary servitude." [9]

The topic of racism in the U.S. judicial systems and in American law enforcement are covered in more detail in a later chapter, but the racially-motivated fear of immigrants and other ethnicities begins to make sense when we place it in the proper context of instinctual terror mixed together with the biological imperatives of male sexual desire. This element leads nicely into the another critical aspect of white hatred – the perceived loss of specialization and the white jealously of racial uniqueness.

"For a people who have been able to take our fundamental Americanness for granted, to suddenly be faced with the realization that we will have to share that designation with people who look different and pray differently and whose primary language may be different from our own, can be quite jarring for some of us. The club is no longer exclusive. The membership rolls are being opened up. In the process, the sense of "specialness" that American identity once held for us is being bid downward by the inclusion of some within its ranks who never would have qualified in decades and eras past. Within perhaps a decade or two, it may no longer be automatic that we envision a white person from the so-called "heartland" when the terms "all-American boy" or "all-American girl" are used; rather, we might envision a first-generation Latina immigrant in the Southwest, a Hmong farmer in Wisconsin, or an Arab Muslim in Dearborn, Michigan. How does that feel? Be honest. Any one of these transformations on its own would be difficult for many of us to swallow, but together they create something of a perfect storm for white anxiety." [10]

If you ask white nationalists why they believe what they believe, you are likely to hear a defense of general sectarianism ("We should have our own country, and they should have theirs.") tied to a righteous effort to preserve the white race. ("If race mixing continues, the white race will disappear.") Interracial sexuality, to them, is ethically equivalent to a genocide of white people. In this way, we are able to see why integration is a perceived threat to the white supremacists. If we integrate too much, they believe their identities will disappear into the mist of history, and everything special, different, and unique about them will no longer exist. Racial jealously and resentment set in quickly, and the buffer white society has enjoyed for ages continues to deflate.

> "For centuries we have defined our status by way of our distance from the racial other. The closer we were to the black and brown, the less status we enjoyed. So a good neighborhood meant a white neighborhood, a good school meant a white school – those were the underlying assumptions of white flight, which began as soon as communities and schools came to have even small numbers of people of color in them. The custom of defining our status by the distance we were able to put between ourselves and racial others is the reason labor unions kept blacks and other people of color out of their ranks for so long. To integrate the workforce would be to diminish what W.E.B. DuBois called the "psychological wage of whiteness," by which he meant the kind of benefit one receives from being able to say that while you may not have much, at least you aren't black." [11]

The rational world must understand the root of this type of thinking if we are to rip it out of the soil. Racial, ethnic, and gender-based hatred typically begins from insecurity, jealousy, and fear. The white racist is scared because they perceive that their own ethnic condition is not as exotic or interesting as their counterparts, and this inspires racial jealously. *How* does anyone negotiate with a scared animal backed into a corner? The only political move left to the white racist in this exchange is to attempt to tarnish the enemy, limit its influence, and remove the possibility of competition with it inside of their own society. The Republicans exploit these anxieties, and thus make their assault on their Democratic opponents asymmetrical. The conservatives have a tool in their toolbox that the Democrats either do not possess, or will not utilize if they did; distortion of the truth and incitement of instinctive racial tensions for political gain. The DNC is forced to bring a knife to a gun fight. If they started to spout nonsense about Mexican rapists, unquestionably, the thinking left would abandon them in droves. Here's another example of political asymmetry in motion; Russian hackers versus Hillary Clinton's and John Podesta's inboxes. The prolonged (and state-sponsored campaign) to slowly drip stolen emails that contained some embarrassing and regrettable emails from inside the DNC left the United States with strikingly few options to return fire. Why? Because, simply, the Russians do not have a free press. Even if the Americans had breached Putin's email system, he could, through the monolithic control of his press, prevent the same kind of damage from being done. It is by nature of virtue itself that sane and rational policy can be easily undercut through treachery. The pressure points that Republicans have been pressing on for decades show no sign of wear and tear. They push because it works, and it works because race *is still a massive problem in the United States.*

> "In this arena the black man acquires quite another aspect from that which he has in life. We do not know what to do with him in life: if he breaks our sociological and sentimental image of him we are panic-stricken and we feel ourselves betrayed. When he violates this image, therefore, he stands in the greatest danger (sensing which, we uneasily suspect that he is often playing a part for our benefit); and, what is not always so apparent but is equally true, we are then in some danger ourselves – hence our retreat or our blind and immediate retaliation. Our dehumanization of the Negro then is indivisible from our dehumanization of ourselves: the loss of our own identity is the price we pay for the annulment of his. Time and our own force act as our allies, creating an impossible, a fruitless tension between the traditional master and slave. Impossible and fruitless because, literal and visible as this tension has become, it has nothing to do with reality... Today, to be sure, we know that the Negro is not biologically or mentally inferior; there is no truth in the rumors of his body odor or his incorrigible sexuality; or no more truth that can be easily explained or even defended by the social sciences." [12]

Not all racism or sexism originates from a position of inadequacy, or a position of real or perceived weakness. Plenty of sexually satisfied people are racists, and this is not a complete or comprehensive explanation in and of itself. Ignorance, willful or otherwise, as well as calloused self-interest are other primary causes. There is something of a communicative purpose and functionality to racism, and much of white-to-white language can conceal exclusionary thought through the use of code words. Racism always seems to be on the periphery, and usually is at its worst on the fringes. A motivational thought for me, after the Michael Brown riots, was to let the world into the universe of white conversation. What's shared in the confines of white-on-white racial speak is revealing. Occasionally, the racism is subtle and under spoken; *"Make sure you lock the car doors if you're driving through that part of town"* is a common refrain that many white Americans grew up with, and is the sort of coded language that most of us can readily identify. We know what kind of people they're really referring to, and we know what they're really afraid of. Other times, it can become crass and overt. One such instance happened to me while I was out drinking with an Asian friend. A white man stumbled out of the bathroom, glanced at my friend, then wobbled over to me and literally whispered in my ear: "I didn't know they let Ninjas in here!"

Why do you think he chose to whisper that phrase to me? Did he lack the courage to say it to my Asian friend? Probably. Did he want the non-white person next to me to hear it? Certainly not. But the message wasn't for my friend, was it? The message was for me. It was for the other white guy. He was doing his part by sending up the smoke signal. *There's someone different here,* I think, was the subtext of his half-drunken whisper to me. Social justice, in general, is often met with the rolling of eyes and the gnashing of teeth. It's easy to see why intercessory politics can become wearisome. I can understand why white people often become beleaguered by the concepts of unconscious racism or sexism, or exclusionary speech, or anything that, at first glance, seems to operate below anyone's ability to control it. But to deny that there is something pernicious in our instinctive communication is foolish. There are smoke signals. There are dog whistles. They'll both keep getting used until we completely deal with the issue at the root. To that end, if racism or sexism is present in the mind of a person because they do not know better, or because have not been taught otherwise, then we can conclude it was erected in response to a threat that is not legitimate. If left to their own devices, children don't often develop racial partitions (the cliché is probably true here, too, that racism is a learned behavior) so after accounting for the instinctive aspects of exclusion, we are now left to account for the volitional mechanisms of sexist and racist speech and behavior. Put another way; the racism of a plantation owner in the 1800's has an entirely different *source* than the racism of the closeted, Alt-Right homosexual man who can't admit he secretly likes black cock. The plantation owner fears egalitarianism because he imagines a threat from it that will hurt his prosperity. This type of racist might even believe inwardly that all humans are equal, and could understand the complicity involved in the participation of slavery (this explains, to me, the popularity of slave-owners like Jefferson freeing slaves in their will upon their death. Which, more or less, says they believed the practice was wrong *while they partook*, but not wrong enough to justify losing money.) White supremacy and male supremacy are attractive ideas because they have broad appeal, and as such, some are drawn to it because of immaturity, compulsion, self-interest, or a lack of education. In our modern era, the moral equivalent of the slave trade has been reinvented in the form of massive and widespread incarceration of black and Latino men:

> "More evidence of the modern-day racial bias manifests in the criminal justice system. Back in 1964, about two-thirds of all those incarcerated in this country were white, while one-third were persons of color. By the mid-1990s, those numbers had reversed, so that now, two-thirds of persons locked up are black and brown, while only a

third are white. This shift was not the result of a change in who commits crime – the relative rates of criminal offending didn't change significantly in the intervening years – but rather stemmed mostly from the disproportionate concentration of justice system resources in communities of color, especially due to the so-called War on Drugs. Although whites comprise roughly 70 percent of all drug users (contrary to popular perception), nine in ten people locked up each year for a possession offense are people of color. Black youth are nearly *fifty times* as likely as our (white) youth to be incarcerated for a first-time drug offense, even when all the factors surrounding the crime (like whether or not a weapon was involved) are equal." [13]

Indeed, the 'war' on drugs was little more than a method of social control that was intentionally aimed at black men:

"Ronald Reagan's approach to crime followed the tradition of Nixon and J. Edgar Hoover. Reagan became a strong voice for law and order, linking the harsh punishment of "offenders" to a broader political agenda of conservative values laced with the rhetoric of patriotism. Once in office, he immediately adopted a warlike approach to crime, launching a renewed War on Drugs and expanding funding for law enforcement. Reagan's administration was the key period in the shift to more punitive legislation and prison expansion. When he took office in 1980, there were just over half a million people in American prisons and jails. By the time of his departure in 1988, that population had more than doubled. The passage of the 1984 Federal Sentencing Guidelines laid the groundwork for expanded prosecutions and lengthy sentences, ensuring the continuing growth of prisons and punishment." [14]

"While African Americans make up only about 13 percent of the U.S population by 2012, Blacks constituted nearly 40 percent of those in prisons and jails…The prison population has changed from about 30 percent people of color in the 1970's to roughly 70 percent in 2012." [15]

"In 1973, after 50 years of stability, the rate of incarceration in the United States began a sustained period growth. In 1972, 161 U.S. resident were incarcerated in prisons and jails per 100,000 population; by 2007, that rate had more than quintupled to a peak of 767 per 100,000. From its high point in 2009 and 2010, the population of state and federal prisoners declined slightly in 2011 and 2012. Still, the incarceration rate, including those in jail, was 707 per 100,000 in 2012, more than four times the rate in 1972. In absolute numbers, the prison and jail population had grown to 2.23 million people, yielding a rate of incarceration that was by far the highest in the world." [16]

The American judicial system, in conjunction with the American law enforcement community, has created an unmistakably racist society in which black Americans exist as second-class citizens (this, too, is covered in greater depth in a later chapter.) Indisputably, African-Americans are far more likely to be jailed by police, and, tragically, far more likely to be killed by them as well:

> "Protesters also targeted excessive use of force on the population in general, citing the killings of young Black men – the strangling of Eric Garner in New York, the shooting of John Crawford in a Walmart in Ohio, the fatal armed attack on Ezell Ford in Los Angeles, and the gunning down of twelve-year-old Tamir Rice, who was playing with a pellet gun in a Cleveland park. A survey by ProPublica found that from 2010 to 2012, police fatally shot 1,217 people and that Blacks were more than twenty times more likely to be shot than whites…In England and Wales, which have a combined population of about 56 million, many police don't even carry sidearms while on foot patrol. From 2009 to 2012, police in all of England and Wales opened fire only eighteen times, killing nine people, about one-twenty-fifth of the level of fatal police shootings in the United States." [17]

Let's return, momentarily, to the boorish complaints of the irritated whites who assure us there is no such thing as 'white privilege' and that minorities are exploiting white guilt. Black Americans – when compared to white Americans – are fifty times more likely to be imprisoned for a first-time drug offense and are twenty times more likely to be killed by a police officer. While African-Americans only represent approximately 13 percent of America's total population, they comprise 40 percent of our prison population. At some point, the numbers become impossible to argue against; minorities are plainly and irrefutably targeted by the very infrastructure of our society. Arguments or implications to the contrary are flatly untrue and easily disproven. Occasionally, a stymied conservative will begrudgingly concede this point when challenged, and they will often retreat to questioning openly the work ethic of minorities to explain these discrepancies:

> "Are we to believe that blacks would choose to remain three times as likely as whites to be poor, rather than work harder? That they enjoy the excess mortality that derives from their current status at the

bottom of the nation's racial and class structure – currently 100,000 black folks die each year who wouldn't if their mortality rates were level with those of whites – and opt to continue down that road, rather than work harder to survive? Can differential work values really explain why African American households today have median incomes that are one-third lower, adjusted for inflation, than what white households today were bringing in forty years ago? Are gaps such as these realistically the outgrowth of differential willpower alone? Along the same lines, do Latinos, so many of whom work in hot fields picking fruit, or clean up after us in hotels, and who generally work long hours at some of the most demanding jobs in the nation – need to be taught how to work hard by white people?" [18]

White paternalism strikes yet again; *the uncivilized savages are in need of our condescending advice*, the white world exclaims with a smirk. This obnoxious pretentiousness is at its worst when it comes to welfare.

"The perception that many current welfare recipients should not be receiving welfare is widespread...only 31 percent of Americans believe that most welfare recipients who can work try to find jobs. On the other hand, two out of three Americans say that most people who receive welfare benefits are taking advantage of the system, and only one in three believes that most welfare recipients are genuinely in need of help. Americans are not shy about expressing their strong opposition to the use of welfare by people who could be supporting themselves. In a survey of Indiana residents, respondents were asked whether welfare benefits should be indexed to the cost of living. Although they were asked only whether or not they supported or opposed this idea, many respondents spontaneously expressed to the interviewers their feelings about welfare, and many of these feelings involved criticism of welfare recipients who did not really need government help...Race coursed just beneath the surface of the welfare debate, and 'welfare' and 'urban' have often been used as political code words that really mean 'minority.'" The Star Tribune goes on to quote John Powell of the University of Minnesota Law School as saying, "A lot of this discussion is racism in drag...When you talk about welfare, vouchers, urban strategies, crime, poverty, you're really talking about race." Since the mid-1960s, poverty and race have been closely linked in the public mind. Where "the poor" once conjured up images of southern European or Irish immigrants, or of white dust-bowl farmers, urban blacks now dominate our perceptions of poverty. The most salient contemporary images of the poor – the homeless beggar, the welfare queen, the teenage ghetto gang member, the heroin addict shooting up in the abandoned building – are strongly associated with minorities in both the mass media and the public imagination." [19]

When President Trump campaigned on a promise of building a wall on the southern border in 2016, his strategy was no different than the Republicans who poisoned the well when it came to welfare. Anyone who has done as much as skim through a single issue of *The Economist* (let alone run a multinational) will know that the most pressing threat to the American labor market is automation, not a negligible amount of illegal immigration. Donald Trump, by the virtue of what *must* be the bare minimum of his business prowess, has to have understood that the trucking industry (one of the nation's largest sector of unskilled labor) is only a decade, if not less, away from large-scale autonomy that will replace many American workers. We can conclude Mr. Trump *cynically* stoked white anxieties for his own personal gain, and this strategy worked in 2016 as it did in the decades of the past. And this hatred, this stupidity, and this broiling anxiety was, *in and totally of itself,* one of his most effective selling points:

> "Donald Trump did not make his mark with tax credits or education reform proposals or bold ideas to balance the budget. He did it by trashing Mexicans and endorsing the mass-deportation of illegal immigrants. No worries about whether getting 11 million people out of the country would be complicated, let alone cruel. He told ABC News' George Stephanopoulos: "George, it's called management…They would be out really fast, immediately." He said he'd build a border wall with Mexico – and make Mexico pay for it. He did it by condemning the leadership of the United States in terms everyone could understand. "We are led," he declared, "by very, very stupid people." He criticized Carly Fiorina, the former CEO of Hewlett-Packard and the only woman in the Republican presidential contest, for her looks. "Look at that face!" Trump said. "Would anyone vote for that?" [20]

As Mr. Trump dragged the national dialog into the sewer, (who could have guessed the party of Jesus Christ would meet this depravity with raucous applause while simultaneously forbidding their children from watching the Presidential debates on account of their sudden vulgarity?) insults became an acceptable replacement for policy that made basic sense, baseless slander of minorities became routine, and impossible promises became iron-clad assurances. The appeals to white purity were impossible to overlook; the Mexicans are sending rapists, Muslim immigration needs to be shut down, and the inner-cities were warzones. White consciousness was accustomed to the dog-whistle versions, but what we got in 2016 was plain, overt, and shameless racism. Now, the landscape was drastically different, and instead of talking *around* racial resentments, Trump simply said them *outright*. This bolstered his message with his base for two reasons: it was easier to understand, and it gave him the illusion of being "tough" to his overwhelmingly male supporters.

> "Consider the perverse logic of Rush Limbaugh's suggestion that President Obama was deliberately trying to destroy the American economy as some form of "payback" for slavery and racism, or Glenn Beck's charge that health care reform is really just Barack Obama's way to obtain reparations for slavery. Both allegations seem the stuff of absurdist and paranoid fantasy, and yet, in an era of white racial anxiety and resentment, they couldn't be more rational. They serve, almost perfectly, as triggers for our racial angers and insecurities. That black guy is trying to harm us, to take our money and give it to them, to make us hurt the way his people were hurt. Obama "hates white people," as Glenn Beck infamously said in 2009, which means, white America, he hates us. As an indication of how he intends to exact his racially motivated revenge, one need look no further, according to Rush Limbaugh, than Zimbabwe, where dictator Robert Mugabe has confiscated white farmers' land. Mugabe, according to Limbaugh, is Obama's "new role model," and "the next thing to look out for is for Obama to take the farms." [21]

Even to hardline conservatives, this nonsense must seem very silly in retrospect. Eight years of President Obama's reign came and went without anything even remotely resembling this insipid drivel. But what was the *subtext* of Mr. Limbaugh and Mr. Beck's prolonged attack campaigns on President Obama? It doesn't take a microscope to read between these lines; both men intentionally wiggled the loose teeth of anxious white men. They inflamed the pangs of their insecurities and played to their psychological shortcomings; and they do this cynically, hatefully, and viciously for their own financial gain. This type of agitation is effective because it relies on the existence of human error. It relies on our vices. More to the point, the Republican Party has been dog-whistling racism like this for so very long that occasionally overt racism bubbles up to the surface instead of the coded-language they typically utilize:

> "Here's an illustration from the 2012 Republican primaries. While stumping in Iowa, a videotape caught Rick Santorum saying the following about food stamps: "I don't want to make black people's lives better by giving them somebody else's money. I want to give

them the opportunity to go out and earn their money and provide for themselves and their families." Challenged over these remarks, Santorum subsequently denied that he had said "black," instead lamely claiming he had stumbled over another word – as Charles Blow reported, "Now he's saying that he didn't say 'black people' at all but that he 'started to say a word' and then 'sort of mumbled it and changed my thought.'" Blow's response: "Pause as I look askance and hum an incredulous, "Uh huh." Santorum surely regretted blurting it out, but the tape is clear, and in addition the statement corresponds to standard rightwing thinking: of course he said "black people." But more interesting is how Santorum's audience reacted, both immediately and as the controversy gained steam. The crowd in the room did not gasp or object: instead, after Santorum gaffed, the all-white audience reacted with applause. It's unlikely they intended to cheer a racist statement. Instead, they probably failed to note the Freudian slip, instead merely hearing what was already in their minds as the minute talk turned to food stamps…criticizing the government's welfare policies in race-coded terms has become a staple of dog whistle racism, so routine that the occasional use of express racial language can easily pass by unnoticed." [22]

Growing up in the heart of Missouri, I understand completely why these appeals work on latently-racist white men. What confounds me is just how easily weasels like Santorum can display such *cowardice* and still preserve robust support from white conservative men who are obsessed with the concept of toughness and virtue. One of the central paradoxes of the conservative manifesto itself is that of *psychological projection*. This is, in my view, quite a substantial part of its appeal. When President Trump boasts of his business prowess, it doesn't matter that rotting casinos in New Jersey and multiple bankruptcies flatly disprove his claim. He projects a falsehood as truth, and in this new and unquestioning atmosphere, his followers can do it without consequence, too. As the old saying goes, Americans are never broke, they're just temporarily embarrassed millionaires. President Trump has cut the finicky nature of reality out of the loop entirely, he is anything he says he is, and his disciples can emulate him with ease. Equally chilling, in hindsight, was the intentional pivot the Republican Party made, post-Romney, to stimulate white voter turnout:

> "After Romney's loss, some conservatives argued that there was nothing wrong with the party that couldn't be cured by an even higher share of the white vote. On its face, this seems absurd, given that the white vote will continue to decline as a share of the electorate…but there is a strain of something important in this line of analysis, as the

respected voting analyst Sean Trende has shown. One of the most important facts about 2012 was the decline in white voting. Trende estimates that some 5 million fewer whites voted in 2012 than in 2008. Most of them lived in the North and were less well-to-do. Trende's analysis pointed, first, to the downside of nominating a venture capitalist after a Wall Street-induced crash, the costs of Romney's "47 percent" comment and other statements that made him appear out of touch, and the success of both his Republican foes and the Obama campaign in branding him as an enemy of working-class aspirations." [23]

To make a lengthy story very short, American culture, over time, reduced the academics of political debate and public discourse about civil issues to sound-bite punditry. Americans grew bored with the monotony of governance and demanded the sweet relief of celebrity, glamour, and entertainment. Debates became competitions of gaffe-avoidance and proving grounds for catch phrases. For decades, American politicians have been dumbing down their messages to increase appeal, and there are, and will continue to be, serious consequences to this approach. When demagogues like President Trump can secure power by stepping on the insecurities of scared whites, the nation is in real trouble. Combine this wave of apathy with the runaway growth of American religious disenfranchisement, and both sides become more galvanized:

"The decline of traditional religious authority is contributing to a more revolutionary mood within black politics as well. Although African Americans remain more likely than whites to attend church, religious disengagement is growing in the black community. African Americans under the age of 30 are three times as likely to eschew a religious affiliation as African Americans over 50. This shift is crucial to understanding Black Lives Matter, a Millennial-led protest movement whose activists often take a jaundiced view of established African American religious leaders. Brittney Cooper, who teaches women's and gender studies as well as Africana studies at Rutgers, writes that the black Church "has been abandoned as the leadership model for this generation." As Jamal Bryant, a minister at an AME church in Baltimore, told The Atlantic's Emma Green, "The difference between the Black Lives Matter movement and the civil-rights movement is that the civil-rights movement, by and large, was first out of the Church." Black Lives Matter activists sometimes accuse the black Church of sexism, homophobia, and complacency in the face of racial injustice. For instance, Patrisse Cullors, one of the movement's founders, grew up as a Jehovah's Witness but says she became alienated by the fact that the elders were "all men." In a move that faintly echoes the way some in the alt-right have traded Christianity for religious traditions rooted in pagan Europe, Cullors has embraced the Nigerian religion of Ifa. To be sure, her motivations are diametrically opposed to the alt-right's. Cullors wants a spiritual foundation on which to challenge white, male supremacy; the pagans of the alt-right are looking for a spiritual basis on which to fortify it. But both are seeking religions rooted in racial ancestry and disengaging from Christianity—which, although profoundly implicated in America's apartheid history, has provided some common vocabulary across the color line." [24]

The number of cards left in the deck are beginning to shrink for everyone at the table. White men, now increasingly unassociated with religious organizations, are becoming gradually more inclined to accept nationalist or openly racist rhetoric as political doctrine. They have, simply, fewer cards to play when it comes to identity-based politics. Black activism, by unfastening itself from the yoke of Christianity, started to search for a spiritual high-ground that could galvanize African-Americans against white supremacy without having to swallow sexism as a cost of doing business. The yearning for non-Judeo-Christian spirituality within black communities should not be underestimated; I saw this first hand amongst several African-American co-workers in Florissant, Missouri. Occasionally, it takes the form of a rather militant black-liberation theology that is only tangentially related to Christianity, ("Jesus will come back in all his glory," a black-liberation preacher chirped at me from a street corner with a bullhorn, "And he will put all of you white people back into slavery!") or it becomes entangled with ancient Egyptian mythology or Masonic-styled paganism. The appeal of these religious alternatives is quite easy to understand; should my religious texts condone the institution of slavery that had decimated my people throughout history, I would not be so eager to adopt it, either. The end result, in my view, widens the chasms between these groups and makes the already-difficult issue of race in America even more disorienting. The vocabulary (as Peter Beinart rightly says) has shifted underneath everyone's feet, and the perception of religious homogeny begins to splinter. The collective discomfort rises. The resentment and polarization swells to a fever pitch. The white nationalists and Republicans are gifted with even more ammunition; they can tell the Evangelicals that progressive politics lead to a godless society. The left drifts further to the left, the right drifts even further to the right, and the chasm between all of us begins to widen.

This galvanization can often drive individuals into rabid institutional worship. The mechanisms necessary to uphold civil life – chiefly the military and law enforcement – instill wholesome and rightful reverence, respect, and gratitude among Americans. This only becomes a problem, and a cause of exclusionary thought, when this normal admiration escalates into mindless worship and devotion to these institutions.

Recent history is littered with textbook examples of this troublesome behavior: rabid defense of police officers who put bullets into the backs of unarmed black men, or the conservative defense of torture when performed by the American military. When these institutions are held in such high regard that no offense, however egregious, could possibly tarnish them, exclusion is certain to follow in many forms. After September 11th, American mosques were attacked and vandalized by fanatical bigots. Even Sikh temples (The Sikh religious in not associated with the Islamic faith and had nothing to do with the terrorist attacks) were not exempt from the violence. Once the threshold of near-perfection is reached in the minds of the institutional worshippers – the police may shoot anyone that they like for whatever reason they like, or the military can main and kill any combatant for any reason they like – we let reason sleep. As always, the support for arguments of this nature appeal to a predictable subset of Americans:

> "If you learn that someone is in favor of a strong military, for example, it is a good bet that the person is also in favor of judicial restraint rather than judicial activism. If someone believes in the importance of religion, chances are he or she will be tough on crime and in favor of lower taxes. Proponents of a *laissez-faire* economic policy tend to value patriotism and the family, and they are more likely to be old than young, pragmatic than idealistic, censorious rather than permissive, meritocratic than egalitarian, gradualist than revolutionary, and in a business rather than a university or government agency. The opposing positions cluster just as reliably: if someone is sympathetic to rehabilitating offenders, or to affirmative action, or to generous welfare programs, or to a tolerance of homosexuality, chances are good that he or she will also be a pacifist, an environmentalist, an activist, an egalitarian, a secularist, and a professor or a student." [25]

One of the most irritating rebuttals I receive when I discuss politics with other Americans is that of disinterest and fatigue. *Politicians are all crooks. Neither party can get anything done. Politics are nothing but gridlock.* The apathy only serves to worsen the conditions they bemoan, and Americans are tired of this war of attrition because all of us break off into predictable camps at the slightest disagreements. Conservatives worship authority and hierarchy; liberals adore empathy and activism. By the very *nature* of our political sympathies, we all stand to oppose each other from the start, almost without consideration to the context of the issues entirely. Whenever there is an American institution, conservatives almost always race to defend it. Whenever there are people maligned by an American institution, liberals almost always race to intercede for its victims. The conversation about systemic racism in our law enforcement communities has to begin from the right position:

> "Whenever America attempts to have a conversation about policing and state repression, it starts with or ends with victim-blaming. Black folks are asking police for the bullets, the chokeholds, the batons to the body, the volts to the heart. Look at how Rodney King was aggressively attacking the dozen or so police around him! If only Michael Brown had just followed Officer Darren Wilson's orders, he would still be alive. It's past time for white America to acknowledge that policing looks different in our communities, that police generally treat black people differently. In this case, differently means worse. The conversation cannot start with whites denying the reality of policing because it differs from theirs. Start with the question, "Why is policing different in the two communities?" *Now* we can have an intelligent conversation." [26]

Earlier in this chapter, I spoke briefly about a mugging I experienced about ten years ago. It was one of the worst days of my life, and I'm still pestered by nightmares and other mild PTSD-related symptoms. The incident occurred outside a hotel in rural Pennsylvania at night. I was attending a college trip to Washington D.C. and the group had stopped at a hotel for the evening. I wasn't paying attention, and was just outside my room, talking on the phone with my fiancé. I heard two men approaching behind me, turned around, and immediately had two pistols shoved into my face. In that moment, I was sure that I was going to die. Those who have experienced a similar level of terror and have felt the chilling effect of a genuine *fight or flight* response understand that no matter how well trained, well prepared, or mentally or physically strong, the experience is damaging and deeply traumatic. It's for this reason that I am not completely unsympathetic to the Darren Wilson's of this world. When you truly believe your life is in danger, it happens more quickly than you can imagine, and it is incredibly easy to make a mistake in the space of a millisecond. When I make a mistake in my desk job, no one will die; but for those who work in law enforcement and the military, often this is not the case. Their work involves life and death, fight or flight, and I sincerely believe that on account of this reality, both communities deserve some deference. Both communities deserve *elevated* levels of immunity and *lowered* levels of liability. An honest mistake made in the blink of an eye shouldn't put a public servant behind bars for a lifetime. Civil society depends on the members of these institutions to offer their very lives as a barrier – as protectors of the innocent from the criminal – and I speak with sincere respect towards them. My personal safety, security, and liberty doesn't exist without their service, and I am profoundly grateful for it.

With all of that said; at the moment they take their first paycheck, comprised of taxpayer money, we have every right to expect them to be *expertly* trained when situations require violence and deadly force. We have every right to expect them to wield this power with accountability, and it is not tawdry nor ungrateful to demand that these institutions operate openly and fairly. We *must* demand that all of our communities are policed with the same level of professionalism and respect. Our black communities, often, do not have the luxuries of restraint that are extended to white suburbs. To go one step further; as a white man, I have received preferential treatment in the same jurisdictions that abuse black men.

When I worked in Florissant, my apartment was a little under a block away from my employer. When the weather cooperated, I would save the gas money and elect to walk to work instead. The main artery of traffic that separated my home from my workplace was Highway 67, (known internally as "Lindbergh," its name usually followed with an angry sigh by St. Louisans who are familiar with the annoyance of its constant traffic) and I would jay-walk across that highway several times a day. This is, and was, illegal, and not entirely safe on such a congested roadway, but unfailingly, I would break this law routinely. I would break it with impunity; on a couple of occasions, I would be jay-walking in front of a Florissant police cruiser.

At no point was I detained for this behavior. At no point was I even graciously instructed to use the crosswalks. Jay-walking as a white man in front of a moving police car didn't even earn me a lazy *whoop* of the sirens from a cop too apathetic to leave the vehicle. They shrugged, unfailingly, at what was a minor traffic infraction and went on their way. Michael Brown jay-walked *once* – a behavior I did multiple times per day in the same general area – and it was one of the last things he ever did. Tell me, now, that I am not privileged. Tell me, now, that I didn't have it easier than Mr. Brown. When I jay-walk as a white man in St. Louis, I get shrugs. Do it as a black man, and you had better make sure your affairs are in order first. How did we let things get so bad, and why is it such a debate when we try to talk plainly about how bad things really are?

The inappropriate adoration of law enforcement and the military will let outrages like these slide and will be happy to slip them under the rug. Attitudes like these always lead to an unhealthy disdain for the other civil mechanisms that are bound to keep both of these institutions in check: the freedom of speech, the freedom of assembly, and the freedom of the press. These mechanisms are pieces of armor for the common man; and we let others degrade them at our own peril. What was the response from those in power when Chelsea Manning leaked the sordid details of the military's behavior? She was jailed, branded as a traitor, and sour politicians complained about that the press was irresponsibly publishing information that could endanger Americans across the globe. When the police and the troops need our support, and not our brains, suggestions, criticisms, feedback, and participation, what they're asking for is blind obedience, and if we give this to them, we will have abdicated our responsibility as citizens entirely.

The victims of these institutions – to return to the central theme of this chapter – are not white men, but women, minorities, and all others who find themselves cut out of the Ethnostate. They have been, indisputably, used to enforce vicious legislation and racist ideologies throughout American history. Police worship, especially when considering their scandalous history of brutality towards African-Americans, is incredibly dangerous and distasteful. However, we must not demonize these servants of our nation, either. They are neither inherently good or bad, but morally and ethnically capable of both honor and evil. When James Meredith was unable to safely attend university during the heat of the Civil Rights movement, it was the American National Guard that protected his life with deadly force. There is no sane American who does not appreciate these arms of our democracy. In fact, I like these functions of fair and impartial law enforcement and judiciary that *I want to see them expanded to all Americans.* I want to see all American institutions serving black men with the same quality and vigor that they have served me. Right now, we don't have that kind of service for everyone, but we can get there together.

Targeting Women

‡‡

CHAPTER 3

"THERE WILL NEVER BE A WOMAN OF MEANS WITHOUT CHOICE ANYMORE. THAT JUST SEEMS TO
ME SO OBVIOUS. THE STATES THAT CHANGED THEIR ABORTION LAWS BEFORE ROE ARE NOT
GOING TO CHANGE BACK. SO WE HAVE A POLICY THAT ONLY AFFECTS POOR WOMEN, AND IT
CAN NEVER BE OTHERWISE." – RUTH BADER GINSBURG

The year is 2003, and I'm standing just outside of the chapel on the campus of Lincoln Christian College. It's fantastically early in the morning and bitingly cold, but I dutifully arrive a few minutes early, and tuck my hands into my pockets after slipping in my iPod earbuds. I was a devoted Evangelical Christian at this time, and I was majoring in Pastoral Ministries. I wanted to graduate and become a Christian preacher. At Lincoln Christian College, all students are required to partake in a regimen of classes they refer to as "Interdisciplinary Studies," and the semester culminated with a class trip. Occasionally, these were acts of service to local congregations or missions trips. Others seemed to resemble a typical field trip a high school might put together, like taking an entire class for a sight-seeing tour of Gettysburg, for instance. A hopeless history buff, I eagerly signed up for a trip to Washington D.C. I wanted to see the monuments and museums. Lincoln Christian had other motives; they wanted to send a group of students to a national protest against abortion. A few days before we're scheduled to depart for the capital, we are given a mystery task to perform on campus. So, I'm standing outside on that day, shivering, awaiting the arrival of the professor who was designated to lead the trip.

His pickup truck rumbles down the parking lot, and attached to the hitch is a seven-foot trailer. He kills the engine, steps out of the vehicle, and opens the twin doors to the trailer. Inside are several hundred white, picket-fence-crosses. We're told to unload the trailer, and instructed to drive the eggshell-white crucifixes into the frozen soil that surrounds the chapel. He had brought with him a specific number of crosses (the exact figure escapes me) which were meant to signify the average number of abortions per day in the United States. The professor waited until the trailer was empty and drove off into the distance, leaving the students to finish the job. The aluminum back of my 32GB iPod (a real treasure in 2003) started to condensate, stuck in a thermal purgatory between the body heat radiating from inside my pocket and the sub-zero temperatures outside. I didn't mind this chore, however, even I was inwardly beginning to waiver on my support of the anti-choice movement. I wanted to see D.C. for the history, and little else.

This trip would be the final nail in my Evangelical coffin. Protesting against abortion taught me all I needed to know about the anti-choice ideology. It was vicious, condescending, judgmental, bone-headed, and unfailingly mean. My stomach would quickly turn against Christianity itself, too. I went to the capital a Christian, and would return as an atheist. Why did an abortion protest finally push me over the edge? Primarily, it was the Harvey Milk effect; I had finally put some faces to the name. Right before the march began, we queued up behind an outdoor stage that overlooked the National Mall. A gaggle of women were preparing to climb the stairs to speak to the crowd, and fastened around their necks were signs that read "I REGRET MY ABORTION."

The looks on their faces haunted me. They were pensive, nervous, stoic, with their bottom lips pursed, preparing to revisit their shame and emotional trauma in full view of this very sizable crowd. It was menacing, pernicious, and I felt a sharpened pang of nausea race through me. From that point on, I knew that the anti-choice movement didn't just hate women, but, remarkably, made women hate themselves. Don't be fooled by the deceitful words of the anti-choice movement; *women* are their intended targets, not Roe vs. Wade, nor Planned Parenthood, but young American girls and American women. Our sisters, our wives, our daughters, our nieces, and mothers are in their crosshairs. Our entire society has been configured to decimate them, to strip them of their rights, to subject them to violent assault, to commodify their sexuality as a possession, to pass ownership of their own bodies to supervisory men. We cannot talk about abortion without talking about the role of women in the United States, and we cannot speak of this role without mentioning the war of attrition waged against feminism's every advance by the bloated patriarchy that has opposed it at every opportunity.

To millions of Christian Evangelicals, there is no greater crime than the surgical procedure known as abortion. In their view, fetal life is sacred (often from the very moment of conception) and a terminated pregnancy, to them, is morally equivalent to the murder of an innocent child. Abortion is the backbone of American conservatism. It is often the largest bone of contention between the two predominant political parties, and for good reason; the fate of the nation itself is inextricably tied up with how the United States deals with this vexing moral issue. The religious and conservative challenge to reproductive rights originates primarily from a position of ethics. Conservatives believe abortion is tantamount to murder, so we find Republicans arguing fervently against a medical procedure they believe is in violation of human rights.

The political left must advocate for reproductive rights if they are to create an egalitarian society. The conservative right must preserve the traditional family structure of one man, one woman, bound to the natural cycles of reproduction and fertility if the status quo is to be maintained. This is a battle for control of the nation's rudder. Will the United States adopt the values of Topeka or Paris? How, exactly, half our population will be allowed to medically function is of the upmost importance to both of our philosophies. Before I embark upon this defense of abortion – I should make it clear that I, in all sincerity, respect the ethical perspective from which a typical conservative approaches this issue. If it is true that abortion is the moral equivalent of a murder, it would rightly be its own Holocaust. I fully accept this premise, without reservation or modification. If abortion is murder, we are wrong to perform it, wrong to write laws condoning it, and wrong in our support of it. Abortion - scientifically, medically, and ethically - is not equivalent to the act of murdering an innocent person. The two primary charges I make against anti-abortionism are quite basic: the anti-choice dogma is an aesthetic ethic, and it lacks the courage of its own conviction. Those who oppose abortion on the basis that they believe it to be ethically equivalent to a genocide lack the courage of their convictions. If this statement was true, and the government denied any legal means to halt the bloodshed, then the only proper response is an armed resistance. Only the most crazed members of the lunatic fringe have been brazen enough to get the blood of abortion doctors on their hands, so what does that tell us about the sincerity of the non-warring majority? Quite a lot, I would say. The urgency in their actions do not match the urgency in their speech. If it is a moral Holocaust, lead us into battle. Prove to yourself – and to the world – that a fetus is a life worthy of violent defense. There is a reason why American conservatives don't take up arms *en masse* against Planned Parenthood. It's because they know, inwardly, that abortion isn't a murderous crusade against defenseless humans, and their moral support of this cause is for appearances only.

There are not many issues (this may be the only one, in fact) that I first attack the sincerity of my opposition. For example, I don't have much trouble accepting that someone like Paul Ryan genuinely dislikes financial regulation. I'm quite happy to take him fully at his word. In fact, nothing in his behavior, or in the content of his speech, would make me suspect otherwise. Because of this, I believe, at least in some fashion, when Mr.

Ryan discusses financial regulation, he does so from the perspective of an impacted party. Or, said another way, I believe he negotiates publically in good faith. He represents a plethora of varied special interest groups that dislike regulation, and speaks out for the concerns of wealthy Americans everywhere. I might disagree with Mr. Ryan, but in so doing, never develop a need to question how sincerely his beliefs are held. When anti-abortionists talk about their qualms with reproductive medicine, often, they are really just talking about their personal discomfort with sexual promiscuity or women in non-traditional roles.

Abortion was a keystone issue in my family. I was born into an incredibly conservative household (conservative enough to ban animated Disney movies after the company hosted a gay pride parade through one of its parks) and my parents did much more than merely talk about abortion. My mother volunteered for years at a Crisis Pregnancy Center, and on several occasions, housed pregnant teenagers at our home. It was presented to us, as children, that the parents of these girls had 'kicked them out of their homes' because they refused to have an abortion. I grew up believing abortion was an abhorrent thing, and the development of my own morality and faith was built upon that belief.

I remember watching the early election returns of the 2000 Presidential election with my family. Bush was declared the winner of Florida at some late point in the evening, and my family was elated that Bush had won. I turned to my mother (as she cried tears of joy) and exclaimed, in my naiveté, 'Is that it? Is abortion over?' The look on her face – and the silence that followed soon after - betrayed a certain cynical knowledge that I will never be able to forget. No, of course, she knew abortion won't ever be over, no matter what laws we make, and she knew we can't ever stop it from happening. If this statement is true, and abortions are permanently unavoidable, what's the point in trying to ban them? Ask a typical conservative why firearms should never be banned, and they'll tell you criminals will get guns no matter how many laws you write, so why are the rules different for abortion?

> "Abortion takes place in Canada and Greece and France, where it is legal, performed by medical professionals, and covered by national health insurance, and also in Kenya, Nicaragua, and the Philippines, where it is a crime and a woman who terminates a pregnancy takes her life in her hands. According to anthropologists, abortion is found in virtually every society, going back at least 4,000 years. American women had great numbers of abortions throughout our history, when it was legal or not." [1]

The acknowledgement of this reality is not equivalent to permissive acceptance of unethical behavior, ('murders will happen no matter what, too, and we make laws prohibiting them' conservatives love to riposte at this juncture) but a tacit admission that a policy that would make abortion illegal could not put an end to abortion. In fact, good evidence shows it often has the opposite effect:

> "Many countries that have outlawed abortion have *higher* abortion rates than countries where abortion is legal. Brazil, Chile, and Peru – in which the predominant religion is Catholicism – are among these. (It's worth noting that the church wasn't always pro-life. Until 1869, even the Catholic Church supported legalized abortion until quickening, at approximately nineteen weeks of pregnancy, which is when it considered the fetus was given a soul.) The truth is that when abortion is outlawed, women don't seek services less frequently; they just survive them less often. This has been true in the United States (when abortion was illegal) as well as in many countries abroad today." [2]

The old cliché rings true – if a law is not easily enforceable, it is probably not a good law – and even if we accept the premise that abortions are wrong, conservatives aren't advocating for fewer abortions, but for a higher number of more dangerous abortions. Americans have specific experience in this manner of legislative logic: Prohibition. It didn't stop drinking, and all the country had to show for its moral crusade was a higher number of people killed, maimed, or blinded by toxic bathtub liquor. This is not a prudent approach to problem-solving at a national level, and every American ought to know better. If we concede that use of alcohol or tobacco are wrong, or dangerous, or unhealthy, but choose not to ban them, does it make us complicit in the deaths caused by these industries since we chose not to outlaw them? Nearly every American would say no – people are responsible for the consequences of their own actions – and making a personal and private choice to partake in any activity burdens that individual with the risks and rewards inherent within them. This is acceptable, and ethically neutral, so long as an individual acts within their own consent, is not coerced into any action, and most importantly, does not remove the aspect of choice from any other humans. Here, we come to the other primary point of contention in the debate: personhood.

> "The bedrock argument of the anti-abortion movement is that intentionally ending new life at any point after conception is murder, or close to it. A fertilized egg is as much a person as Pope Francis. Not a potential person, but a person at that very moment. People who try to be 'fair to both sides' tend to wave away this conviction because it sounds so bizarre, but it is essential to the anti-abortion position.

Because they oppose all abortion as morally wrong and want to ban it, abortion opponents can't allow that some abortions are less evil than others – for example, that terminating a pregnancy at six weeks, when the embryo is the size of a pea, is qualitatively different from having one of those mythical day-before-birth abortions on a whim...If abortion opponents were to accept abortions for reasons that majorities find acceptable – in cases of rape or severe fetal defect or to preserve the woman's physical or mental health – they might gain support from those who want to see abortion greatly restricted but not banned entirely...Once you admit that embryonic or fetal life can be sacrificed for one reason, you're admitting that it is not equivalent to a born person, so why stop there? Moreover, once the door is opened a crack – say, by permitting suicidality to count as a risk to the woman's life, as in Ireland's new law – desperate women will try to push through and sympathetic people in authority will do their best to help them. The potential for wiggle room is one reason abortion opponents tend to deny that abortion is ever necessary, even to save a woman's life." [3]

I've always considered these concessions, especially when espoused by conservatives, to be incurably trite. Those who are fundamental enough to deny exceptions for rape, incest, or the potential life of the mother may hold those views (at least, partially) cynically, as a *tactical* measure to solidify their argument. If the anti-abortionist accepts that there are occasions where it is ethically acceptable to terminate a pregnancy, then the ability to claim there is a moral absolute evaporates. They can no longer claim that life is wholly sacred from the moment of conception if it can be acceptably destroyed under certain conditions. Necessity, not merely in medical terms, but in economic ones as well, play a critical part in underlining the immaturity and short-sightedness of the anti-abortion movement. To accept a position of total abolition, one must conclude that no other possible outcome is worse than ending an embryonic or fetal life. This statement is a vast and sweeping one, and it takes a fair amount of arrogance to believe it sincerely. The death of the mother does not rise above this edict, nor does the conditions of the conception (however violent or unspeakably horrific), nor does the realities of grinding poverty. I do not possess the empathetic apathy required to shrug off the concerns of a woman made to be pregnant against her will, or a woman who cannot afford to feed another child, and I think no one else should, either. I find myself, all too frequently, coming back to the notion of short-sightedness when describing the conservative movement. Occasionally, this lack of intellectual rigor is a result of vice, or proof of a poor education, but most of it has no excuse. It is usually motivated by a dogged unwillingness to see the bigger picture, to engage with the total problem, to go any further rhetorically than their pastor on a painful social issue. The worship of institutions strikes here yet again; but instead of the military or the police being the focus of their adulation, the *family* and the precious values found within it are sacred virtues, worthy of eternal defense. These are not defensive maneuvers, but offensive ones; a woman choosing whether or not to have a surgery is perceived as a *threat* to the lifestyles of Christians. These are expansionist aims – this must be said plainly – and it isn't good enough that the conservatives don't want abortion, but they have to take the option away from everyone else, too.

One of the basic tenets of a democratic society is autonomy. The word, in English, is derived from the Greek *(auto* for 'self' and *nomos* for 'law'), and it means that those who are ruled establish, for themselves, their own order. If we momentarily set aside The Bill of Rights and the Constitution, it seems that among the most basic ethical statements anyone can make is that individuals should have the ability to have a reasonable degree of self-determination. In challenging a woman's right to control their own body, opponents of abortion are chipping away at the spine of our free society by targeting autonomy itself. This is a greater danger than abortion, and with every new legal restriction levied against abortion clinics in Republican states, the teeth of the sawblade drives ever-deeper into the trunk of the tree holding all of us up. It is not hyperbole to claim the fate of our free democracy hangs, literally, in the balance. Despite what the religious anti-abortionists might say, it is, in fact, very possible to hold a fervent and impassioned belief without ramming it down the throats of everyone else. Vice President Biden, himself a devout Catholic, admitted that he believes abortion is always morally wrong and fully accepts the Vatican's position on the issue, but *refuses* to impose that opinion on anyone else. This humility and maturity is hard to find in the right-wing on the abortion issue, and it is truly a shame that Mr. Biden's position is uncommon. The unintended consequences of outlawing safe access to abortion are deeply disturbing. All of us are best served when all women have unfettered access to safe and professional abortion providers. I support abortion because history has taught me what a society looks like without it, and that image is putrid, inhumane, and reprehensible.

"In her important book *When Abortion Was a Crime,* Leslie Reagan documents the ten decades of U.S. history when abortion was outlawed. According to Reagan, the lack of established institutions forced many women to do it themselves…Word of solutions was passed along informal and often unreliable networks. Introducing bleach was one all-too-common and often fatal method tried by women. Reagan cites the cases in Chicago in the 1950's in which young women had been 'injected with lye' to induce abortions. 'One woman described taking ergotrate, then castor oil, the squatting in scalding water, then drinking Everclear alcohol. When these methods failed, she hammered at her stomach with a meat pulverizer before going to an illegal abortionist. Before *Roe,* some women tried to induce abortions with whatever they could find, including the infamous coat hanger." [4]

Forget about the risks of intentional inducement; what about false positives, accidents, mental illness, or miscarriages once abortions are fully illegal?

"In Iowa in 2010, Christine Taylor, mother of two, fell down the stairs, and while in the hospital to make sure the fetus was all right, confessed to a nurse that she had considered adoption or abortion because her husband had left her when she became pregnant this time, and she worried about raising three kids alone. The nurse called the police. In the end, Taylor was not charged – but only because she was still in her second trimester and the state 'feticide law' covered only the third. In Indiana, Bei Bei Shuai was charged with murder and attempted feticide on the grounds that the rat poison she took to commit suicide while pregnant killed her newborn daughter. Interestingly, Shuai tried to kill herself after her boyfriend, the father of her baby, announced that he was married and was returning to his family. For Shuai, Taylor, and many other women prosecuted or threatened with prosecution because of their behavior during pregnancy, the fact that her male partner abandoned her and their child-to-be is of no legal interest. Producing that healthy, live baby is all on her. A true believer would not only applaud all these prosecutions – as many do – but to be logically consistent, they should also want to vastly expand the range of these laws to cover the earliest miscarriages, and the loss of embryos and fetuses due to such legal activities as drinking, smoking, failing to control diabetes, and exposing oneself to domestic violence and stress." [5]

How many Christian, anti-choice women, do you think, are currently overweight or diabetic? No pregnancies for them until they shape up! Or, if they get pregnant, we'll need to put them in prison. Once we ban abortion, and place *legal* protections on fetal tissue health, then *they themselves* will fall under the umbrella of their own stupid laws. On what basis would the law enforcement and judicial communities delineate between an innocent trip down the stairs and an intentional one? How will doctors determine which miscarriages were deliberate and which were not? In whom are we placing the trust to judge which circumstances are criminal and which are tragic?

"Of course, in an illegal environment, the other problem is not with abortions, but with aftercare…caring for a patient who suffered after a clandestine abortion was dangerous for physicians too. A doctor could be held as an accessory to a crime. Doctors were pitted against their patients, and the implications were far-ranging. Even miscarriages were suspect. Was a miscarriage perhaps really an illegal abortion? A lot of physicians just didn't want to have anything to do with providing care even *after* an abortion because of the risk of prosecution. A woman might have induced her own abortion, and shown up on a doctor's doorstep hemorrhaging and near death. If she died, the doctor could be in trouble. 'Police arrested physicians simply because they were the last physician attending the patient and they had not made their report to the coroner,' says Reagan. In our current climate, in which refusal to provide medical services is becoming more common (remember, pharmacists can refuse to fill prescriptions for even birth control), it's easy to imagine physicians could refuse care for women who are miscarrying either naturally or unnaturally." [6]

I can scarcely imagine a more despotic state of affairs. All pregnancies carried out to the end of their term, without exception, on the orders of the state? If this is the decree, then it will have to backed up with the muscle of our law enforcement, investigated and monitored by our intelligence agencies, and the punishments will have to be adjudicated by our judicial system. Every mechanism of civil society, as strained and stretched as they all already are, will have to be fully applied to this insane ban, and it will be more costly than many realize, both in terms of human life and economic expense. The horrifying prospect of losing the protections afforded to American women by *Roe vs. Wade* is deeply troubling. Romanian dictator Nicolae Ceausescu issued "Decree 770" in 1966, an edict that officially made abortion illegal nation-wide. This horrific legislation stood until 1990, but not until lasting and avoidable damage was done to the country as a whole. During this era, birth rates peaked in 1967 and the children born within this baby boom would make up the revolutionary forces that ousted him from power (and would later execute him and his wife via a firing squad) a few decades later.

"Ceausescu's ban on abortion was designed to achieve one of his major aims: to rapidly strengthen Romania by boosting its population. Until 1966, Romania had one of the most liberal abortion policies in the world. Abortion was in fact the main form of birth control, with four abortions for every live birth. Now, virtually overnight, abortion was forbidden. The only exemptions were mothers who already had four children or women with significant standing in the Community

Party. At the same time, all contraception and sex education were banned. Government agents sardonically known as the Menstrual Police regularly rounded up women in their workplaces to administer pregnancy tests. If a woman repeatedly failed to conceive, she was forced to pay a steep "celibacy tax." Ceausescu's incentives produced the desired effect. Within one year of the abortion ban, the Romanian birth rate had doubled. These babies were born into a country where, unless you belonged to the Ceausescu clan or the Community elite, life was miserable. But these children would turn out to have particularly miserable lives. Compared to Romanian children born just a year earlier, the cohort of children born after the abortion ban would do worse in every measurable way: they would test lower in school, they would have less success in the labor market, and they would also prove much more likely to be criminals." [7]

The minutiae of the law reads quite similarly to what American fundamentalists advocate for today. Prison sentences were handed out to medical practitioners who performed abortions illegally. Trite concessions were given out to children conceived by rape or incest, as well as women over the age of forty-five, or when carrying a child threatened the life of the mother. The scandalous reach of the state extended, quite literally, into the genitals of every Romanian woman. Ladies unfortunate enough to work for the state were required to undergo examinations on a yearly basis to prove they had not had an abortion. Miscarriages – an unspeakable tragedy for any mother – were now the official business of the state, and had to be proven to not be the result of intentional action. Beyond the creation of a ghastly police state, this decree produced results too terrible to fully catalog here.

We should start with the most revolting figures first – between 1966 and 1990, approximately nine thousand Romanian women died on account of complications caused by illegal abortions. Orphanages became inundated with unwanted children as child abandonment soared. Patients subverted the law by seeking back-alley abortions or by purchasing black market contraceptives, and doctors falsified legal exemptions for women in an attempt to shield women from the fetid dangers of illegal abortions. Beyond the deadly effect this law had on women, the children born were equally hamstringed. Those maligned by botched or failed abortions, or those whose prenatal medical ailments didn't rise to the level of a legal exemption were known as the *decretei* – the Romanian word for "decree." The economy, already saddled with the default corruption of communism, buckled under the strain of a new influx of children. Schools were filled to capacity, and even parents who wanted to keep their children left them at orphanages because they couldn't afford to keep them fed.

"The children born in the wake of the abortion ban were much more likely to become criminals that children born earlier. Why was that? Studies in other parts of Eastern Europe and in Scandinavia from the 1930s through the 1960s reveal a similar trend. In most of these cases, abortion was not forbidden outright, but a woman had to receive permission from a judge in order to obtain one. Researchers found that in the instances where the woman was denied an abortion, she often resented her baby and failed to provide it with a good home. Even when controlling for the income, age, education, and health of the mother, the researchers found that these children too were more likely to become criminals…The (U.S.) Supreme Court gave voice to what the mothers in Romania and Scandinavia – and elsewhere – had long known: when a woman does not want to have a child, she usually has a good reason. She may be unmarried or in a bad marriage. She may consider herself too poor to raise a child. She may think her life is too unstable or unhappy, or she may think that her drinking or drug use will damage the baby's health. She may believe that she is too young or hasn't received enough education. She may want a child badly but in a few years, not now. For any of a hundred reasons, she may feel that she cannot provide a home environment that is conducive to raising a healthy and productive child." [8]

This law, equal parts pernicious and empty-headed, is likely to continue to ravage the Romanian economy well into the future as the abortion ban has produced a massive generation that will depart the working force and head into retirement nearly simultaneously. The losses keep compounding, and all of it stems from the same dopey moralizing that is just as commonplace in the United States. Ultimately, those who campaign for restricted reproductive choices are advocating for more unloved children, for more deaths related to amateur abortionists, for even more strain on public infrastructure, and for more power for a government they claim they would like to see diminished in size. Their political beliefs are chosen almost entirely *ala carte* and without any desire for consistency. One of the most menacing aspects of the anti-choice manifesto is the latent (or open) self-hatred or woman-on-woman hate that it inspires within women:

"What drives abortion bans and restrictions? The belief that women who have sex for pleasure rather than procreation are sluts. Low-income women more than anyone else are profoundly hurt by obstacles to abortion access. Andrea Grimes, an investigative political reporter who now advocates for the right of women to have access to safe and legal abortion, had been an ardent pro-life supporter when she was growing up in Fort Worth, Texas. She reveals that punishing women for having sex rather than concern over fetuses was the engine driving her pro-life rhetoric:

"Because while I said it was about the babies, it wasn't. It was about slut-shaming. I absolutely loved slut-shaming. Because I was saving myself for marriage – well, oral sex doesn't really count anyway, does it? – I knew that I would always be right and virtuous and I would never be a murderer like those sluts. The issue couldn't possibly be up for real debate, to my mind: either you were a baby-killer slut, or you behaved like a proper Christian woman and only let him get to third base. Babies were simultaneously women's punishment for having premarital sex and beautiful gifts from Jesus Himself. That didn't seem like a contradiction in my mind. It was just another one of God's perfect mysteries…In private, my anti-choice friends and I would laugh and laugh…about how stupid women were for having premarital sex. How evil they were for not being able to control themselves. How great I was for not having sex with my boyfriend."

If those who want to outlaw abortion were truly concerned about fetuses, then why are women alone singled out for punishment – why aren't the men who created unwanted pregnancies also taken to task for their sexual activity?" [9]

Once the door of casual judgement opens, it is incredibly difficult to shut. Furthermore, sex itself becomes another vector of female shame that is openly not applied, in the slightest, to men. Women, as luck would have it, are excellent judges of their own ability to rear children, and the government interfering in this nuanced algebra could only make the situation worse. The "values-voters" never stop offering their empty opinions about the reproductive choices of strangers, even though, if enacted, those policies would likely result in the deaths of their own loved ones. These ideologies find their origin in religion's near-universal subjugation of women:

"In Christianity, the people coming to Jesus were all men. Which woman was allowed to follow Christ? Jesus did not select a female disciple and the Christian church has always upheld this as the main reason why only men should be ordained priests. The idea of apostolic succession is enshrined in Catholicism which to this day, has no female priests. In the Church of England, there is huge outcry every time the subject of female bishops crops up, and many adherents either threaten to become Catholic or actually do so, in protest. There are no women at the head of any traditional religion or church." [10]

In a basic reading of the Bible, Quran, and the Torah, one will find a unifying feature between them all; a biological revulsion of the female body. Menstruation is a shameful – so shameful, in fact, that menstruation-management must literally be codified into law – and thus the routine functions of the female body are worthy of disgust. Modern-day versions of this ancient impulse manifests itself in the form of odd aversions to sanitary products or mentions of menstruation being viewed as impolite or improper in normal conversation. In general, society has no qualms with similar routine functions of the body; the common cold, allergies or the flu do not stray into an unspeakable realm, but the cycle of a woman certainly does. This cultural revulsion powers the counter-productive, anti-abortionist philosophy that abhors abortion but has virtually no interest in pursuing the only methods that have been proven to reduce and prevent abortions: proper sex education and contraceptives.

> "Most unintended pregnancies occur because birth control is not used properly or at all, according the Guttmacher Institute. Currently, half (51 percent) of all pregnancies in the United States are unintended. Nearly all (95 percent) of unintended pregnancies are caused by inconsistent use (43 percent) or nonuse (52 percent) of birth control. Forty percent of all unintended pregnancies in the United States end in abortion." [11]

There you have it – the answer to abortion is staring us all in the face – but the only words out of the mouths of the anti-abortionists are *repeal Roe v. Wade* and *teach abstinence*. This is an irrational proposal, and conveniently enough, the people who support it are simply not interested in rationality. And like many (if not all) irrational ideologies, it becomes less tenable as time passes. Fighting against the onslaught of female liberation is battle that is lost from the start; abortion is the windmill to the conservative Don Quixote. What value will a ban on this procedure have when Plan B pills can be ferried by drone to needy women across unfriendly borders? (Pro-choice activists occasionally use this method to circumvent Ireland's abortion ban.[11]) How can legislation stop a University like UC Davis from offering the morning-after pill in a vending machine? [12] The fight is infinitely unwinnable, the result of the battle is a foregone conclusion, and its only true variable is the number of women that will be needlessly killed before the nation comes to its senses. You might be familiar with the down-south English idiom "If it was a snake, it would have bit you." When it comes to the unintended consequences of making abortion illegal, the conservatives won't notice the snake *until* it bites them. I can spill gallons of ink outlining in meticulous detail all of the grotesque aspects of a society under the yoke of an abortion ban, but it lacks the emotional impact of watching your own daughter bleeding to death in your bathtub. It doesn't rile as much outrage as watching your wife land behind bars because she was unfortunate enough to have a natural miscarriage mistaken for an illegal attempt to terminate. Maybe this is really what the country needs; a new bloodletting, a new plague, a new epidemic of purposeless deaths in order to wake us all up.

Unfortunately, the problem with a great number of anti-choice people is that they have largely never considered the question beyond whether or not they personally *feel* abortion is wrong. To many – if not most – that is as far as the can gets kicked down the road. The potential problems are not just unintended, often, they are not considered entirely. I feel disgusted by a great number of things: Christian rock music, James Dobson, and Rupert Murdoch, just to name a few, but the answer isn't to ban or outlaw them because they upset me. The initial reaction has to transcend our immediate emotional response. Chris Mooney's work on the Republican brain is incredibly instructive at this juncture; the heightened sensitivity to disgust comes directly into focus. I understand that abortion *feels* wrong to a Christian mother when her experience with a nuclear family has been so rewarding. I can empathize with the conservatives when they express genuine concern about whether or not fetal tissue is alive, and whether or not this medical procedure ends another life.

The first objection is emotional, the second is intellectual, and when the emotional response infects the cognitive one, the conclusion will always suffer. And the selective nature of their empathy is illuminating, too. Who gets covered under their umbrella of concern is enlightening; those who march the streets of Washington D.C. to protest abortion do not always return to those same streets to protest against poverty, homelessness, and food insecurity. They are almost always focused *obsessively* on the act of abortion rather than the external forces that cause it. Conservatives are repulsed by the thought of a terminated pregnancy, and while it is their right to hold this view, I wish they wouldn't. I *wish* they were as passionate about ending violence against women as they are about opposing abortion. I *wish* they took their own convictions to heart and vigorously supported the two things that have been shown to reduce abortion the most: sex education and birth control. I *wish* religious women had the basic decency to support their fellow sisters during the most trying times in the lives rather than snidely judging them as harlots from afar. I don't hesitate to use the word 'immature' as an adjective for the anti-abortion movement for this reason. We don't need to speculate as to what will happen once abortion is outlawed, again, history is our guide. We know what sorts of misery this will cause, and we know that it will amplify, rather than diminish, human suffering. This suffering, of course, would not be for men to bear, but women. It would be yet another female-only burden for women to bear exclusively, and would expand the universe of oppression most men *never* come into contact with, even for a single moment.

"The US Surgeon General has declared that attacks by male partners are the number-one cause of injury to women between the ages of fifteen and forty-four. According to the standard nursing textbook, more than 1 million women seek medical care each year for injuries related to abuse; this makes up about 100,000 days of hospitalization and 30,000 emergency room visits. One-third of all female murder victims are killed by an intimate partner (compared to about 3 percent of male murder victims). More than three-fourths of these victims were stalked by that partner first. Murder ranks second (after accidents) as the leading cause of death among young women – and it is *the* leading cause of death among pregnant women. Beyond spousal homicide, or what is known in the field as "femicide," nearly six hundred thousand women are beaten by an intimate partner (husband, ex-husband, or boyfriend) every year – that's a little more than one per minute. It's the single most common reason that women go to the hospital emergency room. The threat to women extends beyond actual murder or battery – to simply eliciting fear in the lives of women. More than a million women are stalked in the United States every year. In two-thirds of the cases where a woman asks for, and receives, an order of protection from the police, that order is violated." 13

The number one cause of injury to women is *men*. This reality should knock the breath out of everyone's lungs. *Fifteen year-olds* are not safe from the violence of the men in their lives. How on earth did we let this happen? Why is it happening on such a large scale? To add insult to this constant injury, women are often slandered in the court of public opinion; they exaggerate the extent of their wounds, they imagine oppression where there is none, and they are lazy leeches, lying around the house, wanting alimony and sole custody of children. We do not say that victims of stroke or cancer were 'lazy' or suffered from a 'persecution complex' but female victims of assault are often looked upon with a suspicious eye.

This insane dynamic, again, finds its origin in the artifacts of our shared history, in the construction of the American state that gave unchecked and unchallenged power to white men for hundreds of years. Women, like minorities, were property of white men, subjected to their every whim, built for industry or pleasure, another aspect of the planet in which God had granted man dominion over. The portrait of who, exactly, perpetrates these offenses often bears the same likeness to the inadequate, insecure, sexually challenged, sexually intimidated, and above all else, angry white men. In their twisted perspective, women *owe* them loyalty, and are obligated to offer their bodies as sexual instruments, and their act of even existing is a crime of barbaric cruelty to their sensitive dispositions:

> "Think, for a moment, about the words we use to describe women's beauty, women's sexuality, women's attractiveness: they're words of violence and injury – to men. Women are ravishing or stunning; she's a bombshell or a knockout; she's dressed to kill, a real femme fatale. Women's beauty is perceived as violent to men: men use violence to even the playing field – or, more accurate, to return it to its previously uneven state that men thought was even. Men who have been convicted of rape and domestic violence tell a similar story – about how they got even with women, how they got revenge. Men's violence towards women does not happen when men's power over women is intact and unthreatened; rather, it happens when men's power breaks down, when his entitlement to that power is threatened and insecure." [14]

Violence against women occurs on such a large scale because feminism is working. The abuse is often punitive in nature, and stems from male insecurity, which backwardly views the vicious outbursts of violence as a method of preventing a loss of power in a relationship. These two events are plainly correlated, and the efforts to stop the bleeding and slow female progress share a common goal; to deny women the basic ability to control their bodies, to select what surgeries they can and cannot have, what industries they may or may not work in, and in so doing, the status quo is defended from an outsider assault. It is precisely this reality that gives me such pause when I encounter anti-feminist rhetoric in the open; how could anyone approach this movement with such calloused cynicism? Women have bought and paid for every civil advance in American society with *blood*.

I understand, at least in part, the pangs of insecurity that cut deep into a man's heart when a woman says or does something against our wishes. Almost all of our masculinity is defined by women, and we judge others, and judge ourselves, for how successfully we operate within these relationships. It is challenging to accept a woman as an equal; even more so when she is our superior, and our fathers, uncles, and grandfathers have taught us that when this occurs, it is as a result of a man's failure somewhere in the chain of command. We are naturally raised to look upon career-minded women in the workplace with suspicion, still harboring within our reptilian brains the notion of the primitive order of society, as hunter-gatherers whose men went to hunt, and whose women stayed to rear offspring. Those mental chains don't come off easy, and sometimes, they never come off at all.

In the same way I admit to being racist in the past, and simply attempt not to be in the future, I think I can make the same confession about being sexist. I have certainly been sexist in the past; for this, I repent, and resolve to do my best not to be in the future. And much like my unconscious, subconscious racism, my sexism strikes in the same sort of ways, too. It is difficult to squash the sort of gendered-pejoratives that arise in your brain when bruised by a woman in the workplace. When she is assertive, your vocabulary almost instinctively turns sour, but when a man behaves in an identical fashion, he takes no prisoners, he turns the ship around, and he doesn't suffer fools gladly. We needle our female counterparts in increasingly smaller ways; a collective chuckle amongst a group of men when she makes a misstep in the office, however slight, sends the covert message of hostility that all of us acknowledge but would never say outright. The proper image of femininity often does not exist in the male consciousness; women get pigeonholed into neatly compartmentalized roles, and when they don't fit, men become uncomfortable.

> "The three stages of women, as Anna Quindlen defined them – pre-Babe, Babe, and post-Babe – have now been expanded to four: pre-Babe, Babe, Botox Babe, and Cher. A few years back, some Hollywood TV producers I know were thinking about making a sitcom with Cher. Before they committed, they wanted to be sure that, after all the work she'd had done on her face, Cher could still actually move it. They went to her house and secretly tested her ability to react, asking questions to elicit various emotions. They ended up not doing the show." [15]

When women attempt to explain to men that they are exposed to discriminations, pressures, and expectations that men do not largely experience, male eyes begin to roll. The appearance-obsession American society has with women ("Does she have wrinkles? Then she's too old! Is her face too rigid because she had work done to fix the wrinkles? Then her face isn't versatile enough!") is utter nonsense. The rhetorical cycle used to defend it is always the same; first comes incredulous denial, followed by concession saddled with dismissiveness and condescension. Once the wounds can no longer be denied, and the impacts of them no longer marginalized, then the opposition starts to scour the planet for *anything* that counters the narrative; false rape allegations, female-on-male assault or rape, poor child custody verdicts, women taking advantage of legal systems, alimony, or child support rulings, or female sexual harassment in the workplace. Once the counter-narrative gets established, the crowd tightens their focus on an individual, or a group of individuals, who can be slandered with impunity, who can become scapegoats at the drop of a hat. Crucially, they can become, in the eyes of their detractors, incontrovertible evidence that proves all women operate this way secretly, and polite society is simply too squeamish to say this openly. When I write about violence against women, this, more than anything else, is spat back into my face. Angry white men sprint to cast aspersions upon feminism, and trip over their own feet to find *anything* that will invalidate their stories:

> "Women complaining about harassment? Actually, it's *men* who are the victims of harassment. "The way young women dress in the spring constitutes a sexual assault upon every male within eyesight of them," writes William Muehl, a retired professor at the Yale Divinity School. Warren Farrell argues that "consensual sex among employees," as he euphemistically calls it, is "courtship" when it works and "harassment" when it doesn't. If there is a problem with employer-employee sex, Farrell argues, it's because it "undermines the ability of the employer to establish boundaries because the employer often feels needy of the employee." See, the employee, the beneficiary of the sexual attention, is actually the one with the power...How about rape and sexual assault? Rape, Farrell argues, is not, as feminists have argued, simply a crime of violence. It's about sex. Younger, more attractive women are 8,400 percent more likely to be raped than older women, we're told. The general point that rape has a sexual component is, of course, not entirely wrong, despite the hyperbolic statistics. But to suggest that rape is a crime of sexual frustration implies that if only women would put out a little more often, rape rates would go down. (The reason younger women are more likely to be raped is also because they are more likely to be unmarried and out in the public sphere "unescorted," going to parties and on dates – and, of course, because the vast majority of sexual assaults are committed by a boyfriend, date, or someone the young woman knows.)" [16]

In these circles, I often find myself having to listen to inane and boorish lines of reasoning. Forced to verify my adherence to near-universal ethics. Yes, rape is always wrong, regardless of what gender perpetrates the act. Yes, assault is always wrong, no matter who is doing the assaulting. No one believes otherwise, except for the militant examples they are so skilled at dredging up. The mental gymnastics of the men's rights groups are so exhausting that they have to put everyone else through them, too. As an epidemic of women land in emergency rooms; their bodies bruised, battered, and blistered from an onslaught of savage violence, and these men *intentionally and with malice* block the bigger picture from their view, and focus their empathy on the exceptions rather than the rule. The metaphor I always return to at this juncture is simple: our house is on fire, and these men's rights firefighters want to put out the fire in the toolshed first. Is the fire in the toolshed a concern? Sure. Is it in any way equivalent to the scope of the entire house being set ablaze? Absolutely not, and to imply that it does impugns the character of innocent women everywhere. Drawing equivalencies at all *denies* the suffering of women, and gives the benefit of the doubt to weak, scared, and infantile men who would rather put the women that love them into a hospital bed than deal with their own mental, emotional, or psychological shortcomings like adults. I also must object to the notion that feminism represents a cultural toxin; occasionally this is submitted in the open, but usually, it is an implication, an undercurrent, pulsing underneath the surface of quasi-sexist language. The accusation is often simple; feminists criticize everything apart from themselves, and lack the basic self-awareness to act in a manner that men (again, placing themselves in a supervisory role over women) will accept. This blithely ignores the blistering and incisive criticism feminist intellectuals direct at their own cause:

> "Looks are the new feminism," says Alex Kaczynski, a reporter for the Times Styles section who has a new book on the volcanic "rejuvenation" industry called *Beauty Junkies*. "In order to have power, you've got to look as if you care about yourself. It's a banner way of advertising your competency. Look at Oprah – she's awesome, totally styled every day. I talked to high-powered women in New York like Peggy Siegal, the publicist, who told me 'Who has time to have kids?' Just taking care of her looks is a full-time job. Our looks now take up a huge space in our lives." Materialism has defeated feminism as well. In a sign of the times, Gloria Steinem was on the picket line when the first American De Beers store opened on Fifth Avenue in June 2005, protesting the evictions of Bushmen in Botswana to make room for diamond miners and the charges that the company dealt in "blood diamonds" used to finance civil wars in Africa. Her presence meant nothing to young Hollywood beauties who are pleased to shill for the diamond industry in magazine layouts and personal appearances. As Steinem stood outside, Lindsay Lohan was inside the party, gushing over the possibility that she could get to wear one of the big rocks. Asked by reporters about the Bushmen controversy, she shrugged it off: "I don't get involved in any drama." [17]

I won't have it said that this movement is one that turns a blind eye to its own shortcomings when powerfully moving work like this exists for all to read. To speak of feminism – as its detractors often do – with one solitary word, drained of nuance, complexity, and context is a crime. The United

States is chronologically not that far removed from slavery, and American women only gained the ability to fully vote in 1920. The artifacts – from slavery, from sexism – are still present in our world today, and in every aspect of life, women are being targeted by men. In their professional lives, they are paid less than men, passed over for raises and prestigious promotions in favor of less-qualified men, and are subjected to perverse campaigns of sexual harassment and violence.

> "When it comes to incomes from all sources including investments, men still make out better than women. Men's median income in 2010 was $1.54 for each dollar women received, my analysis of census data shows. The median income – half make more, half less – for men was $32,137, but for women just $20,831. Ignoring investment income, the pattern still holds. In 2010, men averaged $1.29 to the dollar earned by women. Men averaged $47,715 a year, women $36,931, a difference of $10,784 for the year. That's $207 per week less for women workers. A married opposite-sex couple with each partner at the average would make 12.4 percent more money – the equivalent of more than six weeks of extra pay – if both husband and wife earned the male average. The pattern of more pay for men is not just because men may choose more lucrative occupations or not take time off to bear children. Data disclosed by nonprofit organizations in the annual reports to the Internal Revenue Service (on form 990) show that among executives and managers men make much more than women." [18]

Men's rights activists are deluded enough to believe the "wage gap" for women is nothing more than a figment of the SJW imagination; the numbers, the data, the facts, of course, say otherwise, and damningly so. These variances cannot be explained away by saying the averages are skewed by stay-at-home mothers, or that more high-paying lines of work requiring physical labor are to blame. Let's call this *precisely* what we all know it to be; women get paid less because many of the men in charge decide to pay them less. This is the theme from which no critical thinker should ever depart. Women get beat because men choose to beat them. Women get raped because men choose to rape them. Women get sold because men decide to sell them. And, in the past, women didn't vote because men didn't let them. The violence against women will stop when men stop hurting them. Full stop. The responsibility is ours, men.

I have grown increasingly weary of having to dive into the sewer to drag confused, anti-feminist men out of their conspiratorial rat holes. The MRA's scurry around, digging into the trash, trying to find a glimmering piece of evidence that will once and for all invalidate the suffering of an entire gender. First, let us ask what *on earth* could motivate them to behave this way? Imagine the depravity; to hear the *crack* of bone, to see the bruising of skin, sinew, and tissue, and to be preoccupied first with what the man thinks, how the man had his feelings hurt, how a court case didn't go his way, how his poor choice in partner selection resulted in an unfavorable child custody battle, and how at every impasse a woman is somehow to blame for his every conceivable problem.

It comes as absolutely no surprise that these movements are often comprised of men who have been maligned (if only in their minds) by women. Their roster of combatants are overflowing with tired clichés. They are bitter ex-husbands who dislike child support payments and alimony, they are rotund men, of bulbous and bouncy figures, for whom a fulfilling sexual life might never come to fruition, and they are skittish egomaniacs with acrid personalities who have come to blame their constant and embarrassing strike-outs with the opposite sex on the failures of female discretion, rather than their own stunning lack of self-awareness. We know these characters well, all of us, and often, they are so adversarial to women because women are a thorn in their sides, a source of unfailing consternation, a wound that never heals, a sorrow that never dissipates. I don't condone their speech and behavior on account of this, but we should understand their motivations. These men hate women because there is often a score that was left unsettled, again, if only in their own minds.

I understand, too, as a man, the sickly wave of nausea that crashes over your every synapse when a woman rejects your advances. I remember, once, as a teenager, obtaining a phone number from an attractive girl, only to call up and get teased, and told she was too busy 'washing her hair.' It stung, and I have some sympathy for men who get emotionally bruised when they attempt to act on their natural desires. It hurts, and no one is saying otherwise. But this pain, like so many others, requires maturity to manage. This pain is not an excuse to act as you please, and the hurt feelings of a man is not the pinnacle of all human suffering. Women do not owe men their bodies, their attention, their time, or their affection. This presumption is pernicious. Men want women to fawn over them, to tend to their every discomfort and to fulfill every inane desire.

"When Paul Rudnick wrote the screenplay for the 2004 remake of *The Stepford Wives*, the ultimate feminist nightmare about men preferring hot zombies to complicated career women, he told me that he felt the "embedded biology" of romantic fantasies has not changed: "Men only evolve with a gun at their head. Men want a babe and don't care about her earning power. Women want a rugged poet or musician with a private jet." For women, accruing resources has limited value in attracting men, and might even have the opposite effect of scaring them off. "There's still social pressure – everyone looking at a guy with a wife who makes more money, going, 'He's the chick,'" Rudnick said. High-powered women, especially those with children, simply have less time to lavish attention on their men. A few years ago at a White House correspondents' dinner, I met a very beautiful actress. Within minutes, she blurted out: "I can't believe I'm forty-six and not married. Men only want to marry their personal assistants or P.R. women." I've been noticing a trend along these lines, as famous and powerful men took up with young women whose job it was to care for them and nurture them in some way: their secretaries, assistants, nannies, caterers, flight attendants, researchers and fact-checkers." [19]

It is this impulse, crucially, that informs so much of the female-targeting-mindset. Men who hate women want women to do exactly what they want, and if they don't obey, they will at least make them hurt, cause them some level of pain, some manner of injury, and in so doing, enforce any remaining semblance of their diminishing power:

"Esraa Yousria Saleh was walking down El Hussein, a busy street in downtown Cairo famous for its souvenirs and tchotchkes, when a man in his early 20s made eye contact with her. He followed her, circled her, then suddenly — she felt a hot breath in her ear: "I would like to put it all inside." Saleh, 28, a feminist and activist based in Egypt, was furious. Why did that man feel like he could look at her? Follow her? Say those lewd words to her? A May study from Promundo, an international research group, and U.N. Women sheds fresh light on men's motivations for harassing women on the streets in four areas in the Middle East: Egypt, Lebanon, Morocco and the Palestinian territories. "We know quite a lot about women and girls but [relatively little] about men and boys" when it comes to harassment, says Shereen El Feki, co-author of the report and the author of Sex and the Citadel: Intimate Life in a Changing Arab World. The report found that of the 4,830 men surveyed, as many as 31 percent in Lebanon to 64 percent in Egypt admitted to having sexually harassed women and girls in public, from ogling to stalking to rape…. About half the men surveyed, for example, said they felt stressed, depressed or ashamed to face their families. Perhaps harassing women is a way to assert their power, suggests Barker. These young men "have high aspirations for themselves and aren't able to meet them," he says. "So they [harass women] to put them in their place. They feel like the world owes them." In a place like rural Egypt, the situation is easy to understand, says El Feki. "It speaks to the mind-numbing tedium of being a young man [there]," she says. They can't find work. They can't afford to marry. They're stuck living with their parents. There is nothing to do. "They're in a suspended state of adolescence," she says. The harassment is also a way for young men to "get their kicks," says El Feki. When the men in the survey were asked why they sexually harassed women in public, the vast majority, up to 90 percent in some places, said they did it for fun and excitement. That is not how women see it. "It's not fun at all," says Saleh. "It's a nightmare." [20]

It is for this reason that I don't hesitate to say women are hunted for sport; to the men that stalk them, that molest them, that beat them, that rape them, that is precisely what draws them to those evil activities. Men find solace in the violence, they quell their anxieties through the blood-letting, and in targeting women, they inflate their sense of strength, vitality, and power. There is simply no way to separate this impulse from the vile rhetoric that infects the anti-feminist movement; they harass women for entertainment, and they are fueled by the tears of fearful women and girls. The logic (if one could call it that) applied by these goons is laughable. Perhaps my favorite exchange is found within the trove of documents released by the F.B.I. that detailed some of the harassment the victims of the GamerGate movement received:

> "Another suspect was interviewed around San Jose, California in late 2015. According to the report, he "considered himself to be a 'tech guy.'" who "often plays video games." He was "aware about Gamergate from reading about it on Google News" and recalled posting comments on 4chan mocking someone (likely also Wu) who he "considered a professional victim who *exaggerated the threats.*" He then "admitted to sending [a] *threatening email*" that he admitted "looked really bad." Although details about it are redacted, the report goes on to say that he "does not own a shotgun," which hints at its contents. "[Redacted] understood that it was a federal crime to send a threatening communication to anyone and will never do it again," the report concludes." [21] (Emphasis mine)

Yes, she exaggerates the threats, and for this, her harasser sent her a threat. This is so profoundly stupid it can hardly be believed, and yet, this cabal of internet geniuses are powerfully shaping the digital frontier, and will continue to do so for decades to come. At every second of the day, they are poisoning the internet, and attacking anyone who might dare to oppose them. The dynamic that powers it all, however, cannot be overlooked. The men who hate women attack them, then blame them for being victims: they were asking for the rape because their outfit was so scandalous, women are too stupid to understand sexual consent, women are too cunning and fabricate rape allegations after nights of drinking when there is a possibility of a payout, women deserve to be struck by their husbands when they are verbally abusive to their husbands, and again, at every impasse, what *can never* be said is that men, alone, are responsible for these unspeakable acts and no one else. Perhaps the most salient voice in this issue belongs to the man who helped create the *Violence Against Women Act*, Vice President Joe Biden:

> "This is a cultural problem. A fundamentally cultural problem. What is built into the system? The assumption that you must have done something. You knew him, you must have at least by implication consented to something. You must have led him on. There were laws all over the country that in fact contributed to this notion that there's no need to respect a woman's autonomy because it's just not that important. The other thing is that there are a lot of young men who come up because of that culture that they were raised in and think they have to be tough guys. They think, if you go to kiss her and she doesn't want to kiss you, pull her tight and kiss her anyway: "Be a man, stand up." There are those pressures that are waning, but they've existed. They've existed in society, but none of them justify anything other than parents beginning to teach their children, their boys, what appropriate conduct is, and we have to turn this idea on its head. Being a man means respecting a woman's autonomy, not invading a woman's autonomy. You want to be a strong man? Respect. Anybody who sits in a locker room [where] a guy says, "You know, I was out last night and I reached up and I grabbed her panties and I did this and that," and doesn't turn to the guy and says, "You horse's tail, what the hell is the matter with you?" — if you sit there and you act like, "Oh yeah, man, that's cool," it perpetuates this whole notion, so men have to begin to speak up." [22]

When Mr. Biden speaks here of rape culture, he sheds light on two fundamental aspects that underpin the entire epidemic; a compulsive need to blame the victim, and a cultural disease that has infected American men. In the first point, we see the harm in the MRA-rhetoric; casting obsessive suspicion on abused women *necessarily* leads to blaming them, and will, in the end, will condone the violence or offer its tacit support. In this second point, Vice President Biden offers a sobering indictment of American masculinity. Men, if our idea of strength is coercion, we have lost our way. Actual strength, actual courage, actual character is not found in our physical dominance of women, but in our ability to slay the demons lying dormant within our bones. It takes guts to address your own problems and deal properly with the issues that haunt us, especially when those problems are mental or emotional and so much stigma is attached to them. It takes courage to accept the full responsibility for your own actions and your own station in life. It takes bravery to see yourself as you actually are, warts and all, and focus in improving yourself rather than blaming women for all of your problems. We got lost, somewhere along the way, men, and it is time for all of us to grow up.

It isn't easy to treat all of the women in your life properly. It takes genuine effort not to fall victim to types of idiotic thinking that fuels the male-victim-philosophy. These intellectual diseases are so effective because they prey upon our weaknesses; they feed on the stabbing pains in our stomachs when an attractive woman turns us down, they are aroused by the anger that steams up through our skin when a woman contradicts us in the workplace, and they pounce on our most visceral sexual insecurities. The *real* man refuses to fall prey to these instincts. The *real* man refuses to raise a hand in anger to a woman, and refuses to be a passive spectator to it. The *best* type of men raise their sons to reject these impulses, too, and instead of passing down resentment, bitterness, and anger to the next generation they choose to become a shining example of how great men should act.

I do not, personally, speak about this virtue as if I have obtained it, or as if I have always practiced it perfectly. I have been blessed with an overabundance of devastatingly smart, beautiful, and wise women in my life, and it will be for them to decide if I have lived up to these ideals, not me. I struggle every day with how I ought to treat women, and like every other man, I'm human. I laugh at jokes I probably shouldn't, I don't always act as professionally as I should towards women in my workplace, and the way I treat my wife is never perfect. It is a work in progress, and I try to get better every day. To the women who are victims of men in recovery, I hope it comes as some consolation that there are great men in the world, and that some of us are trying to be greater men every day. We hope we can listen to you more carefully, we aspire to being your best allies as you tear down systems of injustice, and we strive to be the sort of men that we would like to see our own daughters bring home to dinner. A good author always avoids cliché, but here, I cannot resist: *every* woman is someone's daughter. Your daughters are not our property. Your daughters do not owe us anything. It is time we started to break free of these ancient instincts, and it is time to leave the caveman-mentality in the dustbin of history where it truly belongs.

American women cannot be equals in our society until we give them control over their own bodies. Women cannot be equals until they are given a reprieve from our constant attacks. Women cannot be equals until we refuse to create spaces in which they are unwelcome. Women cannot be satisfied until the architecture of our prejudices crumbles by our hands. Women will stop being raped when we stop raping them, men. Women will stop being murdered when we stop murdering them. Women will stop being physically assaulted when we stop assaulting them. Women will stop being harassed when we decide to stop harassing them. Women will make the same amount of money as us when we decide to pay them as equals. It is high time we *manned up* and refused to blame women for our own problems, refused to treat them as punching bags when we encounter big emotions we aren't mature enough to handle properly, refused to treat their bodies as our own property, refused to buy and sell them in human trafficking, refused to commodify their sexuality, and refused to shame them for the way they look, or the clothes they choose to wear. We can be better than this. It can all be better, and we can choose to make it so. We made this mess, men, and it is time we started to make *men* great again.

The War on Art and Education

‡‡

CHAPTER 4

"Never forget, the press is the enemy. The establishment is the enemy. The professors are the enemy. Write that on a blackboard one hundred times and never forget it." –Richard M. Nixon

═══

One could be forgiven for thinking - in light of all of the things American Christianity and political conservatism opposes - that the right-wing had declared war on anything remotely fun long ago. Intoxication, sexual freedom, and secular entertainment are among some of their fiercest enemies. Their desire to soak everything in Christianity puts it naturally at odds with a painting that might question the Virgin birth, or a science teacher that might not believe the Earth is only six-thousand years old, for example. Fundamentally, productive forms of artistic expression and education require some level of free-inquiry. This is a concession many Evangelicals are unwilling to make, and as a result, the Christian and politically conservative worlds are often galvanized against art and education. Both the Evangelical and politically conservative worlds fear, dread, and loathe the artist and the educator. These two vocations, in their view, are responsible for the erosion of their support, especially amongst young Americans. President Nixon said it plainly – if crudely – when he told Henry Kissinger that the professors were his enemies. Universities almost always lean left, and to the right-wingers, the campus is where good Christian Conservatives go to die. This battle is not an inconsequential fight to the Republicans; they spend millions of dollars every year trying to keep things like sex education and evolution out of American classrooms and curriculum. The Evangelicals and conservatives know that the most important front in their cultural war is the children, and they are fighting like hell to keep their influence over them as they mature intellectually and become more exposed to new ideologies and experiences.

I can speak to this experience personally, having grown up in the Midwest with Focus-on-the-Family style Christianity. I spent twenty years of my life as a devoted and fundamentalist Evangelical, and left the faith after four years in Bible college. At first, I studied music as a freshman at what was, at that time, the beating heart of contemporary Christian music; Greenville College. After spending a little under a year there, I switched majors to Pastoral Ministries and followed my fiancé to Lincoln Christian College. I can speak with some authority and experience about how, exactly, the Evangelical world looks on the inside, and how it wages a daily war of attrition against education and artistic liberty. Eve L. Ewing of the *New York Times* wrote an excellent column on why totalitarian systems view art as a threat:

"In 1937, ascending leaders of the Third Reich hosted two art exhibitions in Munich. One, the 'Great German Art Exhibition,' featured art Adolf Hitler deemed acceptable and reflective of an ideal Aryan society: representational, featuring blond people in heroic poses and pastoral landscapes of the German countryside. The other featured what Hitler and his followers referred to as 'degenerate art': work that was modern or abstract, and art that was produced by people disavowed by the Nazis – Jewish people, Communists, or those suspected of being one or the other…Hitler and those close to him strictly controlled how artists lived and worked in Nazi Germany, because they understood that art could play a key role in the rise or fall of their dictatorship and the realization of their vision for Germany's future. Last month, the Trump administration proposed a national budget that includes the elimination of the National Endowment for the Arts. The NEA operates with a budget of about $150 million a year. As critics have observed, this amount is about 0.004 percent of the federal budget, making the move a fairly inefficient approach to trimming government spending. Many Americans have been protesting the cuts by pointing out the many ways that art enriches our lives – as they should. The arts bring us joy and entertainment; they can offer a reprieve from the trials of life or a way to understand them. But as Hitler understood, artists play a distinctive role in challenging authoritarianism. Art creates pathways for subversion, for political understanding and solidarity among coalition builders." [1]

Before I delve any further, I should make clear that I am not interested in comparing the evangelical American right to Nazi Germany (I find the comparison useless and infinitely lazy to begin with,) rather, I am interested in drawing similarities between political or religious systems have enshrined the concept of the sacred. I should further preface my statements here (especially when it comes to the realm of art in any medium) with a broad disclaimer. Too often, vapid people volunteer to act as gatekeepers for art; declaring that one example or another does not qualify as proper art. The internet is infected with this superficial non-sense. Snooty people scour the world for artists who deviate from widely acceptable mediums ("She shoots paint out of her ass on to a canvas and we call it art?" they scoff), or crudely pick on abstract or absurdist paintings as childish. No such judgement will take place here in regards to Christian art, but I will make a distinction, however, if only valid in my own view, between *significant* art and art generated for other purposes.

Take a starlet like Justin Bieber, for example. He is the target of a lot of populist abuse, on account, mostly, of his fame. I have listened to his music, and I find nothing objectionable about it, primarily because I am also aware that his albums are *created for a different purpose* than most others. The art is largely designed for teenage girls, and I'm not part of that demographic. Expecting Mr. Bieber's work to be as intricate and technically proficient as Bach is foolish. In the same way that Justin Bieber writes songs to make money, Christian art creates content for a motive outside of artistic expression; they want to evangelize and tarnish the work of other artists. When I was at Greenville College, one of my closest friends was heavily involved with the art program at the university, and his primary mentor was a professor who made incredibly moving and intriguing sculptures. One recurring theme in his work was creating images of Jesus Christ with a visible erection. On the face of it, you might chuckle or scoff, but to me, the statement he was making was a compelling one; if Jesus was human, did he not tangle with this aspect of our experience? Did he not feel the pangs of romance and arousal? This was art that asked an uncomfortable question of its audience, and reflected the existence that it was created in, and did so at a level of complexity that still strikes me to this day.

It is easy to see why this type of questioning through the artistic process would ruffle feathers within a typical church. In my view, *significant art must ask questions,* and religious communities (as well as totalitarian political authorities) repress inquisition. Religious communities issue mandates and absolutes. Artists cannot create meaningful work under these conditions. Contrast, juxtaposition, and interplay are crucially important to the artist, and when these are stripped away, we are left with shallow art that has little substance. Christians go to war against art because they have something sacred to protect (the Voltaire quote about finding out what is sacred by discovering who you cannot mock is especially potent at this impasse), and because they want to eliminate a competitor and establish a monopoly on human existence. This may sound alarmist, even extreme, but I swear on my life this is completely true and isn't the least bit exaggerated.

It is not enough for Christians to simply believe what they believe. To borrow another phrase from Christopher Hitchens - no, it is not nearly enough - because they have to make you believe it, too. They have a divine mandate to go into the world to make disciples of Jesus Christ in all corners of the world, and I assure you, it is a pledge they take very seriously. It is not enough for them to put Jesus in their heads, they have to put him in yours, too. They aren't content to stay in the church, no, they want to be in the courtroom that governs Christians and non-Christians alike, they want to be in the classroom that teaches Christian children and non-Christian children alike, they want to be in your bedroom, deciding how you can have sex, and who you may have it with, and they want to be in your operating room, and they want to tell you what procedures you may have, and which medical procedures you may not have. Every aspect of life, including music, entertainment, television, art (again, no exaggerating), all of it needs to be centered and grounded in Jesus. *We need Jesus and the Ten Commandments back in our schools,* they blather incessantly; well, do they even know what those Commandments even say in the first place?

> "While Christian nationalists very much want to see the Ten Commandments play a larger role in the United States, they – and the majority of Americans (60 percent) – cannot name even five of the Ten Commandments. Surprisingly, research revealed that only 60 percent of American adults could even identify "thou shalt not kill" as a commandment. Given this, it should not be surprising that most people do not realize the number of commandments that would create an exclusively Judeo-Christian orientation for the government, and that they constitute almost half of God's decrees from the Mount, making the wish for a biblical justice system less than promising for religious freedom in the United States." [2]

This insatiable hunger for cultural domination is precisely why the Christian media machine turns up its nose in snooty judgement of the secular artistic world while simultaneously Xeroxing everything it creates. Americans who never spent time in the Christian church are often surprised to discover the cheesy, cringe-worthy phenomenon of CCM (Christian Contemporary Music) that grabs anything interesting from popular culture and plagiarizes it ruthlessly for wholesome Christian consumption. There is no exception to this rule – kids and teenagers want to listen to popular genres of music, and God-fearing parents worry about all those fucking swear words – so a thriving counterfeit market sprang up organically in these Christian circles. Eminem had a Christian copycat, so did Nirvana, and so does any other notable act you can possibly imagine. The fundamental hole in this logic is unavoidable; the finished product ends up, almost invariably, as seeming like an off-brand cereal from a discount grocery store. It looks the same, sort of, and feels a little bit like the original, but it doesn't really fool anyone. The forgery, which has the added obligation of adhering to the Christian ethos, can copy the blueprint of the original artists, but cannot build on the aspects of the work that require intoxication, vulgarity, androgyny, or sexual exploration. More worryingly, their incessant evangelical message has the loathsome effect of disabling any ability to discuss other issues meaningfully.

In 1988, N.W.A released *Straight Outta Compton*, an album now widely considered to be a timeless classic within its genre. *Fuck the Police*, N.W.A's cornerstone single from that record, was a caustic rebuke of police brutality in black neighborhoods, and contained a powerful political message that spoke to an audience that was thirsty for someone, anyone, to talk about what their lives were like under the yoke of systematic racial oppression. In 1992, Christian group D.C. Talk released a song entitled *Two Honks and a Negro* (the group was comprised of two white members and one black member) whose lyrics dully relayed in acapella fashion that they were "just two honks and a negro serving the Lord." I leave it to the reader to decide which of these examples is trite, juvenile, and valueless.

Of course, there are plenty of terrific Christian artists that simply create their own work without any interest in luring their audiences away from other secular artists. Even as a stone-cold atheist, there are still plenty of Christian bands that I love, and still listen to routinely. The exception to the rule isn't my concern. The rule, to be blunt, is my concern; the plagiarists take to the market in the interest of riding the wave of anything popular, skidding along on the coattails of other more honest and more creative artisans. As mentioned earlier, the Christian world does this for three primary reasons – to compete with the secular world, to protect sacred institutions, and to create a human monopoly – and I'll explain each one in depth.

Competition

People do not go to church simply because they feel it is a righteous duty. As with anything, humans have a multitude of varying motivations for religious adherence, but perhaps the most compelling driver in the American branch of Christianity is the pursuit of *entertainment*. Religion is big business in the United States, and the Sunday morning service of today would be largely unrecognizable to the Christians who worshipped a century ago. The hymnals and pews are often gone, replaced with the stadium-style seating of expansive super-churches. The pipe-organ is gone, too; usurped by the electric guitars, drum kits, and keyboards of modern rock music (usually delivered in a sort of bland, U2-ish fashion). Don't be mistaken – Christians are done with the drab and boring traditional orthodoxy, save for some of the more dedicated sects, and they want every bit of the glamour of secular entertainment.

As a teenager in the church, I was encouraged not to even listen to secular music. Non-Christian music could only steer you away from the Lord, so young and impressionable teens were rabidly advised to prohibit their intake of non-religious media of all kinds. This was a directive I followed up until I was fifteen or sixteen years old (you can only go so far as a guitarist listening to hymns). When you are a dedicated Christian – especially when your dedication reaches to this depth – every single thing you intake is an opportunity to sin. This is no exaggeration, either; Christians are taught that even one single sin would have been enough to stick Jesus to the cross, and by sinning willfully, you are driving the nails into his very skin. This creates mental tension, and every bit of stimuli has to be first run through the filter of holiness. Does this movie edify the Lord? Will the attractive leading actress tempt me with her shapely body? Does this album create feelings of hostility towards the perfect truth in the Bible? The mental gymnastics required for this level of discipline are *exhausting*, and being able to relax in the knowledge that your newly-found source of entertainment is sanctified is a big part of the appeal.

The Christian world, in many pockets, vilifies secular art because it knows that if a person is able to turn off these filters, it might be entertained by high-quality media and might not rely on the church for its entertainment needs. It has to go to battle with non-Christians on principle, anyway. Jesus has 'gifted' his disciples with their talents, so it stands to reason that these cultural warriors should be more highly-skilled than their secular peers. This, like many other Christian campaigns, is a foolish and self-defeating one. There's a reason non-religious television, music, and art are, on the whole, markedly better than these alternatives. They are the originals, not the knock-offs. They are the name brands, and the Christian world makes poor-quality copies.

Protecting Sacred Institutions

When I studied Hebrew at Lincoln Christian College, I was introduced to the concept of the *Tetragrammaton* as it appeared in the text of the Old Testament. In English, it is rendered as "Yahweh" and is the most holy name of God. Orthodox Jews, we were told in class, do not only refuse to pronounce this word out of reverence, but will often cover their ears if they overhear it in conversation. In all religions, there is the concept of holiness, but within the Abrahamic sects, this infatuation is often all-encompassing.

Islam forbids any image of their prophet, Muhammad, and will follow their own pronunciation of his name with a brief praise or blessing. It stands to reason, of course, that within these religious communities lies a strong desire to protect and defend the reputations of the gods they worship. American Christians have the same predilections as their Islamic counterparts; perhaps in less intensity, but the same propensity lies within their bones all the same.

I return, again, to the notion that powerful art is *necessarily* critical, inquisitive, and political. This cannot exist within the walled garden of fundamentalist religion, and it is no surprise that these same devotees lash out at any artist that mocks or blasphemes their gods. Artists don't do well with boundaries or limits anyway; one could argue that the flexing and straining of socially accepted norms are also another indispensable aspect of high quality art in any medium. To that end, Christians are in the business of recruiting new followers. Christian art and Christian media are designed to entertain existing followers and are used as a recruiting tool to recruit new ones. They are eager to give the impression that they are quite laid back, and able to express themselves artistically without restraint. This is flatly untrue, of course, and there is only one unpardonable sin in the Bible that the Lord will not forgive; blasphemy of the Holy Spirit. Don't be fooled by the cheap veneer Christians have pasted over the rotting teeth of their religion – they think you'll go to hell for mocking their gods – and the safe space they build for themselves is suffocating. The Christian desire to be *cool* strikes here again; they, themselves, don't want the stuffy organ music, or the rigid wooden pews anymore. They want electric guitars, they want the illusion of edgier music, they want all of the bells and whistles of modern media without having their religious feelings hurt, or their religious beliefs challenged. It is cowardice that is practiced on a stunningly large scale.

In a modern Christian church, you are just as likely to see someone sculpting, painting, or dancing during a church service as you are to see someone singing. This is all well and good, and in all sincerity, I would rather all Christian artists have a space to express themselves, even if it is latently North Korean in nature. Some expression is better than none at all, but I simply cannot abide with the notion that art can truly breathe in the noxious smoke of unquestionable leader-worship. This environment gives the world Thomas Kinkaid, rather than Pablo Picasso. Which world would you rather live in?

Monopoly

One of the clearest edicts in the Bible (as is often the case) is perhaps the most frequently ignored; judge not, lest ye be judged. Condescension is one of the most attractive and appealing facets of any religion. *You* have the answer. *Your* god is the best (sometimes only) path to salvation or enlightenment. Who could forget the conceded ramblings of Tom Cruise in that now-infamous Scientology video? When an ambulance races past a Scientologist stuck in traffic, Mr. Cruise explained, they are the only ones who can *really* help. Oh, those *stupid* paramedics, trying in vain to help injured people with their silly bandages and street drugs. Can you imagine the kind of self-delusion it takes to reach this advanced level of idiocy and self-righteousness?

The trek to that summit of stupidity is not an easy one, and once you reach the peak, perhaps one of the few comforts allowed to you is a smug sense of superiority. This intellectual phenomenon is alive and well within the walls of American churches, and it is one of the primary reasons, in my view, that religion has such a wide appeal. There is a *right* answer for every vexing problem, and by embracing it, you are now part of something that contains all of the good in life with none of the bad. Is there a reason to partake in non-religious activities after you've accepted the faith? Does the world have anything to teach you once you've reached the answer to all of existence? Pose this question to most Christians, and they suddenly become contrite and humble; they don't have all the answers, but God does. They want Jesus to take the wheel. They are imperfect beings throwing themselves against the holy perfection of God.

Christianity, despite its outward babblings about tithing and charity, is simply not interested in improving this planet. Their treasure, as they will openly tell you themselves, is not stored up on this earth, but in heaven. They have written off our entire existence as a lost cause, and what they are looking to build is a church that casts out sin to draw nearer to God. They want that church to be all, to contain all, to incorporate and to carry all of the value of human life within their monopoly. They evangelize for this purpose – every person is created in the image of God, and the Lord has made a path to salvation for them if only they were smart enough or disciplined enough to just accept it – and their perfect world is a heaven with all of humanity inside of it. Think for a moment exactly what that would look like; all of the culture, color, music, spice, and flavor that this planet has to offer in all of its vastly varied corners, all crushed and smashed together into a bland homogenized grey. Could you imagine anything more drab? Could you imagine anything more hopelessly *boring?* This is precisely why I speak so ominously about this genuinely menacing threat – they do not want dissent, discourse, compromise, or fairness – they want more people who think exactly like them, and won't stop until everyone in existence does. They are openly and actively seeking to crudely separate the world into believers and non-believers. When they can't accomplish this on earth, they pout, and snidely inform us that this is the order of the supernatural world in the next life so we had better get used to it now.

A typical American Christian will tell you that God has a perfect plan for every single one of his children, but humans are too sinful, arrogant, prideful, and indulgent to accept this plan. God's divine plan, they will tell you, without batting a single eyelash, includes the horrors of childhood cancers, genocide, or literally any other human tragedy. God tests us, God knit us together inside the womb, and God is wise in a way that our human brains could never comprehend. Well, what of the Holocaust, then? The Lord, in his infinite wisdom, watches with total indifference as millions upon millions of his children are callously murdered by German fascists? Am I to accept this as just? Am I really expected to have it all explained by God upon my arrival to heaven? This willful release of critical thinking is another powerful recruitment tool for religion. Any problem, no matter how vexing, sensitive, or complex can be explained with a shrug and an extended finger towards the sky. Only God truly knows, only god can truly explain it all, and we're just going to hang on until we all reach those pearly gates. Your wife died? God called her home. Your daughter got cancer? Keep praying and the Lord will answer. The pastor isn't in the business of giving out answers. They're in the business of securing more fervent devotion.

When I made the choice to enter the ministry, I was attending my first year of Greenville College as a music major. I had played guitar for most of my life, and between ice hockey and a slew of teenage bands, I had tried, unsuccessfully, to become a professional at both hockey and music at the same time. On account of my upbringing, I would have always considered myself a Christian first, and anything else second, of course, but I was always drawn to niche kinds of interests, and had trouble accepting popular things. This was, at least in some ways, a result of my own immaturity. I soaked in the same kind of counter-culture condescension I described earlier. I didn't wear name brand clothing as a teenager because I didn't want to be a 'conformist.' As I matured, I started to realize that the humanity was in a constant state of suffering. The single thought that motivated me the most to change my major to Pastoral Ministries was a simple one; I just wanted to help people. Just like Tom Cruise, I thought a spiritual problem was the root cause of all the other problems, and I believed sincerely that if I devoted myself fully to my religion, I would make the world a better place. The monopolistic mentality struck again, and I went out show the rest of the planet what real Christianity looks like up close.

Some of my earliest memories revolve around a ratty truck stop in my hometown of Foristell, Missouri. My father – a devoted Evangelical with Puritan sympathies – would take me along to observe his witnessing attempts with tired and beleaguered truckers. The command in Scripture is clear; Christians are to take as many souls with them as they can to heaven, and my dad took this edict seriously. The highlights of the trips for me were the ice cream scoops served in plastic replicas of baseball helmets. I liked to pick obscure teams with odd color schemes (like the Seattle Mariners) and reveled in the novelty of the helmets, along with other quarter-machine trinkets. I didn't really have the ability to sit still as a child (likely a result of the ADHD I had that wouldn't be diagnosed until adulthood), and my dad likely had his hands full trying to carry on spiritual conversations while I jittered with boredom in the seat next to him.

I can't speak to the content of these conversations (I was far too young) or to how many trips we took, but the purpose, importance, and intensity of this evangelism was not lost on me. This was a war waged against demons, against Satan, against the forces of evil that create every bad thing in existence. It was a somber responsibility, and it was to be taken seriously. The truck stop was just one of his spiritual battleground. He wrote incredulous letters to the management about the availability of pornography in these retail outlets and spent time witnesses to the people who frequented them, but he also used his programming expertise to maintain the early webpages of *MetroVoice*, a far-right Christian online magazine that espoused the virtues of conservative Christianity. As I grew into adolescence, my weekends were often filled with acts of service to members of our church or acquaintances my dad had met at the truck stop.

The differences in our perspectives – both then and now – are striking, and I am compelled to believe these exist above our ability to control them. My mother would often find me asleep underneath an Encyclopedia, knocked out while soaking up as much information as possible. As mentioned earlier, some of my desire was fueled by vanity, I think, even at a young age. Everyone wants to be seen as smart, and I wanted to be respected for my intellect. At the same time, I don't think I could have chosen to be attracted to the pursuit of knowledge. I think it was a predisposition, and one that I had no ability to control. I saw the world, even as a child, as a thing that had something to teach me. When I look at the religious, and how they purport to have eternal answers, I can't help but think the opposite is true; they see the world as something that has something to learn *from them*. I am repulsed by this perspective, and see it as incurably arrogant and profane.

Education

American conservatism roundly opposes proper education, and reviles educators for many of the same reasons that they oppose free expression and art. In their perspective, the traditions of their past are under threat from moral relativism and permissiveness. The enemies of the conservative movement are actively plotting their demise, and are eager to corrupt the children of believers. This is an imagined threat (much like the spooky 'gay agenda' Republicans liked to complain about throughout the 1990's) but the influence they wield over our educational systems is very real.

> "One of the most articulate critics of the philosophical premises for twentieth-century education is Bob Jones faculty member Guenter Salter. Salter, a Vanderbilt Ph.D in philosophy and Dean of the College of Arts and Sciences at BJU, published a series of articles in *Balance,* a monthly periodical published by BJU dealing with various aspects of education. In two articles, Salter has set forth an argument for the superiority of a Christian liberal arts education and a critique of modern secular education...Salter believes that underlying secular education is an insidious philosophy called humanism. Humanism 'embraces the doctrine of evolution; declares heredity and environment to be responsible for a person's value system; dismissed all absolutes, [and] makes man the measure of all things.' Most important, however, humanism is 'entangled in a net of self-contradiction and resultant absurdity.' Among its major fallacies, humanism attempts to ridicule the idea of faith in God while simultaneously affirming faith in man and reason...Salter sums up by observing that 'as a philosophy, humanism simply fails the test because of its inconsistency. The Christian is not surprised; for all things undertaken without God are senseless and utterly devoid of value." [3]

This is Christian nihilism at its most sneering and hateful apex. It should be understood, in the interest of fairness, that Bob Jones University does not represent the median opinion of American Christianity. They are a pariah within Christianity itself, and could be most accurately characterized with the extremist fringe of the conservative Christian world. The excerpt cited above comes from Mark Taylor Dalhouse's superb book on Bob Jones University, *An Island in the Lake of Fire,* and in it, he details the depth of BJU's stunning bigotry:

> "The exclusion of African-Americans from BJU was justified on the grounds that they might date white students, intermarry with them, and thus bring about the 'one-worldism' of the Anti-Christ. So the university administration was hostile to the civil rights movement. Jones Jr. refused to sign an act of compliance with the 1964 Civil Rights Act because, as he wrote to the United States Commission on

Civil Rights, it 'is a subtle and high-handed scheme to force all educational institutions under the control of a federal agency.' Later BJU awarded an honorary doctorate to Alabama Governor George C. Wallace, whom Jones Jr. praised as a 'David, warring against the giant, Tyranny.' The school remained racially segregated. Then, a 1970 lawsuit brought by African-American parents in Mississippi led the Lawyers Committee for Civil Rights to argue that tax exemptions for private schools practicing racial discrimination undermined integration in public schools…In *Green v. Connally* (1971) a three-judge court ruled that private schools in Mississippi that discriminated against African-Americans were not entitled to tax exemption. The court then ordered the Internal Revenue Service to deny exemption to these schools…The IRS proceeded with the revocation of BJU's tax exemption in 1976, making it retroactive to 1970. BJU, the IRS declared, now owed the federal government more than $490,000 in taxes. In compliance with the IRS, BJU filed returns for the 1970-1976 period. The university then paid $21.00 in unemployment tax for one employee in 1975 and requested a refund. The IRS refused, and BJU promptly sued for the $21.00 while the IRS countersued for $490,000. Meanwhile, the original reason for the IRS action, the BJU admissions policy, was no longer an issue. In 1975, the university adopted an open admissions policy. BJU continued to enforce its ban on interracial dating, however." [4]

The ban against interracial dating at Bob Jones University, if you can believe it, wasn't lifted until March 3rd, 2000. As stated earlier, I do not present these bigots as an average reflection of an American Christian, but to claim they (and fundamentalists like them) have no influence or power in the Evangelical world be equally disingenuous. My parents purchased homeschooling curriculum from Bob Jones University, and I grew up reading these textbooks. They were as nasty and vicious as you might expect; they claimed evolution was a hoax, and African poverty was a direct result of worshipping idols.

"Another service and a networking resource for BJU are the textbooks published by Bob Jones University Press. In existence since 1972, the Press publishes textbooks in Bible, English (reading, literature, writing and grammar), social studies, math, computer science, science, and music. In addition, the Press publishes an academic skills evaluation program. Field representatives visit most schools with the textbook offerings…the Press advertises its science curriculum as 'free of distortions of truth such as evolution and humanism." [5]

To belabor the point – my intention is not to draw equivalencies between the racist belief structure of hardline Evangelicals to the more moderate and centrist ideologies of average Christians. The overwhelming majority of American Christians are not extremists, they don't mind drinking a beer at a barbeque, don't mind watching racy shows on television, and don't take issue with basic science being taught to their children. However, the Evangelical fundamentalists cannot be ignored. They exist, they have influence, and they intentionally poison education with malice. The society they want looks every bit as totalitarian and creepy as North Korea:

> "First year students are required to enroll in a year-long orientation class that meets twice weekly. University officials use this class to explain the rules and what is expected of the students…The rules at BJU cover nearly every conceivable situation a college student might encounter. The most obvious offenses, which according to the handbook are 'fleshly living, adultery, homosexuality, sexual perversions of any kind, dishonesty, drugs, drinking, gambling, profanity, obscenity, dancing, card-playing, movie-going and pornography,' are strictly prohibited…Off-campus dating for all students is not allowed unless the couple is accompanied by a faculty member or a married couple. For on-campus dating, the 'dating parlor' is available. The dating parlor is a huge room in the Student Center complete with sofas and love seats where students may talk with, but not touch, one another. Even if engaged to be married, couples may not kiss or hold hands, and in the dating parlor only one partner at a time can have an arm on the back of the sofa. A large desk sits at the entrance to the dating parlor where a monitor enforces the 'no-touching' rule. If, for example, a couple were caught to be holding hands, they would be 'socialed,' that is, they may not see or speak to each other for a week. The crime of kissing carries a penalty of ten demerits plus being 'socialed' for a month…Certain sidewalks on campus are also off-limits after five o'clock because students may not be as readily observed." [6]

Again, in the interest of fair representation, Dalhouse's book was published in 1996. Surely, BJU looks much different now than it did then, and they may not currently engage in such rabid practices on campus any longer. What should not be overlooked here is the *slave mentality* that enables all of this submission. Could you imagine surrendering your every impulse and desire to people like these? Because, to put it bluntly, people like those *are imagining every day* what they would do if they had the power to put you under their greasy thumbs. As any resident of Texas or Kansas can tell you, the extremist right knows how to throw their weight around, and they have become quite skilled at distorting the truth. Their influence is not confined to private Christian schools or universities; the moral majority is coming for your children's curriculum.

> "Of the many barking idiocies to which Kansas proudly affixed its good name over the last decade and a half, the most memorable by far was the 1999 decision by the State Board of Education to delete references to macroevolution and the age of the earth from the state's science standards. So perfectly did the move fit the larger cultural set piece of Rubes versus Reality that the national media could not resist. They descended on the state in multitudes and commenced immediately to file stories alternately deploring and scolding. The cynical mocked Kansas on the late-night talk shows. The moralistic reprimanded Kansas on the editorial pages. The contemplative found in Kansas a timeless illustration of fundamentalism's tragic inability to accept or understand our advanced secular world. As every high schooler knows, fundamentalism had taken this route before. The nation had laughed Nebraska Democrat William Jennings Bryan into the grave for it after the Tennessee "Monkey Trial" in 1925. Embracing biblical creationism has been synonymous with backwoods cluelessness ever since. "It is not often that a single state can make a whole continent ridiculous," wrote George Bernard Shaw after the trial, "or a single man set Europe asking whether America has ever really been civilized. But Tennessee and Mr. Bryan and brought off this double event." To ask for a rematch on this battlefield was to embrace a legacy of folly, ignorance, and humiliation." [7]

The deluded Evangelical censorship brigades often targets evolution in school curriculum. To be blunt, proper sex education and *The Origin of Species* are their most well-worn punching bags, and the rejection of these topics are detrimental to the development of young minds everywhere. I was raised to deplore Darwin as a child; and other Christian homeschoolers likely read from the same Bob Jones textbooks that I did. If given the option, Christian fundamentalists will leave rationality and common sense mutilated, mangled, and obliterated in their wake. Even worse, these attacks on science and reason are often punitive in nature; arising from, or enabled by, the anger of trigged Evangelicals when they feel the secular world has overstepped their proper boundaries.

> "When a high-profile court case ended in June 2003 with the removal of the Ten Commandments from an Ohio public school, the Kansas Conservative Listserv exploded in outrage. Public schools were

"snakepits," declared a former county GOP chairman, and the authorities that caused the Commandments to be removed were "totalitarian liberal judges," "crypto-Nazis" who longed to "ghettoize" Christians. Another participant objected to the very term *public schools*, calling them "government schools" and later upgrading that to "government indoctrination centers." A third helpfully pointed out that "Christian children in public schools are deliberately subjected nearly daily to the leftist pro-homosexual pro-evolution pro-abortion propaganda of the leftist socialist NEA." The consensus eventually reached was that conservatives should have no dealings with public schools at all, although one participant gamely suggested that the kids ought to go as "warriors" against the satanic regime." [8]

These kinds of fiery diatribes against the horrors of the secular world were quite common within the walls of the churches I grew up attending. This type of logic is not confined to the lunatic fringe; there is a clear separatist bend to an alarming amount of religious rhetoric, and doubly so when religious leaders dip their toes into political waters. This should come as no surprise. Evangelical Christianity and political conservatism are not shy about articulating their vision for the United States. They are quite clear with their demands; they want to limit racial and ethnic integration, curb entitlement programs for the poor, and crucially, they want our country to return more fervently to its Judeo-Christian roots. Perhaps most troubling (and most divorced from reality) is the undercurrent that flows throughout this mindset – where the non-Christian world is psychopathically eager to put believers through a Holocaust – and when the Evangelicals don't get their way, the opposition to their proposals serves as incontrovertible proof that the blueprints have already been drawn up, and at any moment, the liberals are ready to pounce. The children must have their minds hardened against the "leftist propaganda" and the best way to accomplish this goal is to influence public school curriculum. And *yet again* we return to another keystone conservative trope; where being denied the ability to impose religious beliefs on others is tantamount to religious persecution.

"For example, Kansas's anti-evolution crusaders insist that it is the science community – not the fundamentalists – that is trying to impose its religious views on everyone else; that it is the science community – not the fundamentalists – that engages in "censorship of contrary evidence"; that it is the science experts who are "dogmatic" and "narrow-minded"; that it is these same experts who are irrational and emotional, unable to face reality; and that the reason no articles refuting evolution are ever published in professional, peer-reviewed journals is that those journals are biased…What's more, these arbiters of professional rectitude wanted no backtalk. "Once you weren't supposed to question God," wrote Gregg Easterbrook of *The New Republic,* clearly caught up in the Kansas spirit. "Now you're not supposed to question the head of the biology department." [9]

Conservatives – religious and non-religious alike – attack the public school system in the United States for a litany of various reasons. Occasionally these motives align, overlap, or diverge from one another, but as with nearly all things Republican, a nasty racial element is never too far removed. The assault on a proper education is fueled by the same ideological backbone of white anxiety and white resentment.

> "The public schooling of children has long been a focus of dog whistle politics. Public education provides easy race-baiting opportunities and in addition it is also a favorite bugaboo of anti-government conservatives. In terms of race-baiting, where once "forced busing" offered a favorite dog whistle, the fact that public schools now are highly segregated by race and in many areas primarily serve nonwhites has allowed public education to be recast as exemplifying white tax money being wasted on unruly youths. Then, in terms of conservative politics, schools constitute both the enemy and an opportunity. They are a natural target as an expensive social service, but the very funds going to education also represent an attractive opportunity to divert public money to private corporations. Schools are also well suited for the more camouflaged form of rightwing racial politics that seeks to push nonwhite faces at the fore: conservatives can argue that they are attacking public education because they care so deeply about protecting nonwhite kids. Consider the pitch on education offered by House Majority Leader Eric Cantor, a Tea Party favorite, put forward after the 2012 elections temporarily motivated the GOP to rebrand itself as committed to serving minorities: "I've talked about a man who is a dad here in the inner city of the District of Columbia who, all he wanted was to find a safe place for his kids to learn...I think what we care about, and what he cares about, is his kids." Cantor's proffered solution? Provide direct funding to parents looking to pull their children out of public schools." [10]

The conservatives gut the Department of Education out of *concern* for the oppressed minorities in the United States. One would need a lobotomy to believe this kind of shameless drivel. Brazen appeals to white purity within discussions of public school policy are far from uncommon, too. One such exchange took place in my home town of St. Louis, Missouri:

"Here in the St. Louis area, this is exactly what parents from a number of area school districts are asking after a court decision this summer ordered school districts to accept students who wished to transfer from schools that had lost their accreditation. That meant that this fall, some 2,000 students in the St. Louis area are now attending schools outside their home districts, some of them are facing long bus rides. And the run-up to the transfers was filled, as you might expect, with some emotion from parents who worry that their children's own achievement would be hampered by newcomers, and others who worried that their children would not be well treated." [11]

Parents of the predominantly white receiving school districts threw insane tantrums, and the dialog quickly devolved into hysteria. Beth Sorami, a parent of a receiving school asked "where the metal detectors are going to be, and I want to know where your drug-sniffing dogs are going to be. And I want – this is what I want – I want the same security that Normandy (an unaccredited school) gets when they walk through their school building. And I want it here." The implications of these questions are barely veiled at all; black students will bring crime and drugs and violent to the white schools. The war on teachers, on education, on public schools is a means that serves a whole lot of conservative ends. We can say two things of the religious and politically conservative movements in the United States without controversy. They are interested in preserving the traditional architecture of power as it existed in the past, and they stand in opposition to progressive ideologies that challenge this order. Conservatism, no matter how gradual or slight in its degree is a wink and a nod and nudge backwards into time. The world, in all of its turmoil, conflict, nuance, and complexity, can be reduced, in their perspective, down to good, old-time religion and family-centered valued. It wouldn't be fair for me to draw a line from Bob Jones University to moderate Republicans, but I can draw a line from the Republicans to Bob Jones University. *That* is where the Republican path, if left unchallenged, ends up.

THE UNITED STATES OF REPRESSION

The Conservative Sex Obsession

‡‡‡

Chapter 5

"Sex education classes are like in-home sales parties for abortions." – Phyllis Schlafly

═══

"This is a piece of simple scotch tape," The youth minister explains, as she peers through the translucent plastic, squinting, with one eye closed. "Look at how clear it is! I can see right through it. Now, I'm going to stick it to my arm." She slaps the adhesive strip on her forearm, presses down gently, and swiftly rips it off her skin after a just few moments. She dangles the tape between her thumb and forefinger, and holds it up high for the whole church to see in the light. "Isn't that gross?" She proclaims, her voice thickened with bemused disgust. "This tape was pure and unblemished before...but who wants to use it now?"

It's with this sneering attitude that children are often taught about human sexuality within the walls of many American churches. Natural urges are shamed, sexual expression is to be strictly confined, and practiced only within the boundaries of marriage. Americans are quite familiar with this drivel; they've been beaten to death with this message for decades. The evidence shows, of course, that abstinence is anything but a solution, but this fact hasn't stopped conservatives from forcing it down the nation's collective throats. This perspective is informed by one of the darkest

96

corners of human sexual history; the edicts found in the Bible originate from eras in which pre-pubescent children were married against their will, where powerful men took hundreds of wives and concubines, where women were traded as callously as property, and where pedophilia was often practiced openly. From this time period, humanity is to derive its sexual ethics, according to the "moral majority." This is insanity, and shouldn't be believed by a thinking person. The Christian sexual *ethos* is much more than just another reprehensible policy in an ocean of them; rather, it is an illuminating look into the typical conservative mind as it struggles with self-repression of hidden sexual urges. The symbiotic relationship between disgust and arousal are on display in this arena. Religion has, historically, a rather strange relationship with sex. It is a stumbling block in ways that other more mundane biological imperatives, like drinking, eating, or breathing, simply are not. Americans are well-accustomed to the typical religious perspective on sexual intercourse; this dirty business is only to take place between a man and a woman and only after they are married.

This prudishness is amusing if nothing else - these are rules that nearly everyone fails to follow anyway - but the stated aims of the conservative sex mantra is duplicitous, even upon first glance. Oddly enough, if one is looking for the height of sexual depravity, one should look no further than the Holy Bible itself: replete with lurid tales of incest, group sex, and temple prostitution, among other forms of debauchery. The conservative world obsesses over sex because it is an important element of social control that, when wielded effectively, represses women, preserves male authority, and subjugates homosexuals. From the perspective of the Focus on the Family-style Evangelicals, alternative sexual orientations and practices are an assault on the nuclear family. To them, homosexuality, polyamory, and non-binary gender identities are an existential threat to the Christian way of life. This, at least in part, accounts for the intensity of their political and religious fervor. All of their values (referred to, with nauseating frequency, as 'traditional' or 'Biblical' values) are under siege by the secular world. The paranoia among Evangelicals is pervasive and incredibly real. Like many other lame Bible-College hipsters, I got two Christian-themed tattoos (an edgy choice whilst attending a Christian university in Central Illinois). Upon showing this brand new artwork to my roommate, he expressed approval, but explained that he could never get similar tattoos because he intended on being an undercover member of the Christian underground resistance when the Anti-Christ rose to power and started murdering believers. This extreme viewpoint is not a unique one in the conservative circles of the Evangelical movement.

The counter-culture warriors of the religious right have drawn the clearest line in the sand around the pillars of human gender and sexuality.

The selection of this point of contention above all others is intentional and calculated – the liberation of women runs entirely contrary to the objectives of religious conservatism. If wives were able to control their reproductive cycles however they wished, the 'traditional' aspects of nuclear family would disintegrate. The male power structure (the man is the head of the household, as God is the head of the church) would erode from the inside out. There are many basic problems with using a centuries-old book as a 'guide' for all of the nuance and complexity of modern ethics and morality, but since conservative Christians in the United States are willing to spike progressive political policies in the name of 'Biblical' marriage, we are obligated to completely explore, exactly, what sexuality during this time period looked like.

> "Other Jewish teachers of Jesus' time, and for generations before, had pronounced certain pagan sexual practices abominable. Among conscientious Jews, only the worship of pagan gods aroused more outrage than pagan sexual behavior. Generations of Jewish teachers had warned that pagans thought nothing of pederasty, promiscuity, and incest. Yet the clash with outside cultures challenged Jewish customs in turn. Many pagans found such practices as circumcision to be peculiar, antiquated, and no less barbaric than Jews found the sexual habits of pagans. Babylonians and Romans, themselves monogamous, criticized the ancient Jewish custom of polygamous marriage, practiced by such venerable patriarchs as Abraham, David, and Solomon, as well as by the wealthy few who could afford it, even in Jesus' time and later. The Jewish historian Josephus, himself apparently polygamous, tried to justify to his Roman readers the ten wives of King Herod the Great (and possibly his own bigamy as well) by explaining that 'among us it is the custom to have many wives simultaneously.' Those familiar with Roman law could also question traditional Jewish divorce law, which granted to the husband (but not to the wife) the often easy right of divorce." [1]

Peering into the historical context of sexuality during Jesus' time on earth, we see anything but clarity. There is everything from state-sponsored pedophilia, polygamy, temple prostitution, and incest. We are to use this cesspool as a foundation for modern sexual ethics? Don't be absurd. Human sexuality during this era was a train wreck, and anyone who yearns for a return to this type of traditionalism is deranged. The sexual practices described above are not, it must be said, a complete list of all outrages inflicted upon humanity during the life of Jesus Christ. Women were routinely used as the payloads of financial transactions (an activity we now refer to as 'human trafficking') and were dealt with as callously as property, worth a little less than cattle, and pre-pubescent girls were frequently used as bargaining chips for kings and royalty to seal political deals and centralize power. Unless fundamentalist Christians are ready to put their own eight-year-old daughters up for sale, I do not believe they are sincere in their stated desired to return to 'Biblical' marriage.

It is quite easy for conservatives to blather on about sexual activity being constrained to marriage within the narrow scope of 'one man and one women' which, hilariously, was not a prohibition that even the most revered men in the New and Old Testaments followed themselves. Forget about having a handful of wives, imagine having a stable of concubines! Why any man, however egotistical, would enjoy disappointing several hundred women on a regular basis is well and truly beyond me. I like to joke, when asked about sex in the Bible, that I believe in Biblical marriage, and that's why I have seven hundred wives and three hundred concubines. King David had eight wives (securing one of these, infamously, by murdering her existing husband in an act of extreme cowardice), Abraham had two wives – Sarah and Hagar – and one concubine, Keturah, which he married after the death of Sarah. King Solomon outdid both by maintaining a stable of seven hundred wives and three hundred concubines. The primary sin of Solomon is not this brazen act of sexual promiscuity, mind you, but the fact that his exotic wives, extracted from all corners of the globe, drew him to worship new and exciting gods. I won't be lectured on the ethics of sex from people who find this disgusting behavior permissible, and neither should anyone else.

What sort of prohibitions do the modern American Evangelicals advocate for now? As with all things conservative, there are deepening degrees of severity. Typical Christians (perhaps more relaxed or casual) might not have much of a problem with their son or daughter moving in with a partner during their twenties (when I did this with my own wife, who was then my fiancé, I got six months of angry silence from my own family, and we both worried they would refuse to attend the wedding as a form of protest.) More devoted Christians might exile family members who 'live in sin' by cohabiting with their romantic interests. Couples who have children 'out of wedlock' are also often equally ostracized by their religious or familial communities. What should not be overlooked at this impasse is the *voyeuristic* aspect of this sexual judgement, gawking, and gossip. Your religious peers have absolutely no restraint or shame in issuing judgements about your own private sex life. They act as if they are entitled to a seat at this table, and have long since pushed any caution about inappropriate behavior out the window.

Individual sexual exploration is often off-limits, too. Even the healthy practice of masturbation is a common target for aggressive Evangelical rebukes. Practically speaking, churches operate 'men's groups' as a codeword for 'accountability' sessions where men 'hold each other accountable' for normal sexual expressions like pornography viewership and masturbation. In one Bible camp I attended, the topic of gawking at women while in public was mentioned - this culminated in a field trip to a public pool in which we all traveled as a group and muttered the Spanish word for eyes, *Ohos*, when an attractive woman came within eyeshot. As you might imagine, keeping teenage males from harboring sexual thoughts is a fool's errand, and like all of these religious prohibitions, it only serves to aggravate more violent and devious sexual activity by removing safe and healthy sexual outlets. Let's say – as is more often the case than many realize – a Christian couple manages to drag themselves into marriage without falling prey to their natural urges. What happens after the chore of sexuality is successfully delayed until after marriage as God intended? Is this truly the nirvana of human sexuality?

As many abstinent Christian men and women eventually discover, this virtue often does much more harm than good once it is fully achieved. Men, having been forced to store up every ounce of sexual desire until the wedding night, frequently harbor unreasonable sexual expectations due to their lack of experience. They might assume that the woman will always be available for sex after marriage, and is sorely disappointed when this is not the case. When the wife is sick, or not in the mood, she defaults on this promissory note and bitterness often sets in. Even worse, when the wife declines intercourse, the man now has no sexual recourse left, because he cannot seek sex outside the marriage, nor can he view pornography within it. Women are hemmed into a repulsive sexual role, where they are expected to completely fulfill every sexual need the man might ever have. Further compounding this difficulty is the philosophical underpinning of typical conservative sexual values (if they are fundamental enough to remain abstinent until marriage, they will usually believe, also, that sex is only to be practiced within the possible bounds of procreation) that force women into years of consecutive child birth. Add all of this on top of the normal stresses of living with another person, tending to the emotional needs of your partner and your children, along with these odd sexual rules, and you can see quite plainly that it is a recipe for disaster. This definition of 'traditional' and 'Biblical' marriage (separated, as if by magic, from the pederasty, human trafficking, and polygamy inherent within both of these definitions) at this juncture now informs conservative political ideology regarding reproduction, and the divine edict against abortion.

"It shouldn't matter what the Bible says about abortion – or indeed anything else. The United States is not a theocracy. Still, given the certitude of abortion opponents that abortion violates God's Word, it might come as a surprise that neither the Old Testament nor the New Testament mentions abortion – not one word. Abortion opponents have to extrapolate from passages about quite other things: prophecies of women eating their young, or massacres in which pregnant women are ripped apart, or someone wishes he had died in his mother's womb. God tells Jeremiah, 'Before I formed you in the womb I knew you' (so Jeremiah existed before he was even conceived?)" [2]

This manner of Scripture-bending is very common in the Evangelical community, and abortion, much like prostitution and intoxicants, have existed for as long as human history itself, and the Bible does not directly prohibit abortion.

"The New Testament was a second chance for God to make himself clear about abortion. Jesus had some strong views of marriage and sex – he considered the Jewish divorce laws too lenient, disapproved of stoning adulteresses, and did not shrink from healing a woman who had 'an issue' (vaginal bleeding of some sort) that had lasted twelve years and would have made her an outcast among Jews. But he said nothing about abortion. Neither did Saint Paul, or the other New Testament authors, or any of the later authors whose words were interpolated into the original text." [3]

This same line of reasoning was brandished remarkably well by the delightfully witty and cantankerous Christopher Hitchens, who loved to remind believers of the Judeo-Christian persuasion that the Ten Commandments failed to prohibit even the most basic moral statements – slavery is wrong, rape is wrong, and genocide is wrong – despite having plenty of space within sixty-six books (more, if you count the un-canonized books of the Bible) to have done so. Biblical marriage doesn't need to have its tenets informed by the Bible, you silly pagans. We just *interpret* the words of Jesus to say whatever we want, without any need for evidence, they tell us. Well, if the Christian sexual lifestyle was merely presented as an innocuous cultural choice – not lauded as superior to secular predilections, just as an alternative – I might have less of an issue with its practice. Their sexual ideology is not even slightly humble, no, on the contrary, they make it quite clear that these are divine edicts, handed down from God himself, and they require our complete obedience.

"There is enough hatred, bigotry and lust for violence in the pages of the Bible to satisfy anyone bent on justifying cruelty and violence. Religion, as H. Richard Niebuhr said, is a good thing for good people and a bad thing for bad people. And the Bible has long been used in the wrong hands – such as antebellum slave owners in the American South who quoted from it to defend slavery – not to Christianize the culture, as those wielding it often claim, but to acculturate the Christian faith…the Pat Robertsons, the Jerry Falwells, and the James Dobsons – clutching to the cross and the Bible, offer, like Mephistopheles, to lead us back to a mythical paradise and an impossible, unachievable happiness and security, at once seductive and empowering. They ask us to hand over moral choice and responsibility to them. They will tell us they know what is right and wrong in the eyes of God. They tell us how to act, how to live, and in this process, they elevate themselves above us." [4]

There is a pernicious streak to this kind of repression – both of personal sexuality and general individual autonomy – and it succeeds only when we choose to allow it to do so. What the conservative right wing is asking for is by no means inconsequential. They want control over who you sleep with, they want control over what medical procedures you are allowed to have, and they want control over who you can marry, and who you cannot. On what basis would they making these judgements? The contents of a two-thousand year old book that harbors all of the ignorance and prejudice of the Dark Ages:

"The Old Testament is not abrogated by Jesus at any point in the New Testament, and there are similar reminders of this in other parts of the Gospel As such, Christians are stuck with it as half of the Bible, despite the fact that it is often difficult to explain, and, indeed, justify. Further, many bedrock beliefs of Christian nationalists – creationism, that homosexuality is a sin, and that the death penalty is based on Biblical principles, for example – come directly from the Old Testament, along with a strong ethos of judgement and punishment that are central to their worldview (and are difficult to support using only the New Testament). Relativism is evil, and relativism is used to describe anything that weakens the black-and-white assertions about sin in the Old Testament – some of them, anyway. It is interesting, really: The Old Testament fits far more easily with Christian nationalism but it is so problematic to defend that they often retreat from it when pressed." [5]

At this point, the believers will often say they are the ones who are marginalized by secular society unfairly. They are ridiculed for their personal religious beliefs when it extends to marriage and the bedroom, and both the politician and the professor have in their sights the helpless religious devotee, and both are determined to outlaw their religious freedom and destroy the faith of their children in the classroom. When there is no persecution of Christians in America, (drop them in North Korea with a Bible and see if they can return with a proper definition of 'religious persecution') they are quite keen to lie and invent it where there is none. In this perverted way, *not being able to impose your own bigoted beliefs* on everyone else is defined as religious persecution. This is a horrifying insult to their Christian brethren who are actually being murdered and tortured because of the faith.

Oddly enough, what stands between American Christians and this dystopian future that they fear, is the thing they hammer away at on a daily basis: the separation between church and state. The reason that American democracy has lasted for as long as it has can be entirely attributed to the religious impartiality it has maintained. Unlike our counterparts in the United Kingdom, the United States does not have an official church (like the Church of England), and as such, does not concern itself with the kicking down of church doors. American law goes even one step further – churches in the U.S. are not required to pay taxes on their income – and the religious protection offered by the state is precisely the safeguard they'd most like to obliterate. It is a self-destructive desire that goes largely unexamined within Christian circles.

In my personal view, the most American principle found across all of our founding documents is that of *autonomy*. You are free to select a church of your own choosing, you are free to select a religion of your own choosing, or you are free to select no church or religion at all. The press (outside of fraud and libel) are free to select and print words of their own choosing, and individual citizens are similarly uninhibited in their speech (outside of fraud and libel). You are free to congregate and assemble with people of your own choosing, and you are unencumbered in your personal choice of vocation and recreation, so long as your choice does not prey upon, or unfairly interfere with the liberty of others. It is not hyperbolic to say that when the fundamentalists take aim at this principle, they take aim at the pillar that holds all of civil society upright. In so doing, they take a pickaxe to the platform that allows them to speak openly. This does not offend their sensibilities, because autonomy is the very thing that stands in the way of what they want the most: a Christian theocracy where God is the King. To be fair, conservative Christians are not entirely nor uniformly opposed to a separation between religion and the state. Among their most pressing (and delusional) fears is the possible implementation of Sharia Law, a different flavor of theocratic rule found most commonly in Islamic nations. When it comes to competing religions, they are very much in favor of a secular and impartial government, but not when it comes to their own.

The liberal position is not incompatible with the practice (or reverence of) basic family life. I am, personally, the beneficiary of a 'traditional' family structure, and I'd be lying if I said that my own life wasn't greatly improved by the presence of two loving parents. I have no interest in attacking the family life of American Christians. What I would like is for them to stop attacking the personal and private choices of others. To borrow another quip from the inimitable Christopher Hitchens – focus on your own damn family!

The secular world is *completely* disinterested in kicking down the doors to American churches to impose our ideas upon Christian congregations. We haven't yet invaded your places of worship, with Darwin and condoms in hand, but the *Christian* invasion of secular culture is a multibillion dollar industry (that, in case you've forgotten, has the added advantage of not paying any tax). We have absolutely no motivation, for example, to modify the drivel taught to Christian children in Sunday 'Schools' nationwide. We are quite content to let you say and do whatever you like in the walls of your own church – but the same respect is not given to our secular institutions of law, education, and government. States like Kansas and Texas have a well-oiled lobbyist machines that crudely modifies textbooks and curriculum to include religious fairytales, or to promote the religiously-fueled idiocy of abstinence. Secular society has given American Christianity safety, security, and respect, and has not interfered in its practice of religion as the law commands. This, of course, is not enough for the fundamentalists. They're not content to keep their churches, because they want our schools, hospitals, and courthouses, too. What would Jesus himself think of such a judgmental and sneering political movement?

> "For starters, Jesus would never hang out with Christian nationalists. They would have nothing in common, and he would likely find them annoying. They are modern day Pharisees: judgmental rather than understanding, capitalistic rather than socialistic, hateful rather than loving, and militant rather than peaceful. In short, they are the antithesis of everything Jesus stood for…Christian nationalists are fighting a war in this country, and they are winning a lot of the battles because the other side is largely absent from the field." [6]

What upsets me the most – especially when it comes to the American brand of religious fascism – is that if society truly disintegrated, and the government started to come for the Christians, they'd find ardent allies in the secular humanists they loathe. If they came for the Christians tomorrow, well, tomorrow, I'm a Christian right alongside you. That is *precisely* the way it needs to work. When American society starts to bend the law that rules everyone on account of the religious beliefs of one group, the mechanism that is designed to protect us all is damaged in the process. American religious fundamentalists are trying every day to puncture the parachute that keeps everyone safe. It is any surprise that this religion purports to 'store up treasures' in heaven, not on earth? Is it any surprise that Christians believe that the rest of us are destined to be tortured forever in hell? Don't be fooled; it is the Christian and politically conservative world that views the secular world with condescension and disgust.

"Peter Ditto is a collaborator with the aforementioned University of Virginia social psychologist Jonathan Haidt, who is a leader in applying an understanding of motivated reasoning to our views about what's right and what's wrong. To that end, Haidt has identified five separate moral *intuitions* that appear to make us feel strongly about situations before we're even consciously aware of thinking about them, and that powerfully guide our reasoning. These are 1) the sense of needing to provide care and protect harm; 2) the sense of what is just and fair; 3) the sense of loyalty and willingness to sacrifice for a group; 4) the sense of obedience or respect for authority; and 5) the sense of needing to preserve purity or sanctity. Here's the thing: in surveys, Haidt finds that liberals tend to strongly emphasize the first moral institutions (harm and fairness) in their responses to situations and events, but are much weaker on emphasizing the other three (group loyalty, respect for authority, and purity or sanctity). By contrast, Haidt finds that conservatives more than liberals respond to all five moral institutions. (Indeed, multiple studies associate conservatism with a greater disgust reflex or sensitivity. In one telling experiment, subjects who were asked to use a hand wipe before answering questions, or answer them near a hand sanitizer, gave more politically conservative answers.)" [7]

One of the first books I ever read was Laura Numeroff's *If You Give a Mouse a Cookie* – a cautionary tale about the incessant nature of granting concessions. Let the theocrats have a cookie, and they'll want some milk to go along with it. Give the theocrats a say in how two consenting adults express their love and affection for one another, and who knows what we'll have to give them next? Much like the greed of the one-percent class in the United States, the expansionist desires of religious fundamentalism is limitless, and it will always be bound by the partitions we set in place.

This war of attrition the Christian world has waged against the secularists is sharpest at its most worn-out spots: homosexuality, gender, and hedonism. These are three of the most existentially dangerous pressure points for the Evangelicals, and they have never stopped attacking them. If same-sex relationships are to be permitted, then the holiness of sex-as-procreation is completely destroyed. Androgyny – another symptom of sexual liberation – is equally dangerous as it threatens the role of men and women within the nuclear family. Hedonism is not reviled by Christians because of the pleasure it provides (talk to any minister for more than a few minutes, and they will likely pummel you with all of the sordid details of their sinful life 'before they came to Jesus'), but because 'opening' the mind might include listening to other explanations of the origin of life and existence, and could lead someone into the arms of a 'false' god or prophet.

Having gone to Bible College, I understand the culture that subsists within Christian circles. It is not entirely corrupt or money-grubbing (as those who never attended church often believe from watching the gyrations of televangelists on television) and in my life, while I was a Christian, the church brought me comfort and joy. It is often said that Christian apostates were embittered by the church, but in my personal case, this was the furthest from the truth. My family lived in a house about an hour's drive away from St. Louis, in the truck-stop town of Foristell, Missouri. My parents were (and still are) very religious, and I was homeschooled up until I went to college. The church, to me, was not stuffy and boring. It was, for the exceptions of playing music and participating in sports, my social life in almost its entirety. Beyond providing a desperately needed social outlet, the charitable wings of Christianity fed my family through food banks when my parents got into financial trouble. My parents took the Gospel message to heart, and when they came into a bountiful harvest, gave back by taking several less-fortunate people into our home. I hope it is understood by my readers that my disdain of organized religion does not originate from a place of spitefulness or bitterness. Indeed, if my religiosity was solely predicated upon the quality of treatment I personally received by the church, I would still be a Christian to this day.

The reason, of course, that my experience within the church was so stellar is simple: I am a white man. Nobody obsessed over my virginity. No one appraised my outfits and clothing for their sexual modesty. No one told me I had to be subservient to another gender – I was to be the future head of my house, just as God is the head of his church – in fact, I was being taught on how, exactly, I was to be the *leader* of the church and the world. American Christianity, apart from more left-leaning denominations, is inherently sexist.

"Christianity has treated women terribly since its creation, beginning with the actual story of creation, in which Eve is made as a subservient helper to Adam, and then is used as the scapegoat for the expulsion of humans from the Garden into a world of pain, toil, and death. Feminist scholars have subjected the story of Eve to tremendous efforts of interpretation and reinterpretation to address this apparent indication that men are superior to women, but I see no need to enter that particular fray, since it seems clear that it is fiction written by men with a vested interest in keeping women subservient…Women are viewed variously as deceitful, untrustworthy, sexual predators, unclean, the fall of mankind, spoils of war, and above all, subordinate and inferior to men." [8]

This is not to denigrate all that comes from religion – there are some wholesome values mired somewhere underneath all of the murder, war, sex trafficking, and slavery found in the pages of the Bible – but start turning over logs in your church and you'll find no shortage of repulsive things. One of my sisters was literally assaulted by a church elder, (she mouthed off to him, and he responded by cracking a clipboard over her skull, putting her in the hospital and giving her a concussion) and my mother was dragged into a meeting with a senior pastor at a church in Wentzville, Missouri, and told she was an 'unfit' mother because she had asked to play more contemporary music during Sunday morning services. There are too many outrages (even within the experiences of the women in my own family alone) to catalog them completely in this book, but after two decades in the American church, let me tell you plainly and with some authority: women do not have it nearly as easy as men.

"The hyper masculinity of radical Christian conservatism, which crushes the independence and self-expression of women, is a way for men in the movement to compensate for the curtailing of their own independence, their object obedience to church authorities and the calls for sexual restraint. It is also a way to cope with fear. Those who lead these churches fear, perhaps most deeply, their own internal contradictions. They make war on the internal contradictions in others. Those who are not subdued, who do not bow before the church authorities, are seen as contaminants. Believers are driven into a primitive state, a prenatal existence, a return to the womb and a life of submission. The assault on freedom, human equality, and reason, however, also engenders feelings of omnipotence. Death and decay seem to be overcome. All are empowered by God, promised a utopian paradise and immortality. The movement feeds off of power and powerlessness, off of subjugation and control. It induces mass delusion. And the crowd, stripped of personal initiative, soon projects its dreams and aspirations for power through the leader. The surrender of personal power allows believers to indulge in fantasies about becoming instruments of a limitless, divine power. As the spiritual vacuum grows, as fear increases, violence in the name of God becomes not only seductive but imperative. The movement, to compensate for the loss of personal power and submission, fosters a warrior cult and feeds its hapless followers a steady diet of battles, wars, and apocalyptic violence." [9]

As we wrestle with the concept of civil 'definitions' of marriage, law, and religious freedom, the American people will have to confront what masters they wish to keep. If your pastor has control of how you use your sexual organs, are you your own person? If the church can tell you which surgeries and medical procedures you may or may not have, what *can't* they tell you to do? Isn't this less of an issue of law and more of an issue of attraction? *Why* would anyone enjoy intellectual serfdom? *Who* in their right mind would be permissive enough to allow the priests and preachers of the world to stand in judgement over their most intimate moments? *Why* does humanity need a master, and why, exactly, do those bound by religion wish so desperately to apply those shackles to my ankles, too? What difference is it to them if I join their club? In the *Statute of Virginia for Religious Freedom*, it was Thomas Jefferson who wrote that 'it does me no injury for my neighbor to say that there are twenty gods, or no god. It neither picks my pocket, nor breaks my leg.' Proselytization has the dubious habit of taking issue with the independent choices of others, and, crucially, imposing the decisions of one's own group upon the rest of the world.

"George Marsden, in his *Fundamentalism and American Culture*, provides a useful model for understanding the often paradoxical nature of fundamentalism. Marsden observed that within fundamentalism there was a tendency to 'identify sometime with the establishment and sometimes with the outsiders.' Among the groups to which twentieth-century fundamentalism can trace its roots, two of the most significant were the nineteenth-century revivalists and the seventeenth-century Calvinists. The revivalists provided a heritage of 'individualistic, culture-denying, soul-rescuing Christianity.' Revivalism also provided the fundamentalists with, in Marsden's words, the presupposition of a 'radical separation between the unconverted and the converted.' Since the stakes involved spending eternity in hell, there was no time for the luxury or theological debate and hypothesis...Viewing the world divided into the converted and unconverted heightened the separatist mentality." [10]

When I focus on the entirety of my Christian life, I see a lot of good intentions undercut by intellectual immaturity. In my view, if I didn't talk about Jesus to those I cared about, I was negligent in my duties as a Christian. I was ordered to go into the world, baptizing men and women in the name of Christ for the sole purpose of saving them from an eternity of torture. It appealed to my naïve sense of compassion and justice. I believed every word of it with sincerity, and never truly stopped to question it until I got into university. I can't fully accept every consequence of my actions as a Christian – I was raised into this mindset, and the choice wasn't genuinely afforded to me – but there are things I've said and done that I now deeply regret. I told a bi-sexual friend that his urges were sinful, and were likely caused by sexual abuse he experienced at a young age. He confided in me, and I used his pain as ammunition to strengthen my argument when he challenged me. It was shameful, manipulative, and cowardly. I pressured my Christian friends not to express their sexuality in a healthy way, shaming them for watching pornography and encouraging them to abandon masturbation. I stewed in abject rage when I first encountered an openly gay Christian at Greenville College, calling his analysis of the Scriptures 'malicious and self-serving' (he was right, and the courage he displayed defending himself in front of a hostile classroom went entirely unappreciated by me in the moment). The point of my confession here is to illustrate something that the secular world often overlooks. It's *painful* to crawl your way out of intolerance, and when you start to leave extremist views behind, you are forced to face up to all of the awful things you said and did. It isn't easy, and while discomfort is no excuse for bigotry and hatred, I think we should understand the sensitivity of the things that we rightfully challenge. When the political left pressures the Christian right wing, we're asking them to change something they *feel* is more important than anything else in their life. I am not asking for crocodile tears, but if pressure and shame could have changed their traditions, it would have done so many years ago. Political polarization is taking place now because we have lost the ability to have any empathy for our counterparts. Faith – however ill-informed or immature – still means a great deal to Americans, and it is deeply traumatic when the world seems to be conspiring to take it away.

Cost-Effective Compassion

‡‡‡

Chapter 6

"Pro-life conservatives are obsessed with the fetus from conception to nine months. After that, they don't want to know about you. They don't want to hear from you. No nothing. No neonatal care, no day care, no head start, no school lunch, no food stamps, no welfare, no nothing. If you're preborn, you're fine; if you're preschool, you're fucked." – George Carlin

═══

The conservatives are attempting to preserve a way of life that has existed for hundreds of years without meaningful challenge – white men in positions of power, with women and minorities serving them in subservient roles. All that remains for Americans to determine now is if this approach is ethically acceptable, and, crucially, if such an approach would deliver the results that the conservative right has promised. What should be abundantly clear after the election of President Trump is just how varied Americans' personal sense of ethics and morality differ from one another. It is far from unified, and it rarely (if ever) adheres to basic logic or common sense. This is true of basically everyone, anyway, no matter how well educated or intelligent.

Our basic sense of good and bad are *visceral*, informed by our predispositions and development first, rather than the cerebral and even-keeled approach we like to believe we have. I concede that all humans are flawed in this way, some more than others, but there comes a point where arguments for egalitarianism can only go so far. To continue hammering away at the ethics of one political issue when it has been well established that no such sympathies exist in the target demographic is foolish on many levels. Setting aside (momentarily) the moral and ethical implications, there are several major cornerstone policies in American politics that can be *objectively* improved by following the left, rather than the right. Ignore the pesky and nuanced nature of morality for just a few minutes, and let's focus

111

on just the numbers and how, selfishly and self-interestedly, the United States can drastically improve its own economic results by adjusting its approach to law enforcement, military spending, the death penalty, prostitution, and immigration.

Drug Enforcement

The decriminalization of all drugs – long met with snooty scoffs from both sides of the political isle – is now beginning to pick up steam, both within the far-left and the more right leaning libertarian communities. In 2016, the Drug Enforcement Agency gobbled up $208 million taxpayer dollars (and is requesting an increase for 2017 of $23 million more) and these funds are largely used to disrupt smuggling networks and incarcerate drug users and distributors. Sub-billion dollar expenditures, when compared to the enormity of other types of monolithic spending in the federal budget, may seem inconsequential, but the devil is always in the details. The price that the American people pay for the endless war on drugs is staggering, and it could be drastically improved by simply decriminalizing usage and possession of all illegal substances. This position strikes many as a radical one, and substance abuse, in all of its forms, is one of the worst tragedies to have ever infected mankind. To campaign for the end of prohibition might seem, at first glance, to be a cruel and calloused proposition – millions of people have dropped dead on account of deadly substances – but after decades of 'fighting' drugs, the one thing that should be abundantly clear is that compulsive drug use is often a *medical and neurological problem, and not a criminal one.*

> "No man treats a motorcar as foolishly as he treats another human being. When the car will not go, he does not attribute its annoying behavior to sin; he does not say, 'You are a wicked motorcar, and I shall not give you any more petrol until you go. He attempts to find out what is wrong and to set it right." [1]

The horrors of drug addiction; meth addicts with jagged teeth or the track-mark-laden arms and appendages of junkies everywhere should soundly confirm to us all that no sane human would wish to remain in this condition if given the choice. A predisposition to these self-immolating habits could certainly be evidence of a pre-existing mental illness or deficiency that medical science could do infinitely more to correct that a jail cell. More to the point, when we discuss incarceration, we should be talking about a system that *arrests* threatening and criminal behavior from harming the public good, and *rehabilitating* those who commit these acts for later reintegration into society. This, simply, does not happen in the United

States. Criminals go into our correctional facilities as rookie criminals and leave them with their skills honed. They are almost exclusively banned from re-entering the legitimate work force (a felony conviction is basically a non-starter for millions of American employers) and if they leave prison without being murdered, maimed, or sexually assaulted, they exit prison with fewer options than they came in with. This is completely backwards, and the dysfunction of this system makes our society *less* safe.

For the low price of $308 million, the United States is removing millions of working-age and able-bodied men and women from the legitimate workforce (where their legitimate income could be legitimately taxed) and instead, holds them in detention *on the taxpayer dollar* at the average expense of $28,000 a year per prisoner. Again, forget about ethics and just focus on how the math doesn't hold up to basic scrutiny. Who is served by these state of affairs? The private prison industry is making a mint, along with all of the companies that operate in conjunction with them. Here's a truly radical idea: what if, instead of criminalizing non-violent drug offenders, we dealt with the cause of the problem rather than the symptoms? What if we identified the culprit of substance abuse – mental illness – and chose to use public funds to treat it?

Intelligence Squared – a YouTube channel that hosts debates with writers, politicians, and intellectuals – posed the issue of drug decriminalization with one of its panels, and the discussion was truly fascinating. Nick Gillespie, editor of *reason.com,* was far and away the best on the panel. He illuminated an aspect of this issue that I had personally never considered; *pharmacological freedom.* On what basis is the government demanding that adults may not use whatever substances or chemicals they want? We have the right to eat whatever food we prefer, right? Why are the rules vastly different for pharmacological items? The typical reply to this question is a pithy one – drugs are deadly, they'll say, and the government is trying to protect you – but alcohol and tobacco are available around every corner, and both have killed, and will continue to kill, millions. Both substances are completely legal, federally regulated, and the sale of these items are taxed. Let's not pretend these prohibitions are for the sake of safety. If this was the case, it wouldn't just be cigarettes and spirits being outlawed. Sugar causes diabetes. Red meat causes heart disease. Processed foods might cause some kinds of cancers. These would all have to go under the 'safety' standard. This is absurd, of course, and the government shouldn't have a say in the types of things adults choose to put in their bodies; except when it comes to drugs. Why is this the case?

"Drugs, like crime, are socially defined. Lives ruined by cigarettes far outnumber those harmed by heroin, yet, nicotine sellers openly urge more Americans to take up the habit; indeed, by compulsory taxation the federal government forces citizens to aid tobacco growers. Nicotine's physical danger and addictive potential are so well demonstrated that the federal drug control law of 1970 specifically exempted tobacco because otherwise it fit the scientific criteria used to describe banned drugs." [2]

Let's dispose, immediately, with the notion that these chemical prohibitions exist as a form of genteel kindness bestowed upon us by the federal government. The policy is flatly inconsistent, and the classification of illicit substances is entirely driven by the special-interest-influences of the alcohol, tobacco, and pharmaceutical industries. They stand to lose the most from legalization, and they have bent the rule of law to their every whim for decades.

When you encounter outwardly puzzling and inconsistent political policy, most of the time, you are encountering corruption, cronyism, and corporate welfare. Federal legalization of marijuana, for instance, has been largely popular in the United States for the last decade. If a national referendum was held on that topic alone, legalization would almost certainly win a popular vote in a landslide. State-level decriminalization, like the programs enacted in Colorado, have been resounding successes. So much so, in fact, that Colorado taxpayers had to vote on a proposition that determined where billions of dollars in new, marijuana-related tax revenue should be allocated. If this was implemented on a national scale, the American budget would be injected with tons of new capital, so why isn't such a policy in place already?

If Americans had open access to powerful substances – both for recreational and medicinal use – several incredibly powerful industries would see demand for their products and services drastically decrease. If an adult can buy marijuana at a corner market, Philip Morris stands to lose business. If an adult can buy Vicodin at that same corner market, Pfizer's earnings will take a hit, too. The (often) unspoken rule in American politics: don't fuck with big pharma, and don't fuck with the DEA's budget. Well, what, exactly, are we getting for our investments into these companies as a nation? We get an epidemic of pain-killer addiction that puts our loved ones in early graves. We get outrageous price surges for life-critical prescriptions. We subsidize the sordid private profits of tobacco companies like Phillip Morris who have pivoted towards developing markets like Thailand and the Philippines who, conveniently, have little to no regulatory structure and have no safeguards in place for advertising cigarette usage to children. What have we gotten in exchange for the corporate welfare offered to these giants? Death, extortion, monopoly, and apathy. Surely – no matter what your political leanings might be – everyone must recognize that this entire ecosystem exists *at our own detriment* and could be reversed by a simple injection of common sense. This economic infrastructure does much more than just line the pockets of executives in the pharmaceutical and intoxicants industries. The power vacuum that has sprung up in the production, sale, and distribution of more potent substances like cocaine, heroin, and methamphetamine has created incredibly powerful cabals of organized crime. By choosing not to federally regulate, manage, and tax these substances (used by the metric ton by Americans every single year) the United States has created a black market where the cartels can operate with near-total impunity. The sword that is bleeding our nation to death is double-edged; we fund, at a loss, enterprises and industries that deal addiction and death to our friends and family legally, and in outlawing some substances over others, drive a billion-dollar market underground, to the benefit of violent and illiterate warlords with no other concern except for their own wealth. I have to return, again, to a bi-partisan appeal. Surely *people in all political parties* must see that this is simply not sustainable on a basic level.

What, besides the influence of special interest groups, keeps America from decriminalizing drugs? Stigma, racism, and religious delusion are primarily responsible for the opposition outside of the boardroom. The war on drugs, a creation of President Ronald Reagan, was objectively used as a tool to monetize the incarceration of black men. This reality is so blatantly undeniable that even a toad like Newt Gingrich admitted openly in the Netflix documentary *The 13th* that the policy he helped design fiercely punished 'crack' cocaine (largely used by blacks) but largely ignored powered cocaine (widely popular with suburban whites) had the effect of decimating the black community. African-Americans constitute roughly 10% of America's population, but make up 40% of its prison population. Primarily, black Americans are incarcerated for drug offenses, many of them non-violent, even though blacks use illegal drugs at a *lower* rate than white Americans. Put simply; drug policy is used as a form of racist repression against black men and women. Religious opposition to intoxication and mind-altering supplements is certainly not new. The degrees of ideological disdain for alcohol, tobacco, and recreational substances can vary wildly between different sects, denominations, and even different religions entirely. Most Islamic teaching forbids alcohol consumption, while Christian, Catholic, and Jewish practitioners have more relaxed attitudes to drinking and smoking. Some of the more extreme belief systems will refuse to take simple medication (Scientologists see prescription medication as no different than 'street drugs' and Jehovah Witnesses will almost uniformly refuse blood transfusions based on a quirky interpretation of a phrase used in the Old Testament that refers to the 'lifeblood' of a human). While there are plenty of exceptions to this rule, generally speaking, religious Americans don't typically resent drinking or tobacco usage, but most will widely object to recreational usage of other substances. Many religiously-minded Americans view any type of drug use as a failure in personal morality, and oppose any potential legalization on that basis alone. More hardline perspectives – usually cut from the same cloth of religious fundamentalists who object to any modification of a 'God-given' state of mind – will portray drug usage as a sinister substitute to more traditional (and, in their view, wholesome and healthy) pursuits. Why have a family and children and a nice job, they might ask, if you can just take a pill that gives one the illusion of happiness? This will erode the moral fabric of the nation, they warn, and this torpid style of moralizing is hugely popular in the national dialog on drugs.

> "Some users of illicit drugs may have a special need. Many people have an imbalance or lack of chemicals needed for normal functioning; physicians prescribe drugs to correct such conditions. Investigators suspect that certain illicit drugs may correct conditions unrecognized by medical science, that some users are medicating themselves." [3]

It wasn't all that long ago that developmental delays, mental impairments, or neurological or mental illnesses were seen as volitional. Your neighbor who couldn't keep a job was lazy, or work-shy then, but today, we would more closely associate that kind of impairment with depression, rather than impugning his character first. If we consider the stunning length and depth of all humanity *does not yet know* about the intricacies of the human mind, it seems silly to race to judgement when it comes to people who step outside of our socially accepted norms to feel chemically comfortable. Instead of seeing the homeless man on the corner as a human who has a disorder that could be treated by medical science, the religious dolt views him as *morally inferior*. They do not see an issue that could be rectified by the breathtaking advances of technology, rather, they see a person who has made poor choices and, if he gained the moral fortitude, could 'choose' his way out of addiction, poverty, and compulsion.

> "If sophisticated chemical analyses of blood and urine are required to identify who is a deviant, clearly nothing in the "deviant's" observed conduct differs from normal citizens. Conduct is not being punished; the status of being a drug user is punished. (Traditionally, U.S. jurisprudence abhors sanctions against status, but that tradition is yet another casualty in the drug war.)" [4]

This aspect is worthy of consideration as well; outlawing the status of a person's chemical makeup is far different that issuing statutes that prohibit an observed behavior, like robbery or murder. The moralizing strikes here yet again – *good* people don't use those substances, *normal* people don't use those substances, *healthy* people don't use those substances – and the cycle of waste, needless imprisonment, and ruined lives churns over and over again. I am certainly not a chemist, but it doesn't take one to acknowledge that socially acceptable prescriptions are often composed of the same types of substances found in street drugs. They are two different derivatives of the same thing; with two *vastly* different consequences for their consumption. If asked, most Americans will accept that certain conditions will require powerful medications to treat – so where, exactly is that line? Is it acceptable to issue a powerful prescription for depression? Most will say so. Is it acceptable to prescribe an opioid for a debilitating chronic-pain illness? Most would not object. How does a person, perhaps unemployed and living under the poverty line, access these substances legally? The short answer is that they can't, and average Americans store up haughty judgement for impoverished people who have fewer options to treat their issues.

Given the popularity of this thick-skulled philosophy, is it any wonder that drugs have decimated Americans for decades? Is it any wonder that a spate of cottage industries have sprung up to profit from our collective suffering? Drug use, of course, is not always a result of sickness or mental deficiency. Recreational use by healthy people is common, and even in those instances, illegal substances have resulted death outside of the bounds of addictive intake. Alright, but what typically causes death within the scope of what we call 'recreational' use? Overdosing on account of unsafe potency, or on account of deadly 'filler' material, could be completely corrected by treating drugs like any other item approved for intake in the human body, with active ingredients measured, labelled, and the finished product inspected, like any food or drink we purchase on a daily basis at any retailer across the nation. Pre-existing medical conditions often cause death when occasional drug use takes place, but these causes are certainly not helped by the currently deregulated black market that Americans use in lieu of a civilized one. *Maybe* it could be argued that operating vehicles or heavy machinery under the influence of powerful intoxicants or mind-altering substances is (or could be) a common cause of death after legalization, but even if I concede this point, the 28 people (on average) killed by drunk drivers in the United States *every single day* scream out to me from the grave.

There is simply no way drug decriminalization could even come close to the damage alcoholism already inflicts on Americans. At least, when it comes to alcohol, we have the basic sense to *tax the sale* of these dangerous items that Americans will buy no matter what laws we set in place to help foot the bill for the consequences. Why does it make sense to make one of these deadly substances legal, but others illegal? The stigma American culture has placed on open drug is powerfully snide and needlessly judgmental. This nasty attitude that views substance abuse as weakness has the ancillary detriment of extending its stigma to mental illness as well. Depression, anxiety, and post-traumatic stress disorder (among many others) become collateral damage; if drug addiction is shameful, then the antecedents of it are also shameful and evidence that these ailments were dealt with improperly before they blossomed into the death-spiral of drug dependency. The calloused moralizing of the religious bigot kicks this entire cycle into motion, and once it starts, *all of society suffers.*

In the United Kingdom, law enforcement has a phrase to describe crimes that result on account of drug addiction: *acquisitive crime.* As anyone who has endured the painful experience of loving someone with a substance abuse problem can attest, as the dependency to substances deepens, the costs begin to rise, and addicts will do whatever is necessary to end the discomfort of withdrawal. So they turn to theft, fraud, violence, anything to get a fix. Returning, again, to the premise I stated at the beginning of the chapter; where we ignore the ethical and moral aspects of this political issue, I am merely arguing from a perspective of cost. Drug abuse creates crime, and law enforcement takes a hefty bite out of our public funds. In addition to requiring the employment (not just a salary, but benefits, medical care, and pensions, too) of police officers and paramedics who are the first responders to acquisitive crime, we are also left footing the bill for the judicial costs, as well as the correctional ones (to the tune of $28,000 per prisoner per year as mentioned earlier). Taxes aren't the only bit of your own pocketbook that are impacted by acquisitive crime. When a junkie breaks into your car or home, you pay an insurance company *a recurring fee* privately to help finance the repairs and to help mitigate the full impact of the damages. Let's say instead of theft, you find yourself down the barrel of a gun during a mugging. Provided you manage to survive this incident, you will incur medical costs if injured, and if not, the psychological trauma will take its own toll financially. Is it really all that radical to suggest that subsidizing mental and medical care for this dangerous demographic might just be far cheaper in the long run? If it was your son or daughter on the street corner, would the answer be different? Would you suddenly see the value and virtue of setting aside some tax revenue for some of your less-fortunate peers? The perception of criminality in American consciousness itself is fundamentally broken and needlessly cruel. Not only is imprisonment expensive and counterproductive, but it does nothing to solve the underlying issues that create a need for incarceration in the first place.

"Michael Treadwell sat at the back of a courtroom in New Hampshire. He wore a windbreaker and khaki pants and leaned over his work boots with his elbows on his knees. At first it looked like he was chewing gum — a bold choice in a courtroom. But when he spoke it was clear: He wasn't chewing gum, he was chewing his own gums. Michael doesn't have any teeth. Taxpayers in Hillsborough County, N.H., have spent $63,000 over the last six years keeping Treadwell in jail for little more than trespassing. For years now, his life has looked like this: Trespass in an apartment building, spend 30 days in jail; bother restaurant customers, spend 42 days in jail; panhandle aggressively, spend 30 days in jail. "When you live in a town like Nashua, there's not a lot of homelessness there, and it kinda like focuses, puts you in the spotlight," Treadwell says. "Especially if you drink alcohol and stuff." [5]

This carousel of imprisonment does not seem to be an effective use of sixty-three thousand taxpayer dollars. In fact, I'd argue it represents a tremendous amount of budgetary *waste*. Putting Mr. Treadwell in jail didn't create any deterrence. Nor did it create any benefit for the community as a whole. It was a stagnant expense, one that recurred and compounded, and did nothing to solve the larger problem. This is the risk we run when Americans moralize political issues; the "values-voters" wouldn't hesitate to shower Mr. Treadwell with moral condemnation at this point. He's making bad choices, and he should be punished, they'd likely say. Well, it makes little difference if Mr. Treadwell's actions are moral or immoral. The *responses* to these actions are literally benefiting no one in either case. It does not benefit Mr. Treadwell, and it does not benefit taxpayers in Hillsborough Country. Our sneering moral condescension does nothing but lock us in a stalemate, wherein we create policy not based off common sense and frugality, but out of inane, bitter, and quasi-religious principles.

Had Hillsborough County introduced a measure on the ballot to help their tiny homeless community get state-funded social services, you can be certain that the budget-hawk Republicans would have attacked it with the force of a thousand suns. They loathe government handouts, and men and women like Mr. Treadwell need to pull themselves up by their own bootstraps and work harder. And so, chained to these insipid notions of "limited government," this municipality turns a blind eye to Mr. Treadwell, and in so doing, *spends more* to incarcerate him than it would have spent to help him. In this way, the decision is both fiscally unsound and needlessly cruel all at the same time. Let's return to the concept of acquisitive crime, and apply it to Mr. Treadwell. It is probably safe to assume he struggled with substance abuse and mental illness (as many homeless do) and in order to fund these kinds of habits, for the sake of argument, let's say he participated in some manner of criminality in order to finance his addictions. We've moved beyond the sixty-three thousand dollar price tag now, and every loss incurred by his criminal activity over the course of those six years will get tacked on to the overall cost to society. Being "tough" on crime might feel good, and it might make for good television ads for judges trying to get re-elected, but it doesn't save taxpayer dollars, and it doesn't fix the problem.

This snidely judgmental mindset fully extends to federal assistance programs like welfare or food stamps. This is seen by many conservative as government waste, only used by the lazy or work-shy. A popular viewpoint in Republican circles is that these programs are rife with fraud, or that these assistance programs are inordinately expensive. Neither claim is true; welfare programs in the United States had a meager 4.7 percent rate of fraudulent payouts in 2013, and the $481 million allocated to welfare in 2017 pales in comparison to both defense spending and Medicare and Medicaid (all three of which are popular expenditures with aging Republicans). The right-wing objections to welfare extend far beyond budgetary concerns, however. At its core, the conflict (as many others are in the conservative playbook) is a moral and philosophical one. *People shouldn't get money for free*, they claim. It is a question not just of finance but of righteousness.

Their suffocating moralism is inescapable, and yet again, it clouds our collective judgement and locks our society into poor decisions that get progressively worse over time. Food insecurity is a huge problem in the United States – 16 percent of all American households suffer from it – but instead of dealing with this problem dispassionately, as one might deal with a cold or a flu, conservative Americans turn up their noses at any attempt the federal government makes to help alleviate this problem. This fissure, at a fundamental level, divides American conservatives from the rest of the country. The role of government, in their view, should not concern itself with the welfare of its weakest and most impoverished citizens. How did the party of Jesus Christ become so heartless and devoid of compassion? *Obama isn't that dark-skinned, socialist, giving away free healthcare*, read one protest sign at a demonstration in D.C a few years ago, *you're thinking of Jesus*.

Defense and Military Spending

My position on this issue is largely atypical in the political left. I think a robust budget for the armed forces in the United States is not just desirable, but necessary. I believe, wholeheartedly and sincerely, that secular democracy ought to be an exportable commodity, and when other democracies come under attack, we should defend them with all our might. I wish, as Christopher Hitchens did, that President Kennedy's pledge to oppose any foe and support any friend in liberty was actually true and not just a platitude. I wish it was true for the subjugated women in Saudi

Arabia, I wish it was true for the millions of enslaved North Koreans, and I wish it was a virtue that the United States took seriously. Unlike many on the left, I politely disagree with the sneering sort of outlook that dismisses foreign outrages with a shrug ("We're not the world's police" they'll say.) Well, what's the point of having a military at all if it is not used in defense of the helpless?

It is this perspective that enables me to say openly that I support a massive budget allotment for the military and defense industries. I am comfortable going even one step further: the United States should *lead the planet* in military spending. That proposition is acceptable to me. If this makes me a bit of a nationalist, so be it. What is not acceptable, to put it bluntly, is for the United States to spend more on its military than China, Saudi Arabia, Russia, The United Kingdom, India and France *combined*. This is waste on an astronomical scale (hang on, where are the Republican budget hawks who can't stop talking about food stamps?) and it is a dangerous and irresponsible expenditure. The reason our free society cannot tolerate runaway defense spending of this nature – set to increase under the Trump administration by another $54 billion dollars annually – is that it is a budget completely removed from reality. We are being misled about the very nature of warfare in a modern world by the people who are supposed to be experts on the topic. This outrageous spending wouldn't have been justified, even at the height of the Cold War, and it makes even less sense now.

As nuclear weapons became more common, and proliferated equally to superpowers and moderately influential states alike, the scale and scope of warfare changed, too. The ground wars of the 1930's are ancient history, replaced with the policy of mutually assured destruction. Nuclear nations no longer take to an open battlefield against one another. They fight proxy wars over resource-laden chokepoints, fund insurgencies, or they might orchestrate a *coup de 'tat* against unfriendly governments. There's a reason that Russia and China refuse to spend half of a trillion dollars annually on their armed forces; there is no additional capacity to be gained by increasing the expenditure to such an absurd scale. In modern warfare, two nuclear nations might prop up one regime in an non-developed or non-nuclear state in a war against another, funneling arms and resources in the interest of getting a return on that investment at a later date. If the objective is significant enough, two developed nations might go to war with one another covertly through their intelligence services or special forces directly. No matter how adversarial two nations might be with one another, a nuclear exchange between two nuclear powers has never taken place.

This has been the status quo for good reason – a nuclear war is in no one's interest – and outspending the seven-nearest nations combined in defense spending cannot prevent all-out nuclear annihilation, and does not provide a competitive advantage in the very limited scale of insurgencies and proxy wars. This runaway spending gives us no tangible edge over any adversary, and is driving the nation to bankruptcy. At the time of this writing, the United States spends $614 billion dollars annually on its military. This represents roughly 3% of the nation's entire gross domestic product, and depending on the source you consult, constitutes anywhere from 50%-57% of every single American tax dollar. This expansive budget, even by the most conservative estimates, *is fifty times larger* than the budgets for the Department of Education, the Department of Housing and Urban Development, the Environmental Protection Agency, and the State Department. It does not make practical sense to spend on this scale. This cannot be said enough. Imagine what our schools could be like if we spent $300 billion on the education of our children. Imagine the health care we could offer to Americans everywhere with a fraction of the budget the Pentagon gets every single year. Imagine the progress we could make against – as President Kennedy called them – the common enemies of all mankind; poverty, disease, famine, and war.

As someone who has spent nearly a decade working in technology, I am amazed at the speed of technological progress and innovation. The depth of complexity found in computation that Americans now find routine is staggering. It inspires me with genuine awe, and it advances in sophistication at an alarming rate. The most revealing and illuminating thing about technology is what humans choose to use it for first; war and sex are almost always the first implementations of bleeding edge tech. The contrast of usage should stick out like a sore thumb to everyone. An American drone pilot in Las Vegas can fire a missile that lands in Yemen with total ease. All of the technical kinks and issues that this capacity presents have been soundly solved. Humanity has perfected the art of killing, and has used every single advance in technological capacity for this purpose without exception. Cancer, diabetes, muscular dystrophy, and any other disease currently incurable still manage to confound us. We would rather first use our knowledge for the vulgar purposes of dealing death rather working for the common good.

I feel it necessary to reiterate that I am not arguing for pacifism in the slightest. The American military can have the biggest budget on earth. I would be happy to write the check myself – but the size of that check should be reasonable, defensible, and must fall within the bounds of a fair appraisal of future military expense. It must be said simply; when we give the military half-a-trillion-dollars a year, we are harming America domestically by neglecting sectors equally as important as the common defense. What is the purpose of having the most well financed and sophisticated military if our highways and bridges are left to rot, collapse and decay? What, exactly, is gained by outspending the rest of the planet in military expenditures if our children are forced to spend every day in underfunded and dilapidated schools?

The Death Penalty

There's always a pocket of subversion in every community, and as my stomach started to sour on the haughtiness of the Bible college demographic, I took some joy in finding them. Some of my favorite classmates were two exchange students from Haiti, and you would be hard-pressed to find kinder humans on the face of the whole planet. I never heard them speak a negative word about anyone or anything during the course of several years. Maybe these differences were cultural, or maybe they were just extraordinarily nice. They seemed to never stop smiling. Both men were intimidatingly smart, too. You can't graduate with a degree in the Bible without learning to translate the original text from Hebrew and Greek, and these Haitians learned both languages through the filter of English, which was their second language. The mental gymnastics this must have required would have made lesser men melt. They endured it all quite gracefully.

On one lazy, weekend afternoon, I started to gab with them while leaning on the doorframe to their dorm room. Our particular wing of this dorm was largely populated with students pursuing a pastoral ministries degree (we liked longer quiet hours) and was replete with the typical, guns-and-God American conservatives. The topic of the death penalty came up, somehow, and I expressed to the Haitians that I did not believe capital punishment was ethical. I'll never forget their response; their brows began to furrow, and they replied with some incredulity that they shared my view as well. "Voltaire says only God makes life - who are we to take it away?" They exclaimed. Who are we to take life, indeed?

But in the spirit of this chapter, I will present the abolition of the death penalty as a cost-effective measure first; the United States chooses to execute people at tremendous expense to the taxpayer, and there is no return on this investment in the slightest.

"For example, a new study of the cost of the death penalty in Colorado revealed that capital proceedings require six times more days in court and take much longer to resolve that life-without-parole (LWOP) cases. The study, published in the University of Denver Criminal Law Review, found that LWOP cases required an average of 24.5 days of in-court time, while the death-penalty cases required 147.6 days. The authors noted that selecting a jury in an LWOP case takes about a day and a half; in a capital case, jury selection averages 26 days. In measuring the comparative time it takes to go from charging a defendant to final sentencing, the study found that LWOP cases took an average of 526 days to complete; death cases took almost four calendar years longer – 1902 days." [6]

There is simply no debate here; the death penalty is extravagantly expensive, and it consumes an enormous amount of time to prosecute. Productivity is lost in the process, and the expenditure for executions far exceed the costs of life imprisonment. There are usually two reasons offered to justify this madness; the death penalty deters future crime, and it gives the families and friends of the victim necessary emotional closure.

I first saw this argument on Penn and Teller's terrific HBO series "Bullshit," and it's stuck with me ever since: the criminal mindset, in nearly all cases, cannot be meaningfully deterred by the existence of the death penalty. If we examine three common causes of death-penalty-worthy crime, we can this dynamic in action.

First, we have the crime of passion; a man comes home, discovers a stranger in bed with his wife, and in the heat of his anger, he murders the stranger. Could it be reasonably said that in this scenario, the man committing the crime of passion will have the presence of mind not to commit a murder because he might get the death penalty? Certainly not.

Second, let's talk about the crimes of rape and murder that are committed from a position of illness or compulsion. For an example, let's use a serial killer with an untreated mental ailment like schizophrenia. He murders his victims as a result of a mental deficiency or disability, and while this factor does not indemnify him in the slightest, deterrence, again, could not enter into the equation. The killer might well be aware that his actions might result in a death penalty verdict for him, but his compulsion overrides his ability to make rational choices. In the second position, the death penalty as a deterrent fails again.

Lastly, we come to the crimes of rape and murder committed intentionally, with no mitigating circumstances. For this example, we'll examine the motivations of a husband who murders his wife for the insurance money. The husband commits the murder, predominantly, for the financial benefit it gives him. He is not motivated, primarily, by passion, or by illness, or by compulsion. He has a financial motive to commit the crime. He premeditates the act, makes preparations for the murder, and with a sound and sober mind, carries out the crime successfully. The risks of jail time, or the death penalty, if applicable, have already entered his mind during his premeditation, and he decided to commit the murder anyway. Capital punishment did not deter him. In this argument, like the rest, the existence of death penalty provides no hurdle to the criminal. It serves no practical purpose. It has no measurable benefit for crime reduction:

"Assume for a moment that the death penalty is a deterrent. How much crime does it actually deter? The economist Isaac Ehrlich, in an oft-cited 1975 paper, put forth an estimate that is generally considered optimistic: executing 1 criminal translates into 7 fewer homicides that the criminal might have committed. Now do the math. In 1991, there were 14 executions in the United States; in 2001, there were 66. According to Ehrlich's calculation, those 52 additional executions would have accounted for 364 fewer homicides in 2001—not a small drop, to be sure, but less than 4 percent of the actual decrease in homicides that year. So even in a death penalty advocate's best-case scenario, capital punishment could explain only one twenty-fifth of the drop in homicides in the 1990s. And because the death penalty is rarely given for crimes other than homicide, its deterrent effect cannot account for a speck of decline in other violent crimes. It is extremely unlikely, therefore, that the death penalty, as currently practiced in the United States, exerts any real influence on crime rates. Even many of its onetime supporters have come to this conclusion. "I feel morally and intellectually obligated simply to concede that the death penalty experiment has failed," said U.S. Supreme Court Justice Harry A. Blackmun in 1994, nearly twenty years after he had voted for its reinstatement. "I no longer shall tinker with the machinery of death." [7]

I argued this point (loosely) in a philosophy classroom at Greenville College and was lightly heckled by a classmate who sternly asked if he had shot my mother "in the face with a crossbow" if I would still argue against the death penalty for him. I said yes; I might want to kill my mother's murderer in the moment, but basing a judicial system off how we feel moments after violence seems to be the definition of imprudence. My argument, painfully, did not carry the day or win the room, and I remember sharing a rather fitful walk to a nearby convenience store with a sympathetic acquaintance to soothe my sorrow with chocolate milk. Therein lies the core incompatibility with humans and the death penalty: it doesn't feel cathartic. It seems egregiously unfair. Instant and bloody revenge always plays better to a crowd, and rationality doesn't win many popularity contests. Critically, the religious crowd has traditionally thrown its support behind "tough" laws and sentences for criminals, too:

"Retributive justice in the form of the death penalty can also be seen in numerous biblical stories. For example, after judging the actions of the inhabitants of Earth and finding that only Noah and his family were righteous, God punished everyone else with a deadly flood. Similarly, when Lot offered two angels shelter in his Sodom home, he and his family were spared while the people who went

against God's wishes were sentenced to a fiery death by God. Thus, not surprisingly, philosophers, lawmakers, and others, have historically relied upon the Jewish Torah or the Christian Old Testament to justify their support for the death penalty despite the commandment, of the ten found in the Book of Exodus, that direct the same not to murder."
8

Capital punishment is barbarism. It is a vindictive and hateful policy that is wholly unbecoming of a dignified and developed nation. It does not meaningfully deter future crime. It does not rehabilitate offenders. It does magically bring back to life the victims of those we execute. The death penalty is an expensive exercise in futile cruelty, and we would all collectively be better off without it.

The Sex Trade

In the United States, save for Nevada, prostitution is flatly illegal, and this prohibition continues to needlessly claim lives all across the county. Make no mistake; the horrors of human trafficking are unspeakable and not lost on me. I am appalled and outraged by the modern slavery of the sex trade, but outright legalization is the best way to address the problem, and would be the most effective method to end the stranglehold that the criminal underworld has on the market. In the 1920s, the United States amended the Constitution and outlawed the production and consumption of alcohol. During this time period, rival beer distributors would shoot each other dead on the streets. The mafia became enormously powerful in the power vacuum, and a tremendous amount of damage was done with the best of intentions. That sort of violence doesn't spring up around the business of alcohol anymore; and why do we suppose that is the case?

Because the United States legalized the sale and consumption of alcohol, and as a result, Budweiser sales executives aren't engaging in gunfights with their competitors. Alcohol is every bit as dangerous as prostitution, and would be doubly so if driven back underground. Why are the rules different for the sex trade? The qausi-legality of professional prostitution in the U.S. speaks to our collective sexual repression and holy-than-thou attitude when it comes to the unpreventable. The absurdity of it is laughable; open a media production company with the expressed intention of paying women to perform sexual acts on camera, and the federal government will happily sign off on the paperwork and will gladly deduct taxes from the income you generate in the process. Remove the cameras from the equation, and a SWAT team might kick in the doors. Surely, everyone can see the silliness in this state of affairs, but only the lunatic fringe of the religious right are actively campaigning to make pornography illegal. The opposition to legalization is almost always inconsistent in this fashion, and the ones who suffer the most are the sex workers themselves.

The damage, for every victim of the sex trade, is made significantly worse by keeping it in the dark; organized crime syndicates retain their stranglehold on the business, and continue to traffic young girls and women, sex workers are forced to operate in the shadows and without basic workplace safety afforded to nearly everyone else in any other profession, and in a deregulated environment, legal methods of dispute resolution no longer exist, and as a result violence is the most effective way of settling conflicts. This system exists to our detriment, and setting aside ethical concerns momentarily, the same revenue problem rears its head yet again: by making this industry illegal, taxes are not deducted from the revenue generated. The losses compound in the same way our fiscal losses compound with immigration and the drug war. The United States pays to prosecute these crimes, and does so continually, without any expectation that the root cause will ever be meaningfully stopped. These laws are not enforceable, and they are foolish campaigns of well-intentioned moralism that have absolutely no chance of succeeding. Prostitution is inevitable, and will be naturally occurring for the remainder of human history. To pretend otherwise is completely disingenuous.

Immutable problems like prostitution cannot be solved; but they can be managed. To return to the alcohol metaphor, no one asks how humanity can "end" alcoholism with laws and legislation, instead, they ask how this social problem can best be handled. To see these vexing issues in one dimension is immature; and as a result of our squeamishness and repression, sex workers drop dead from preventable diseases and workplace violence. This is a lamentable state of affairs, and it worsens every day on account of our inaction, our stuffy moralizing, and on account of our rigid sexual mores. There are many attitudes that are frequently repeated across the conservative platform, and in this instance, we see the religious undertones pulsating in the same undercurrent; prostitution has a simple solution in the conservative view, men should stop paying for sex, and women should stop exchanging sex for money.

Surface-level judgementalism like this isn't just evidence of poor (or selective) reasoning skill, it is also evidence of a failure (or refusal) to see the bigger picture. Sex workers start in the industry for a litany of different reasons, but chiefly among them is poverty. Where are the Evangelical cultural warriors when we go to the polls to increase federal assistance programs for the needy among us who live below the poverty line? Almost unfailingly, they line up on the side of Republicans, who take perverse pleasure in gutting entitlement programs. When there's little choice left to these men and women, they turn to the seedy underbelly of our economy to get by. For this, we put them in prison. For this, we all collectively spend taxpayer money to house and feed them as prisoners. It doesn't make sense from a fiscal or moral perspective.

Often, apologists of the legalization movement have a tendency to distort the truth. I concede this point fully, and have no intention of ducking or dismissing the undeniable truths about the worst aspects of the sex trade. People (predominately women and girls) are sold into slavery to serve the needs of this industry every day. Proponents of legalization can occasionally view the problem with rose-tinted glasses. They hold up 'best case' examples of sex workers who have other options but choose to work in the industry. Some women, for instance, claim that the experience is sexually liberating for them. I have no doubt that this is true for many sex workers, but intellectually, I believe it is best to reason from the median experience; drawing not from the absolute worse or best case.

"Both the oppression and empowerment paradigms are one-dimensional and essentialist. While exploitation and empowerment are certainly present in sex work, there is sufficient variation across time, place, and sector to demonstrate that sex work cannot be reduced to one or the other…Victimization, exploitation, agency, job satisfaction, self-esteem and other dimensions should be treated as *variables* (not constants) that differ between sex work, geographical locations, and other structural conditions." [9]

This is perhaps a polite way of saying that this issue, like any other, should not be dealt with in absolutes. The experience of working in this trade, as it is in any other, is contingent upon the factors listed in the passage above. It should not be condoned or condemned uniformly because it does not exist monolithically. What's more, the image of prostitution that many Americans often associate with this vocation is that of the woman on the street corner leaning into an open window. While these types of engagements are certainly common, that image has powerfully distorted our collective perception of vast swathes of the industry. "Street level" prostitution, as defined in Ronald Weitzer's book on the legalization of the sex trade, is dangerous work often performed by desperate people who are selling sex to survive, or to maintain drug addictions. "Indoor" prostitution is a different animal entirely:

"It is not the mere fact of being indoors that distinguishes indoor from street prostitution but rather that certain characteristics of indoor settings are preconditions for a work environment that can be superior to the streets. These characteristics include the following:

- Indoor workers are less accessible and hence less vulnerable to street predators.

- Meeting a client indoors allows for more thorough screening than what is usually possible on the street.

- If one works indoors with a manager, receptionist, or other providers, they are available to intervene in the event that a client becomes abusive.

- Working indoors shields one from the elements, which can pay dividends for one's comfort and health.

- If conducted discreetly, indoor work does not present a public nuisance, whereas street commerce is often associated with public disturbance and generates complaints from nearby residents and merchants." [10]

Many of the concerns raised about the safety of sex workers are herein addressed rather comprehensively; and it should come as no surprise that indoor prostitutes report far lower rates of robbery, assault, and rape when working indoors as opposed to their street-level counterparts. [11]

It is at this point I am forced to ask a rather pointed question of the anti-legalization crowd: would you prefer higher, or lower, rates of assault for the sex workers whose safety you claim to be concerned with? Would you prefer higher, or lower, rates of rape for the people who are currently working in the industry? The reduction in violent crime against prostitutes could be accomplished quite easily by bringing all of prostitution indoors, by making it legal, and by regulating the industry as the United States regulates any other industry. Beyond insulating American sex workers from overt attack, legalization would have the added benefit of drastically improving their occupational safety. Legalization would (and where it is enacted, often does) significantly reduce the transmission of sexually transmitted diseases, and gives sex workers a greater ability to screen their clients. To put it bluntly; those who refuse to support legalization on account of the health and safety of prostitutes, either do not know, or do not care, about the improvements in both arenas that legalization provides.

Outlawing prostitution does nothing to stop human trafficking; if anything, it has *precisely* the opposite effect. Driving the sex trade underground only serves to strengthen the power of organized crime. Just as the end of prohibition effectively ended violence between alcohol distributors, so, too, would sensible legislation de-incentivize illicit human trafficking for the purposes of prostitution. In fact, the act of criminalizing buying and selling of sex itself comes at an enormously high price:

> "Criminalization has several consequences. First, arrests and fines have little deterrent effect on the sellers, who quickly return to selling sex. Yet arrest and punishment can be considered harmful because of the stigma of a criminal record. Second, at least some of those arrested present no harm to the public, insofar as their activities occur in discreet private settings between willing sellers and buyers. Third, criminalization is *costly to the criminal justice system, expenditures that could be reallocated to other priorities.* Fourth, criminalization jeopardizes sex workers insofar as they fear reporting victimization to the police. Many prostitutes are reluctant to report rape, robbery, and assault because they want to conceal their illegal activities or because they believe the police will not take their reports seriously." 12 (emphasis mine)

The moralizing of the anti-legalization crowd *accomplishes nothing.* It protects no one. It does not meaningfully prevent the purchase of sex. It does not meaningfully prevent people from being sold into sexual slavery. It does not provide a deterrent to future sex work after incarceration. What it does accomplish is ghastly; it stamps those caught up in prostitution with criminal records that can often blacklist them from future offers of legal employment, it can often make women, who are already fearful of reporting rape, sexual assault, and violence, *even more afraid* to go to the police and press charges, and lastly, all of these counterproductive policies are financed with taxpayer funds. It is a lose-lose-lose situation.

The American prostitute is the wounded man to our passing Levite in Jesus' parable. They lie battered, injured, and maimed along the road, and instead of being the Good Samaritan who lifts them up from the ditch, we avert our gaze, because looking soberly at the problem of the sex trade makes us uncomfortable. It would require an open and honest dialog about human sexuality, a chore Americans have long avoided like the plague. It would require a suppression of our judgmental attitudes, a habit Christian Americans have long been unable to quit. The question, of course, is not "What is best for the sex workers?" but "What are Americans willing to change to help them?"

Judeo-Christian sexual ethics, without question, have only served to aggravate this problem. Both the Jewish and Christian traditions not only condoned slavery – offering instructions in their Scriptures on how a master should treat their slaves – but also gave clear instruction on how sexual intercourse should be bought and sold through the legislative systems of bride prices and dowries. The prostitute is a harlot whose expense is never justified; but a pre-pubescent girl could be righteously purchased for sexual intercourse via an arranged marriage. The buyers, during this historical era, were of course not bound to monogamy post-marriage; they were free to compile harems of girls and women if they were men of means or royalty. At every impasse, any excuse proffered to keep prostitution illegal simply evaporates in my hands at the first moment of scrutiny. I detest, most, I think, the implication that the sex trade is inherently unsafe and thus is immoral to condone. A wholesome activity widely enjoyed in the United States is the consumption of professional sports; or said another way, the act of watching grown men slowly destroying their bodies over time while risking death, dismemberment, and serious injury in the process. This causes these detractors of sex trade legalization no cognitive dissonance. I suppose the objection does not truthfully come from a place of concern after all, does it?

I am not unmindful that innocent people are subjected to unspeakable cruelty in the sex trade; it is precisely for that reason that I so ardently support its legalization. If it was my daughter working in a brothel, I would unquestionably wish for her to be employed in a principality where it is legal, and where more, not fewer, workplace protections exist. I would wish for her to go to work for an employer that she may elect to leave at any time, for any reason, as are the rights of any American employee in an "at-will" employment state. The United States should remove the nationwide prohibition, and take the health and safety of its citizens in the sex trade seriously.

Immigration

Analyzing the total costs incurred by an aggressive anti-immigration policy (like the one proposed by President Trump) is another terrific example of short-sighted conservative action that spends more than it saves. To be clear, immigration from impoverished nations to developed ones *can never be completely stopped.* It was easy to laugh, then, as then-candidate Trump blabbered about his future wall being "impenetrable." Once Mr. Trump was elected, the promises about the wall started to crumble. Republican leadership begrudgingly conceded that in some points, the wall would actually be a fence, and after officials from the Mexican government swore up and down that their country would not pick up the tab for the wall as Trump promised, suddenly another concession came from the GOP; Congress would foot the initial bill for the construction of the wall, but America would be reimbursed through trade tariffs with Mexico. To call this diplomacy juvenile would be an insult to wise youngsters everywhere. Forget about the construction costs (The Department of Homeland Security estimates a price tag of $21.6 billion) and forget about the long-term maintenance and staffing expenditures that the wall will incur over the course of its lifetime. Let's focus, instead, on the economic impacts of slowing illegal immigration and deportation.

"Pew Research estimates that there were around eight million undocumented workers in the US in 2014. That's roughly 5 percent of the workforce. "Deporting 5 percent of the workforce would disrupt business activity," said Yelena Shulyatyeva senior US economist at Bloomberg Intelligence. She also pointed out that the six states with the highest concentration of undocumented workers account for 40 percent of all the goods and services produced in the country." Undocumented workers often fill low-wage jobs such as maintenance and farm work," she said. "Labour shortages could lead to an inflation spike due to severe upward wage pressures." While American workers could undoubtedly use a raise, a sudden and dramatic wage "spike" can have a destructive ripple effect... That could damage the US economy if it dissuades foreign-born students from seeking degrees in the country...A 2011 study by the American Enterprise Institute, a conservative think-tank, found that an additional 100 foreign-born workers in science, technology, engineering and mathematics fields with advanced degrees from US universities created 262 jobs for citizens born in the US. If students feel unwelcome or unsafe studying on US shores, there are other countries where they can earn degrees, and settle down to become job creators. Immigrants are also at the forefront of many cutting edge tech companies. A recent study by the National Foundation for American Policy found that more than half of US start-up companies worth at least $1bn had one or more immigrant founders; a list that includes the likes of Elon Musk's Space X, which employs around 5,000 people. There are those in the economic ecosystem who stand to benefit from Trump's immigration policies. Firms that build and operate prisons could profit handsomely from the executive order instructing Immigration and Customs Enforcement officials to immediately build and operate new detention facilities. But weigh that against all the potential negatives outlined above, not to mention the price tag for detaining and deporting undocumented workers and preventing future entry, which the American Action Forum estimated would cost taxpayers between $400bn to $600bn." [9]

Immigration, contrary to what populist ideology might tell us, is a net gain for economic strength. It is a vital pipeline for the acquisition of both skilled and unskilled labor, and our own internal economic infrastructure is dependent upon the influx of immigrants. We can see clearly what kind of impact switching off the valve would have, but what does it cost the taxpayer to deport illegal immigrants? Depending on the source you consult, ICE (Immigration and Customs Enforcement) spends anywhere from $8,500 to $10,000 for each individual deportation. This is particularly stupid when 'repeat offenders' are factored into the equation:

"Because the security situation in Mexico and Central America has deteriorated so badly over the last decade, citizens of these countries are more motivated than ever to run the risks of the north-bound journey. And it doesn't matter to them how many Border Patrol agents get assigned to the border, or how many miles of fence we build. This is a concept that is extremely difficult for politicians and individuals in the anti-illegal immigration camp to understand...Out of 364,768 illegal immigrants apprehended by the US Border Patrol in 2012, 100,735 had been previously apprehended at least twice, and 21,684 had been caught at least six times. One hundred and forty-five Mexican citizens had been apprehended by agents at least thirty-five time that year while trying to cross the border illegally." [10]

To be fair, in this context, apprehensions do not necessarily equal full deportations, but the point still remains; there is a significant, recurring, and *compounding* cost associated with the large-scale management of illegal immigration. The damage caused by deporting an immigrant is not merely contained just to the mechanisms used to apprehend and transport them back to their countries of origin:

"To understand deportation we must go beyond the numbers and examine what the rise of removals means for deportees. The criminalization of unauthorized migration has turned repeat immigration violations into felony offenses, punishable in some cases by years of incarceration. A congressional mandate requires Immigration and Customs Enforcement (one of the successors to the INS) to detain an unprecedented 34,000 people in immigration detention centers each day. Moreover, the U.S.-Mexico border is more militarized, and unauthorized migration is more expensive and dangerous, than ever before. It was more difficult for deported migrants to re-enter the U.S. in 2013 than at any previous point in history. These factors combined have resulted in an increasing number of families separated by deportation. The U.S. deported more than 200,000 parents of U.S.-citizen children between 2010 and 2012, and a more recent report estimated that 5,000 children have been placed in foster care after one or both of their parents were deported." [11]

Those who re-offend are often incarcerated at our expense. Immigrant children who are separated from their parents by deportation tossed into our foster care systems at our expense. Detention centers are constructed, maintained, and staffed to hold immigrants at our expense. These would all be bad enough, on their own merits, but add to this bill all of the lost tax revenue once working immigrants, however illegal, are no longer having deductions taken from legitimate paychecks. Why does America insist on operating these vast programs at a loss? Imagine, now, adding the expense of Trump's $21 billion dollar wall on top of an expanded deportation system on top of all of this waste.

> "The best evidence indicates that immigrants are a net financial plus to the government. However, comprehensive immigration reform has become an increasing irritant for immigrant-receiving states and cities: the fiscal benefit (i.e., taxes) is disproportionately paid to the federal government by immigrants, even though many of the costs of providing services – public education, public safety, and social services – are borne by the states and localities." [12]

At least some of the angst, fear, and dread white Americans feel when faced with an influx of new immigration can be explained by this dynamic. The federal government reaps most of the financial benefits that a new wave of cheap labor creates, while the state and local budgets foot the bill for their basic needs and services. Fair enough, but minor fiscal disputes do not drive people to commit hate crimes alone. They are blinded by the same white anxiety and racial resentment that causes so many problems in so many other arenas. This anti-immigrant mentality is deeply troubling, especially in the United States, where a majority of our white population comes from Irish, Italian, or German lineages.

> "The immigrant share of the population peaked in 1910 at 14.7 percent, with the vast majority in urban areas and particularly concentrated in the biggest cities. In that year 41 percent of New Yorkers were foreign born. And these immigrants were foreign indeed to the Americans of the heartland. The Irish were considered alien well into the twentieth century: The 1928 campaign of Al Smith, an Irish American Catholic, was greeted with burning crosses." [13]

Almost all of us came to the United States from immigrant families. Our surnames bear the stamp of our foreign origin. Mine in particular – *Steevens* – is ostensibly German (by one account, it was previously spelled *Steevenz*, but my ancestors changed the final letter to an "S" because of anti-German sentiment in the United States after the Great War) and I have some distant relatives who live in Stuttgart, Germany. After chatting with them over the internet, I discovered that one of my aunts suspects our bloodline has some English heritage tucked in there as well. My mother insists there was, in her words, 'a squaw' who married into our family at some point, thereby giving us some Native American heritage in addition to all of our European bloodlines. I simply do not have the ability to turn off my compassion and empathy on the basis of fear or greed. These, after all, are the primary concerns of anti-immigration advocates. *They're going to bring terrorism. They're going to cost too much.*

My hometown of Saint Louis has no shortage of immigrants, and our community is far better off because of them. The International Institute of St. Louis is an organization that operates just a few miles down the street from my apartment, and they help refugees acclimate to life in Missouri. I attended a seminar at the institute, and their Chief Executive Officer gave a lecture that was profound. She explained that the International Institute, at the culmination of the relocation process, gives new refugees a purple bag adorned with their logo before they board their planes. If you see a refugee with this bag at the airport, it is probably safe to assume that *all* of their worldly possessions are contained inside of it. I can scarcely imagine anything more heartbreaking. How could Americans like us; so wealthy, so fortunate, so insulated from famine, hunger, and disease, turn our backs on our fellow humans? The executive went on to explain that after the terrorist attacks of September 11th, the scrutiny of these displaced persons has risen to fever pitch. Refugees have to be approved for entry into the United States by nearly every American intelligence agency. For this reason, families are often split up because military-aged men do not often make the cut, and as a result, women and children often migrate to America alone.

Some vicious myths started to circulate about the size and scope of the program. Rumors were spreading about resettled refugees living like kings off of the taxes of Americans. This couldn't be any further from the truth – the refugees are even required to pay back the American taxpayer for the cost of their international airfare within six months – and the food and housing benefits provided by the government are meager at best, and can only subsidize a fraction of typical living costs. This, too, is another example of what happens when reason sleeps and hysteria is allowed to run unchecked. Great ideas that benefit everyone get trampled in the process. Saint Louis, for instance, owes almost all of its vibrancy to its immigrant communities. The Italians gave us "The Hill," the Bosnians gave us "Bevo Mill," and you can find the finest Vietnamese food in the state at *Mai Lee*, which is another immigrant small-business in a city filled to the brim with them. The International Institute was clear on that point as well; immigrants are twice as likely to start their own small businesses (compared to American citizens) when they arrive to the United States. They don't have much to lose when they step off the plane, so they don't have a problem taking that sacred risk of starting a business that Republicans revere so much. In fact, Saint Louis itself is a textbook example of "white flight," and the city has been actively depopulating for decades. Suburbs started to spring up in the principalities of St. Charles, O'Fallon, Wentzville, and Chesterfield (among many others) and as the tax base started to disappear, the city began to deteriorate. The thing that can fix these dilapidated urban centers is precisely the thing that white, conservative, Christian Americans often fear the most; immigration. We need the small businesses to draw taxable revenue. Landlords need tenants for their properties. Multinational and local businesses alike need a client base that isn't a forty-five minute drive away.

Of course, the *reason* people harbor these sentiments is not because they were reasoned into harboring them. They exist because of fear, or ignorance, or inadequacy, or insecurity. These racist and xenophobic philosophies persist because they are not difficult to understand or adopt. Humans, by their very nature, are social animals with a neurological need to classify external individuals and groups. Some individuals are family, others are friends, some groups are adversaries, some are ambivalent, some are cordial. As such, humans find instinctual comfort in coagulating with similar or identical ethnic groups, and racial tensions are agitated when liberals attempt to integrate communities together when they aren't ready for change. This is a core argument of conservatism, too; societies shouldn't change before they are ready. Forcing them to change creates division. Gradualism is the best method for enacting social change, and those who overlook its importance have no respect for the lasting institutions they tarnish in the process. This is what they'll have us believe – *just let us change when we're ready and we'll get there in the end*, they claim – and if you buy it, I have a bridge to sell you.

> "The fact that the resistance to change has something to do with conservatism – and with psychology – is pretty hard to dispute. History's most famous conservatives have described their belief systems in just this way. Thus, criticizing the French Revolution, Edmund Burke wrote that 'People will not look forward to posterity, who never look backwards to their ancestors.' And describing the purpose of the magazine he founded, *The National Review*, William F. Buckley, Jr. wrote that the publication 'stands athwart history, yelling 'Stop!' It should be obvious how an ideology that is resistant to change would appeal to the need for certainty and stability and the desire to manage fear and threat." [14]

So for the sake of slowing progress, we're to build a wall and make immigration more difficult for poor Central Americans? What kind of effect would such a project have on the people they are meant to deter?

> "I come from a family of Cuban immigrants, and I know from listening to their experiences in the 1960s – along with those of Cubans who have taken more dangerous measures to come here – what fear and desperation will drive people to do. I acknowledge that my family was in a different situation; they were able to come here legally under asylum provisions because of Fidel Castro's communist revolution. Despite that, immigration is still extremely dangerous for some Cuban migrants who try to reach US shores by travelling across the shark-infested Florida Straights on makeshift rafts with little food and water. There are untold Cuban immigrants who have drowned trying to make the ninety-mile journey from Havana to Key West, just as there are untold numbers of Mexican and Central American migrants who have perished in the sand and scrub south of Arizona and Texas. Whether it's Mexicans, or Cubans, or the Chinese, or Iraqis, foreigners will always want to come to the United States." [15]

This, of course, is different than appraising the efficacy of the wall itself; its ability to slow immigration, even at the preposterous scale proposed by President Trump, is dubious at best. The most efficient strategy for stopping illegal immigration doesn't revolve around building a wall, but intercepting the traffic that crosses in the first place:

> "So is the border fence doing its job? Before that question can even be addressed, it's important to understand that the fence was never designed to truly *stop* anyone. My Border Patrol escort in San Diego was very clear about this: "The border fence *is*, however, designed to slow people down long enough so we can respond." While it was good to know agents aren't naïve enough to think anyone will believe the fence is impenetrable, they don't really go out of their way to explain that the response time to an attempted breach can vary from two minutes in San Diego sector to never in places with bad weather, washed out roads, or insufficient agents near the breach site. Back in the early 1990s, the primary fence "by itself, did not have a discernable impact on the influx of unauthorized aliens coming across the border in San Diego," according to a Congressional Research Service analysis." [16]

Is it, really, that much of a surprise to discover that a physical wall is a poor response to the intricate problem of illegal immigration? What should be abundantly clear now is that the wall has little to do with actual immigration policy; it is another racist dog-whistle in a Trump campaign littered with them. It is meant to emotionally destabilize the anxious white voter, meant to inflame latent racist feelings, and plainly designed as an appeal to white purity.

I am not advocating these policies because of their fiscal results alone. In my view, these are the best moral choices our nation could make in each arena. I remain convinced that the death penalty accomplishes nothing more than burying another human being. I remain convinced that America's problems often originate from the fact that 2% of our budget goes to education, while more than half goes to our military. I am firmly convinced that the horrors of the sex trade are made far worse by insisting it operates in the dark rather than the light. I am completely convinced that our nation is almost entirely comprised of immigrants, and to sneer at these new, teeming masses, when our families received kindness is sickening. Other Americans are often equally convinced in the opposite direction on all these fronts; they are entitled to these opinions, but they cannot claim that it is expense or expenditure alone that drives their opposition. The compassionate viewpoint is almost always the cheapest, collectively, and in our post-truth era, these are realities that the United States can ill afford to let conservatives distort.

Pious Prosperity

‡‡‡

Chapter 7

"Where in the Bible does it say I have to drive a Honda?" – Benny Hinn

═══

American culture is too often reduced by outsiders (unfairly, I might add) to the tired troupes of God, guns, and wealth. While this view is simplistic, it isn't, to put it bluntly, untrue. Anyone who's stepped foot inside a church in the United States can likely attest to the depth of the relationship Americans have with religion, but a peculiar sect of Christianity - the "health and wealth gospel" - has enjoyed decades of popularity with American Christians. Super church magnates like Joel Osteen and Benny Hinn have capitalized on this demographic, and promise their disciples the ability to "claim" prosperity or medical healing for themselves in the name of the Lord. This philosophy has permeated all throughout the Republican party, and has welded together the interests of the financial elite with the aspirations of the economically struggling Christians.

This salacious dynamic - one that allows for billionaires to shrewdly abuse the teachings of a Jewish carpenter who told his followers to sell all they had to follow him - powers the Republicans to political victory. Americans have a confusing relationship with God and money. Renown globally for its conspicuous consumption, the United States is home to one of the most vibrant economies on the planet. It should come as no surprise that a nation founded by the expansionist aims of both the missionary and the gold-rusher have developed prickly opinions about how one should worship, and how one ought to make a living. Critically, the religious and the wealthy are more often than not, brothers and sisters in arms in political combat. The glowing praise Mr. Trump received from the likes of Peter

Thiel and Jerry Falwell Jr. is enough to validate the cross-contamination between these two disparate camps, and progressives around the world have long been puzzled by this strange marriage.

The leaders of the enterprise and spiritual industries are rabidly single-minded and hopelessly self-interested. Left to their own devices, the rich would gladly build palaces like French royalty without sacrificing a single cent to the public coffers, and the religious, left unchecked, would build their religion into a monolith that consumes all of governance and society. From the perspective of the progressive, these two interests are toxic and exist at the peril of the average citizen. When they intersect – as they did, rather seamlessly, in the election of Trump – the question of how to reduce their terrifying power becomes significant.

Depending on the research you consult, you may come away with different percentages of wealth distribution among American citizens. Rather than drowning in the specifics, I think it sufficiently safe to say that very few Americans are high-earners, and those who are extremely wealthy wield a disproportionate amount of influence over the American government than their less-wealthy counterparts. Christians, of the politically neoconservative variety, represent a much more challenging appraisal. According to Kevin Phillips' research in his 2004 book *American Theocracy*, 94% of Americans believe in God, 84% believe in miracles, and 75% believe in the Devil or Satan. Perhaps the best delineation for our purposes is this survey question : *Is the Bible literally accurate?* To which 55% of Americans polled replied in the affirmative. Fair enough, plenty of people claim to believe in a God, but a large share of those clearly don't take up the mantle of Christian fanaticism.

The One-Percenters can barely believe their luck, I imagine. At their disposal is a massive bloc of highly-motivated voters who can be cajoled into cheering for Estate Tax revisions that will never, ever, benefit anyone other than greedy millionaires, just as long as one of those millionaires smiles real big and wide while clutching a Bible in one hand. How do we lift our nation out of polarization? How do we break the noxious spell of the pious and prosperous? The beginning of the journey has to begin with identifying the problem as it exists – we live in a society that is tailored to the preferences of the financial elite.

"What are the main principles of a banana republic? A very salient one might be that it has a paper currency which is an international laughingstock: a definition that would immediately qualify today's United States. We may snicker at the thriller from Wasilla, who got her first passport only last year, yet millions of once well-traveled Americans are now forced to ask if they can afford even the simplest overseas trip when their folding money is apparently issued by the

Boardwalk press of Atlantic City. But still, the chief principle of banana-ism is that of kleptocracy, whereby those in positions of influence use their time in office to maximize their own gains, always ensuring that any shortfall is made up by those unfortunates whose daily life involves earning money rather than making it. At all costs, therefore, the one principle that must *not* operate is the principle of accountability…What they put at risk, though, was others people's money and other people's property." [1]

Beyond the passing context of the American bailouts (which is the reference point here for Mr. Hitchens' article,) the foundation of conservatism itself is elitism and the preservation of the status quo.

"Because movement conservatism is ultimately about rolling back policies that hurt a narrow, wealthy elite, it's fundamentally antidemocratic. But however much the founders of the movement may have admired the way Generalissimo Franco did things, in America the route to political power runs through elections. There wouldn't be nearly as much money forthcoming if potential donors still believed, as they had every reason to in the aftermath of Barry Goldwater's landslide defeat in 1964, that advocating economic policies that increase inequality is a political nonstarter. Movement conservatism has gone from fringe status to a central role American politics because it has proved itself able to win elections. Ronald Reagan, more than anyone else, showed the way. His 1964 speech "A Time for Choosing," which launched his political career, and the speeches he gave during his successful 1966 campaign for governor of California foreshadowed political strategies that would work for him and other movement conservatives for the next forty years. Latter-day hagiographers have portrayed Reagan as a paragon of high-minded conservative principles, but he was nothing of the sort. His early political successes were based on appeals to cultural and sexual anxieties, playing on the fear of communism, and, above all, tacit exploitation of white backlash against the civil rights movement and its consequences." [2]

One irritating tenet of the Republican mantra is the necessity of fooling the uneducated. It's the old bait-and-switch. Say what they want to hear, and do what you want to do.

"The trick never ages, the illusion never wears off. *Vote* to stop abortion; *receive* a rollback in capital-gains taxes. *Vote* to make our country strong again; *receive* deindustrialization. *Vote* to screw those politically correct college professors; *receive* electricity deregulation. *Vote* to get government off our backs, *receive* conglomeration and monopoly everywhere from media to meatpacking. *Vote* to stand tall against terrorists; *receive* Social Security privatization efforts. *Vote* to strike a blow against elitism; *receive* a social order in which wealth is more concentrated than ever before in our lifetimes, in which workers have been stripped of power and CEO's rewarded in a manner beyond imagining." [3]

Post-Trump, the intelligentsia on the left and their 'bubbles' were diagnosed as one of the primary problems. If nothing else can be gleaned from this puzzling shotgun wedding, we can at least deduct that the Republicans know how to speak to the lower and middle class whites in the most efficient fashion. This phenomenon has many possible explanations, be they aspirational (the poor don't like to think of themselves as such and like to entertain thoughts of financial grandeur) or otherwise, the wealthy elite have leaned into this strategy simply because it has been proven to work. The political left has far too much variety and disunity for this type of mob mentality, and the one percenters know a good market when they see one.

"Money is the glue of movement conservatism, which is largely financed by a handful of extremely wealthy individuals and a number of major corporations, all of whom stand to gain from increased inequality, an end to progressive taxation, and a rollback of the welfare state – in short, from a reversal of the New Deal. And turning the clock back on the economic policies that limit inequality is, at its core, what movement conservatism is all about. Grover Norquist, an antitax activist who is one of the movement's key figures, once confided that he wants to bring America back to what it was "up until Teddy Roosevelt, when the socialists took over. The income tax, the death tax, regulation, all that." [4]

The divorce between pro-business politics and the political left in the United States is a tale as old as the nation itself. Organized labor and unionization has galvanized bosses against their workers, and the democratic left has, quite rightly, prioritized the plight of the worker over that of the wealthy factory owner. Taxation, then, becomes the point of contention between the financial elite and the government itself:

"In the twenties, taxes had been a minor factor for the rich. The top income tax rate was only 24 percent, and because the inheritance tax on even the largest estates was only 20 percent, wealthy dynasties had little difficulty maintaining themselves. But with the coming of the New Deal, the rich started to face taxes that not only vastly higher than those of the twenties, but high by today's standards. The top income tax rate (currently on 35%) rose to 63 percent during the first Roosevelt administration, and 79 percent in the second. By the mid-fifties, as the United States faced the expenses of the Cold War, it had risen to 91 percent." [5]

The threat of lost prosperity has propelled normally intelligent and innovative people into the arms of brain-dead theocrats and demagogues. This is not a new development; right-leaning politicians have long loathed entitlement programs, and typically view them as outrageous forms of needless welfare.

"Ron Paul was asked at a Republican presidential debate what if "something terrible happens" to some guy who has no health insurance? What do you do? He said, "That's what freedom is all about: taking your own risks." Actually, when the moderator pushed back on this, he backed off and he said that people without health insurance would be taken care of by their families or their church. Then Rand Paul – this is more interesting – said national health insurance is slavery. He said, "I'm a physician, and if there's national health insurance, the government is forcing me to take care of someone who is ill. Why should I be a slave to the state?" Here we're getting capitalist pathology in its most extreme, lunatic form." [6]

Despite how regal President Trump might currently look in the Oval Office, this marriage is an unhappy one, and it is bound to fail. Automation and an exploding technology sector (an industry, by some estimates, that could account for nearly half of all jobs in the space of a few decades) are threatening to reverse this trend. The new money, soaking up sunshine in Silicon Valley, doesn't much care for the right-wing manifesto, and doesn't mind taxation, powerful women, or homosexuality. In my view, the most stunning shot across the neocon bow came in the uproarious protests against President's Trump travel ban. Among the masses of demonstrators crowding San Francisco's international airport was Sergey Brin – the co-founder of Google, and a man whose net worth likely exceeds $40 billion. If he is moved to object to the most wealth-friendly administration in American history, it seems to me safe to assume that the old guard is in a great deal of long term trouble. The present picture, though, is a bleak one, and it will likely get far worse before it gets any better. The conservative establishment has convinced poor whites to vote against their own interests for decades, and that trend shows no indication of declining any time soon.

"Sadly, those of us who have fallen prey to the siren song of the right are lining up behind a political and economic agenda that offers no way out of this mess and indeed would make it worse. Conservatives propose to only slash taxes on corporations and wealthy individuals, or to reduce regulations so as to ostensibly free up more potential investment dollars with which those companies and persons could create jobs. But if these folks are already flush with cash, what good will tax cuts do? How can such policies spur economic development, hiring and growth when incomes for most workers remain stagnant, and have been so for nearly *three decades*, thereby depressing demand? Corporate profitability is at its highest point in fifty years, and nearly 90 percent of the nation's recent income growth has gone to corporate profits (while only about one-tenth of one percent went to worker wages), suggesting that if all such entities needed was more money to restart the engine of employment, they would have done it long ago. If $2 trillion in cash reserves fails to spark a hiring spree, why would anyone assume that another $300 billion or so would make the difference? Rather, such tax cuts would simply reduce revenues for vital programs in education, health care and public sector job creation. They would result in the further evisceration of the safety net at the very moment when millions of people are increasingly in need of it." [7]

The insanity of it all – impoverished whites cheering the scissors that slice their own safety nets to bits – is enough to confound anyone. The shrewd and conniving nature of the wealthy using God and guns to swindle the heartland is repulsive. Lying always works best, and telling the truth is usually the worst thing any politician can do at any time. The phrase I used above got Mr. Obama into some hot water a few years back:

"You go into these small towns in Pennsylvania and, like a lot of small towns in the Midwest, the jobs have been gone now for 25 years and nothing's replaced them," Mr. Obama responded, according to a transcript of the fund-raiser published on Friday on The Huffington Post Web site. "And they fell through the Clinton administration, and the Bush administration, and each successive administration has said that somehow these communities are gonna regenerate and they have not," Mr. Obama went on. "And it's not surprising then they get bitter, they cling to guns or religion or antipathy to people who aren't like them or anti-immigrant sentiment or antitrade sentiment as a way to explain their frustrations." [8]

Obama told the truth and got pummeled for it. Mrs. Clinton did, too, when she accurately (and infamously) described the nature of many of Trump's supporters as deplorable.

> "You know, to just be grossly generalistic (sic), you could put half of Trump's supporters into what I call the basket of deplorables. Right? The racist, sexist, homophobic, xenophobic, Islamophobic — you name it. And unfortunately there are people like that. And he has lifted them up. He has given voice to their websites that used to only have 11,000 people, now have 11 million. He tweets and retweets offensive, hateful, mean-spirited rhetoric. Now some of those folks, they are irredeemable, but thankfully they are not America. [9]

It is perhaps a slight exaggeration (one Mrs. Clinton seems to concede with her preface) to claim "half" of Mr. Trump's supporters fit an extremist mold, but she did, very much, tell the truth about the nature of many his supporters. This was a truth that was undeniable – Mr. Trump did appear on *Infowars* with Sandy-Hook-denier Alex Jones of his own volition – and like clockwork, this became a paralyzing and powerfully stupid media controversy in which Mrs. Clinton was cajoled into insincerely apologizing for telling the truth.

Many Americans, not to put too fine a point on it, simply cannot handle the truth. They are not interested in nuance or complexity. They are not interested in information that takes time to acquire, or requires any amount of work, however small or negligible, to obtain. And what Trump's election teaches us irrefutably is that Americans don't want to hear the truth, they want to hear *aspirations*. They want to hear strength where there is weakness, they want to hear values where there is corruption, they want to certainty where there is doubt, and they want to hear of prosperity where there is poverty. This parlor trick, in my view, won't age well, and public opinion of these ruling conservatives will fall even further through the floor. Republicans once had a sense of proprietary, they once felt public opinion was a valid concern worthy of management, and saw no shame in reaching across the aisle towards their democratic counterparts when the option was reasonably available. Any semblance of this wholesome and altogether sane attitude is long since dead and gone, and the hyper-polarization of maniacal partisanship has replaced it entirely. The hyper-wealthy American elites are burglarizing the nation while the infrastructure decays underneath our feet.

> "I hope you read the findings of the Department of Transportation and the Federal Highway Administration that followed the plunge of

Interstate 35W in Minneapolis into the Mississippi River last August. Sixteen states, after inspecting their own bridges, were compelled to close some, lower the weight limits of others, and make emergency repairs. Of the nation's 600,000 bridges, 12 percent were found to be structurally deficient. This is an almost perfect metaphor for Third World conditions: A money class fleeces the banking system while the very trunk of the national tree is permitted to rot and crash." [10]

The problems become public burdens, and the collective harvest becomes a bounty enjoyed by the group that shrinks and shrinks. There is no ceiling to greed. It is limitless. The wealthy will always take as much as they can, and we should dispose of the notion that their gluttony is reasonable, restrained, or would destroy the economy if it was reasonably reigned in:

"Our current brand of capitalism is an ersatz capitalism. For proof of this go back to our response to the Great Recession, where we socialized losses, even as we privatized gains. Perfect competition should drive profits to zero, at least theoretically, but we have monopolies and oligopolies making persistently high profits. CEOs enjoy incomes that are on average 295 times that of the typical worker, a much higher ratio than in the past, without any evidence of a proportionate increase in productivity. If it is not the inexorable laws of economics that have led to America's great divide, what is it? The straightforward answer: our policies and our politics. People get tired of hearing about Scandinavian success stories, but the fact of the matter is that Sweden, Finland, and Norway have all succeeded in having about as much growth in per capita incomes as, or ever faster growth than, the United States and with far greater equality...So corporate welfare increases as we curtail welfare for the poor. Congress maintains subsidies for rich farmers as we cut back on nutritional support for the needy. Drug companies have been given billions of dollars as we limit Medicaid benefits. The banks that brought on the global financial crisis got billions while a pittance went to the homeowners and victims of the same banks' predatory lending practices. This last decision was particularly foolish. There were alternatives to throwing money at the banks and hoping it would circulate through increased lending. We could have helped underwater homeowners and the victims of predatory behavior directly." [11]

When the housing market imploded, the government subsidized failing private industries under the auspices of preventing further economic damage to low and middle class Americans. What this did, instead, was direct more capital to the people who created the mess in the first place, and we recoiled in shock and alarm when these same bankers shamelessly wrote bonus checks for themselves with taxpayer funds.

"And still, in so many words in the phrasing of the first bailout request to be placed before Congress, there appeared the brazen demand that, once passed, the "package" be subject to virtually no more congressional supervision or oversight. This extraordinary proposal shows the utter contempt in which the deliberative bodies on Capitol Hill are held by the unelected and inscrutable financial panjandrums. But welcome to another aspect of banana-republicdom. In a banana republic, the members of the national legislature will be (a) largely for sale and (b) consulted only for ceremonial and rubber-stamp purposes some time after all the truly important decisions have already been made elsewhere. I was very struck, as the liquefaction of a fantasy-based system proceeded, to read an observation by Professor Jeffrey A. Sonnenfeld, of the Yale School of Management. Referring to those who had demanded – successfully – to be indemnified by the customers and clients whose trust they had betrayed, the professor phrased it like this:

"These are people who want to be rewarded as if they were entrepreneurs. But they aren't. They didn't have anything at risk"

That's almost exactly right, except that they *did* have something at risk. What they put at risk, though, was other people's money and other people's property." [12]

They'll keep on stealing if we let them, and a society that rewards incompetence and theft will always rot from the inside out. Take Russia, for instance, (for the sake of clarity, I should mention a more in-depth look at Russia occurs in a later chapter) while we're on the topic of kleptocracy: It was once widely accepted, in a bipartisan fashion, that any nation that eliminates a free press, murders its opposition leaders, and invades other sovereign states on a whim is a dangerous pariah. Russia fit this bill with remarkable precision. They annexed Crimea, the first such seizure in European history since Adolf Hitler, Boris Nemtsov caught four bullets in the back virtually on the steps of the Kremlin itself, and Russia's state-owned RT is as ethically responsible as the insane ramblings of North Korea's trussed up reporters. Gary Kasparov, one of the most eloquent and powerful voices on Russia (and, it is not insignificant to note at this impasse, a passionate Republican and Rubio supporter, too), is virulently opposed to the moral equivalences and condonations that started to suddenly flow out from the right wing once allegations of a Russian connection started to hover over the Trump administration. In fact, long before this empty-headed partisanship sprang up, Kasparov was taking Russian apologists to task on both sides of the aisle.

> "One person's central role in a singular incident ends up looking more important that the serious issues, which have been building up for a long time, that the incident represents. That was the case of Edward Snowden, a traitor and spy to some and a whistleblower and hero to others. I have no special knowledge about his actions or his leaks, but I would surely feel differently about him had he not taken refuge in Russia, where his asylum request tacitly endorsed the dictatorial regime of his gracious host, Vladimir Putin. My reaction is not only due to Snowden's first statement from Russia, while he was still in legal limbo at Sheremetyevo airport, in which he included Putin's Russia – a police state and patron of despotism worldwide – on a list of nations that "stand against human rights violations carried out by the powerful rather than the powerless." Excuse me? Putin's many political prisoners would disagree quite strongly, as would the many opposition members who have had their emails hacked and their phone calls recorded by the KGB in attempts to discredit them. And Snowden could have been more respectful of the many injured and dead among journalists and his fellow whistleblowers in Russia. One note on Snowden's NSA revelations, however, speaking as someone who grew up under the all-seeing eye of the KGB and who is fighting its modern rebirth under Vladimir Putin: it is exasperating to hear blithe comparisons between the NSA, and other Western spy agencies or law enforcement organizations, and the vicious internal security regimes of the USSR and East Germany. The NSA is to the Stasi what a bad hotel is to a maximum security prison." [13]

Mr. Kasparov is devastatingly right here, and these glib comparisons to totalitarian regimes are tasteless and ignorant of realty. Edward Snowden, when confronted on the point Gary mentioned above, claimed that he did not choose to travel to Russia, but was forced to stay on account of the State Department cancelling his passport. That deflection is quite weak in my view. While I certainly concede Mr. Snowden did a great service to the American people (and we are all indebted to him for it), I too was deeply troubled by the cognitive dissonance he displayed. Often, he video-conferenced into American or European universities to lecture on human rights *from* one of the most repressive political regimes on the planet. During one of Putin's pseudo-town hall sessions, Snowden asked Putin for imaginary accountability on domestic Russian surveillance – Putin replied to his fatuous question with an equally fatuous response. "You and I will talk later," Mr. Putin riposted with a shit-eating grin, and to expect a czar with an ocean of blood on his hands to respond in any other fashion reveals the depth of Mr. Snowden's tackiness and naiveté. He allowed Putin to use him as a prop – the sort of tokenism that bullies love to use to as a veneer of transparency over frightful actions – and all the while the mafia state continued to churn unabated. The state of affairs we can plainly observe in Russia is a glimpse into the future of the United States if the neoconservative pogrom isn't stopped very soon. Corruption, wealth coagulation, the death of regulatory bodies, important government positions being stuffed with those loyal to the leader, and the angry distrust of the free press are all hallmarks of a burgeoning banana republic.

"The Putin regime is and always has been about one thing: money. Specifically, about how to move it into the bank accounts of Putin's allies. Hosting the Olympic Games, a first for Russia, as Moscow's 1980 was in the USSR, was a perfect way to shift tens of billions of dollars from the treasury and state-owned banks into private hands. Everything from infrastructure to venues and hotels to catering was done by companies hand-picked by the Kremlin, and it was no surprise to find the names of many of Putin's closest pals "going for the gold" a bit early in Sochi. The price tag soared far beyond the promised $12 billion (already a record) to an estimated $50 billion, more costly even than the lavish 2008 Beijing Summer Games. According to the *Economist*, the companies of Putin's old judo buddy Arkady Rotenberg alone received $7.4 billion in contracts. The entire 2010 Vancouver Winter Olympiad cost $6 billion. Hosting the games in Sochi was a dubious effort even if the classic old resort town were being turned into Xanadu with Putin as Kubla Khan. But due to epic levels of corruption, most of the money never even made it to Sochi. The construction was shoddy and many of the ambitious projects weren't even scheduled to be built until after the Games. That is, they were never built at all, and they never will be. It is fair to say that Switzerland won the most gold from Sochi regardless of the success of their team." [14]

Of course, as the title of this chapter might suggest, I am not merely speaking here about finance. The best way to cover the filthy stench of greed is with religion, and like the United States, Russia likes to use the same type of old myths as a shield against progress and transparency. Russia's LGBT community is hunted like sport, both by vicious bigots and the state-funded security services alike. If you can stomach it, the videos of homosexuals being beaten within inches of their lives are freely available on the internet. It is the orthodox Russian church that leads the charge against the helpless gays, wielding inordinate levels of influence over law makers, who, in turn, legislate incredibly hateful and idiotic policies. Beyond the scope of sexual orientation, we can also observe that women-hating is a core principle to the Russian right-wing. In January of 2017, a bill that decriminalized some aspects of domestic violence passed with ease in the Duma. Once you're finished beating a defenseless gay teenager in a public park, you can return home to kick the ever-loving shit out of your wife without fear of legal reprisals. The conservative triad is here on perfect display: pro-business, anti-woman, and pro-religion. In plain view, too, is the revolting cesspit all of these loyalties inevitably lead to.

The name of "conservatism" itself certainly implies that there is something traditional in the old order worthy of defense. I don't think it is unfair to claim that "preservationism" would be an appropriate description of this political mindset. *Let's keep the money where it is, let's keep the power where it is, and let's resist progress in the fashion described by our counterparts and opponents.* This, of course, is an easy statement to make when you are the one with the privilege. The inane and paranoid fear that accompanies wealth is a profoundly depressing phenomenon. During my college years, I scraped by on odd computing jobs here and there. One such gig was performing basic database management for an elderly man who needed to archive ancient digital records for a long-defunct business. He had done well for himself, his home was immaculate and beautiful, but I will never be able forget the depth of his anxiety. He physically shook while describing the potential of an audit. On multiple occasions, he would be at the literal brink of tears when he explained the necessity of avoiding penalties from the IRS. He had wealth, and the thought of losing it seemed to him to be worse than death.

When life is good, one supposes, the fear migrates from daily survival to lifestyle maintenance, and as the pro-business cadre rightfully remind us, there is no shame in success. Similarly, the desire to keep the lion's share of one's own work, risk, ingenuity, and creativity isn't unreasonable, nor is it unduly selfish. Barney Frank, the delightfully cantankerous liberal stalwart, claimed in a Netflix documentary that the difference between a liberal and conservative is simply the degree to which one thinks industries should be nationalized or privatized. This definition is a salient one, and I think no one wants to live in a coldly grey Soviet-style state where the government does everything, nor does anyone wish to live in the heartless prison of cowboy capitalism where there's a fee to be paid for collecting rainwater.

What exists now in the United States is not democracy, but some tepid mixture of plutocracy and kleptocracy. The Koch Brothers can vote several million times over. Their resources can be applied to the machinery of American politics and will produce tangible results in a short order. Serfs like you and I get to vote once, or twice, and can demonstrate and cause a bit of a racket, but that is the extent to which our power can be expressed.

As in finance, there is disproportionate distribution of representative political power, and the inherent unfairness of it should drive all normal people up a wall. I think it's fair to claim that no one wants to see the type of blatant corruption and coffer-pillaging that Putin and his jackals have perfected, nor do we want to see a hyper-regulated business environment where hapless small-business owners are taxed to death while the government, riddled with inefficiencies, delivers lamentable services that the private industry could perfect with machine-like efficiency.

What should be coming into focus at this juncture is the depth of the complexities and nuances a vibrant economy requires – by necessity, in order to function, there must be compromise and a willingness to give and take from one interest to another. This cannot come to fruition under the leadership of American conservatives. How do you compromise with a cadre of politicians who would rather shutdown the entire government instead of making a deal? How do you negotiate with an irrational actor? "Mark my word," Barry Goldwater barked, "if and when these preachers get control of the party, and they're sure trying to do so, it's going to be a terrible damn problem. Frankly, these people frighten me. Politics and governing demand compromise. But these Christians believe they are acting in the name of God, so they can't and won't compromise. I know, I've tried to deal with them." The means, both for the rabid Christian fundamentalists and the wealthy, always justify the ends. These factions have absolute mandates. *Deliver more value to your shareholders. Stop the satanic holocaust of unborn children.* There is nothing that cannot be sacrificed to achieve these goals, and it should be noted that these principles are international mandates to American Christians. Put another way, they are not content just to influence domestic policies, but actively look for ways to influence other political systems, too:

> "Foreign policy also found itself in the theological arena. The State Department and other federal agencies took action to block needle-exchange and other harm-reduction programs in United Nations drug-control efforts, to suppress foreign efforts to extend civil rights to sex workers (Brazil persisted in doing so), to defeat international women's treaties, and to keep federal funds from being used to support any international program that funds contraceptive efforts." [15]

Their craven determination and resilience, especially after the improbable election of Mr. Trump, should never again be underestimated. If the sane world wants to defeat these groups, we had better be prepared to work twice as hard as them. One might be inclined to ask just how in the hell Wall Street and the church became bedfellows in the first place. Religion is ostensibly about piety, humility, charity, and unconditional love. Business is about building wealth, succeeding in the pressures of competition, and eliminating your rivals with ruthlessness. Where could these incredibly separate sets of interests ever overlap?

The answer is a bit of a paradox, and the mindset that allows these disjointed unions between religion and outside forces that appear to be outwardly opposed to religious ideology is a difficult one to fully articulate. I delivered my first sermon to a small church in Wentzville, Missouri. This congregation was a diminutive one, too tiny, in fact, to have built their own building, so they rented out a Masonic Lodge for their services on Sundays. The absurdity of preaching a Christian message in the midst of bizarre Egyptian iconography was a unique experience, to say the least. In most non-denominational Christian churches in the United States, there are a host of programs and services that stretch from the early morning on Sunday into the late afternoon. Sunday school for children, pre-service Bible studies, even segregated worship music hours (like any good business, churches appeal to their clientele, and the older folk don't like drums and modern music, while the more youthful members generally enjoy generic-sounding, inoffensive rock music.) Before I was set to preach, I arrived at the lodge early, and participated in a pre-service Bible studied delivered by one of the church's elders. He had copied the transcript of a joke from the popular animated television series *Family Guy* – and expressed his incredulity towards an exchange that took place between Jesus and God in an episode of Seth MacFarlane's show - in which God slithers up to the bar to chat up an attractive woman in a tight dress. He snaps his fingers once and lights her cigarette, she giggles, and he snaps his fingers a second time and accidently kills her with a lightning bolt. "Jesus Christ!" God exclaims, and his son appears. "Get the Escalade, we're getting out of here!"

He spent five or six minutes explaining this joke with a sullen and dour expression, and relayed some tepid outrage at our Savior being mocked by a cartoonist. He concluded his remarks with a gripe that has never been able to escape my memory: "And people, you know, anyone, is free to put this on television where anyone can see it." What was this church elder alluding to? The implication was clear - people should not be able to put things like this on television. In the space of a twenty-minute Bible study, he was advocating for a frightening level of censorship that few sane people would support in the light of day. Who, myself included, objected to this implication in the moment? Not a single soul. Who had the boldness to speak up? Nobody. The frightening reality is that most religious folk will smile and nod at anything, no matter how vicious or vile, *so long as it comes from a brother or sister in arms.*

The faith-based mindset, despite all of its outward intolerance, is a dangerously permissive one inwardly. There is an infinitely longer leash given to those inside the church that those outside of it. We shouldn't be surprised that organized tribalism looks the other way when it shouldn't, and nods and smiles when it should object, so long as the offenses come from a fellow partisan. There are plenty of good Christians who know the Bible calls them to a life of poverty, but still knowingly vote for the greedy elites who make more in a single hour than they will in a lifetime. Ask them why they voted for the snake-oil salesman, and the response is a simple one: they can't vote for abortion, they can't vote for gay rights, they can't vote for the things that they believe the Bible speaks clearly about (it doesn't, for whatever it's worth.) Oddly enough, the topics that Jesus covered zealously and in great repetition and detail – the crime of greed, flipping over the tables of the money-changers in the temple, instructing the rich man to sell everything he had before following him, then joking when he couldn't part ways with it all – are often the first political causalities in the conservative arena. As Christopher Hitchens was always so fond of saying: the sleep of reason indeed brings monsters.

This is not to blame, entirely, the docility of the religious demographic for the overreaches of the business-minded or wealthy. American religion is a thriving business in its own right, and there are charlatans everywhere, out to make a quick buck in the name of God. Most of us are not fooled by the outrageous claims of pseudo-faith healers or televangelists like Benny Hinn or Peter Popoff; those contemptible, shameless snakes whose lurid shtick only fools the most desperate and vulnerable. They are vicious predators, and much like the drug dealer on the street corner, have a fortuitous advantage over the rest of us in that they are not even required to pay taxes on their windfalls. What a joy it must be (and what untarnished sleep it must deliver) to spend one's time as a glorified pickpocket, wrestling the spare change away from senile grandmothers.

The seedy underbelly of the "Health and Wealth" revival circuit was most strikingly captured by the 1972 documentary film *Marjoe*. Following the life of a calloused Pentecostal preacher, Marjoe Gortner, as he demonstrated how the sausage is made behind the closed doors of the church. He rolls gleefully in a pile of bills stacked on a hotel room bed, savoring the take from a productive tour stop. Marjoe compares preaching to the duties of a rock-and-roll front man, delivering entertainment and providing an emotional payoff for a fee. It is a compelling and devastating look into a filthy business, and a salient reminder that if at any point, an adult is willing to suspend their disbelief and critical thinking, a crocodile is inevitably lying in wait, ready to pounce.

Willful ignorance is so remarkably powerful that even the stupidest frauds can be comprehensively exposed and continue on fleecing without issue. James Randi – the talented slight-of-hand artist and skeptic – launched an investigation that revealed the stunning depth of Peter

Popoff's deplorable sham ministry many years ago. Mr. Popoff, much like Benny Hinn, claimed falsely to be a faith healer. For some time, Popoff puzzled skeptics on account of his ability to be able to transcend some of the more typical "cold-reading" techniques by naming incredibly detailed specifics about members in his audience, down to their individual medical ailments or street addresses. At first glance, it seemed to be telekinetic. Randi was able to reveal through his investigation that Popoff's wife was using a short-range radio to read off the contents of attendance cards members of the audience had filled out before the event. Peter was simply parroting the audio received through an earpiece. This colossal embarrassment didn't stop Mr. Popoff – the video of this fraudulent activity was shown on national television to a stunned audience - his ministry is still going strong to this day, and last I personally checked, he was hawking holy water in direct-mail-friendly pellets.

You might be inclined to believe that anyone with a thick enough skull to be receptive to this type of snake oil deserves to lose their hard-earned money, and on some level, I agree. Ignorance (willful or otherwise) always comes at a cost, and those who fail to learn will always make an easy mark. The reason I don't hesitate to call these practices repulsive and predatory is that their victims aren't solely comprised of garden-variety idiots – many do not possess a sound mind, to no fault of their own. The lion's share are elderly men and women suffering from incurable or degenerative diseases, or the mentally ill, and they have the most to lose and are often lured into financial or medical ruin as a result. If you can stomach it, watch the rallies of Hinn or Popoff on YouTube. Their disgusting circus routine includes encouraging aging men and women to toss their pills, prescriptions, and canes into the isles. The Lord is going to heal them, not some foolish doctor, of course, so pitch that worthless heart medicine, get rid of that filthy walker, and do a jig for your Savior.

Wolves like Popoff and Hinn are shameless, but perhaps their most egregious crime is their boorish stupidity. Smarter charlatans – like Joel Osteen, for instance – have enough basic intelligence to realize that the blatant lies about on-stage healing are counter-productive. The best way to make a killing off the religious is to operate just below the level of faith-healers. The poor and poorly educated are quite receptive to this type of message, they love being told they can 'claim' things in the name of the Lord and wish them into fruition, killing two important birds (prosperity and religion) with one attractive stone. Southern congregations – especially black church-goers – seem to be especially susceptible to this type of exploitation. Look no further for evidence of this phenomenon than *BET Inspiration,* a block of programming etched out on the popular minority entertainment cable channel on Sundays where one can see the up-and-coming religious businessmen and businesswomen pitching and hawking their worthless wares. Among the laundry-list of peculiarities that the business and religious sectors have in common is a disdain for paying taxes. David Miscavige, the head of the sordid pyramid-scheme known as Scientology, famously waged a lengthy and contentious legal battle against the IRS in an attempt to attain tax-exempt status in the United States. It was a war of attrition Mr. Miscavige would shamefully win, as the federal government caved to the whims of a time-share salesman (and, it must be noted, lost, by some estimates, billions of rightful dollars in tax revenue as a result). Germany's legislative bodies, unlike the American government, actually found its backbone when it came to this dispute and ripped the rug of religious protection out from underneath this sham, and famously declared Scientology as a "deceptive business practice(s) masquerading as religion."

But is that really the right approach? How will we, as a society, choose to deal with the predatory industries that spring up in the power vacuums? How do we manage the pious and the prosperous? What sort of policy is fair for both? As the old clique goes, the road to hell is paved with good intentions, and Scientology's swindling of the American taxpayer is a perfect example of this. The IRS, admirably, wasn't interested in kicking down the doors to a place of worship. The hesitation arises out of wholesome respect. Our founding documents were quite clear on this topic, and on some level, it is comforting, at least in passing, that there remains some tangible distaste in the corridors of power for meddling with religion. Terrific, but what about cockroaches like Miscavige who abuse a protectionary system for their own personal gain? If ever there was a slippery slope, the government deciding which religions are valid and which were not is quite a slick one, indeed. I concede that point fully. It is a delicate balance, and culling the populations of religious hustlers shouldn't come at the expense of free religious express for innocent people.

While I believe it necessary on some level to divide and conquer these political foes – the pious and the financial elite - (either by appeasing the new-wave of youthful and left-leaning one percenters with less regulation, in the fashion of the 'Bourbon Democrats' to steal a phrase from Paul Krugman, or by running to the right on civil issues to further isolate the lunatic fringe of the right-wing,) the conflict is probably best distilled to the basic issues of education and influence. If the perspective of the white, uneducated, low and middle class voting bloc is to shift in our lifetime, how will we know it when we see it? How can progressives be sure that their influence is making a meaningful impact? Correlation and causation are finicky mistresses, and while the problem is clear, the solution is far more difficult to find.

This contrast goes hand-in-hand with the war on facts and information currently being waged by the Trump administration. Let's suppose, for the sake of argument, the Democrats are demonstrably correct on an issue of contention with the Republicans. If this current narrative of 'fake' news persists (to the stunningly dire extent that the Associated Press was being called 'fake news' on Twitter by thick-skulled Republicans,) how can these two sides even have a basic conversation if neither one can agree on what things are basically true or false? Some – not all – of these difficulties are directly caused by a lack of critical thinking. In Kentucky, for instance, "Obamacare" is incredibly unpopular and the proposition of repealing it on the campaign trail was met with raucous applause. The Affordable Care Act, however, is highly utilized by low and middle class Kentuckians and is thoroughly well liked. These, of course, are just two different names for the same thing, and to put it bluntly, those duped by the Republican party into this idiocy are dumb enough to be easy marks, or are too lazy or too partisan to research and acknowledge a basic fact available to everyone.

The question left to us is one of praxis. What sort of strategy can be concocted to combat unknowing ignorance? Supposing one existed, would it be as effective at unwinding willful ignorance as well? The nasty root of this lamentable tree is a lack of a proper education that extends to the political arena. Trump's election is an indictment of our current state of affairs – a man who appeals to the absolute lowest common denominator, up to and including the brain-dead ramblings of white nationalists like Alex Jones – and as a result of them, Trump was able to parlay that support into actual power. In simple terms, that means that there are enough of them to ruin the planet. This is an existential crisis; as legitimate a threat to our continued existence as a species as any other.

The uneducated American voter has become weaponized, and no successful countermeasure against them has yet been created. Education is not a quick fix, and is a slow investment that gradually pays out dividends over time. Some political analysts have suggested reinstatement of formal logic to school curriculum as a means of redressing this grievance. This suggestion, while novel, is not the silver bullet to sink the future of demagoguery. The sins of our consumer culture might just be coming back to bite us. Our national obsessions with wealth, celebrity, and fame have made us overvalue inane consumption while dismissing the substantive as boring. But I don't believe the country, as a whole, is destined to remain locked in this stalemate forever. As technology advances, access to previously locked-out social classes and systems become attainable. The mystery of high-finance will eventually fade, and the germ planted in the minds of the American public by the Occupy movement will only bear more fruit as time passes. The religious knot is well on its way to untying itself, which, oddly enough, is actually part of the larger problem:

"How might religious nonattendance lead to intolerance?

Although American churches are heavily segregated, it's possible that the modest level of integration they provide promotes cross-racial bonds. In their book, Religion and Politics in the United States, Kenneth D. Wald and Allison Calhoun-Brown reference a different theory: that the most-committed members of a church are more likely than those who are casually involved to let its message of universal love erode their prejudices. Whatever the reason, when cultural conservatives disengage from organized religion, they tend to redraw the boundaries of identity, de-emphasizing morality and religion and emphasizing race and nation. Trump is both a beneficiary and a driver of that shift. So is the alt-right. Read Milo Yiannopoulos and Allum Bokhari's famous Breitbart.com essay, "An Establishment Conservative's Guide to the Alt-Right." It contains five references to "tribe," seven to "race," 13 to "the west" and "western" and only one to "Christianity." That's no coincidence. The alt-right is ultra-conservatism for a more secular age. Its leaders like Christendom, an old-fashioned word for the West. But they're suspicious of Christianity itself, because it crosses boundaries of blood and soil. As a college student, the alt-right leader Richard Spencer was deeply influenced by Friedrich Nietzsche, who famously hated Christianity. Radix, the journal Spencer founded, publishes articles with titles like "Why I Am a Pagan." One essay notes that "critics of Christianity on the Alternative Right usually blame it for its universalism." [16]

So church attendance is down, generally, and the number of people who openly describe themselves as having no religious preference rises every year. This might well have the counterintuitive effect of loosening typical religious sexual prejudices at the cost of aggravating racial ones. The headaches we experience now, to say it gently, are largely resonating in the latent predispositions of older generations. Trump doesn't win the White House without Florida, and his message was intentionally designed to appeal to the aging Americans who won't think twice about their dormant and ingrained prejudices. These same people, too, won't notice that it's a Republican hand obliterating their entitlements, social security, and Medicare benefits at every opportunity, either. Again, the outlook is a bit grim, but it is brightening with each passing second. Senator Sanders' populist campaign is evidence that Americans could, under the right circumstances, learn to look their real captors in the face, rather than being spooked by the immigrant scarecrow the Republicans shake angrily in front of their faces before every election.

Armed and Dangerous

‡‡‡

Chapter 8

"And it's not surprising then they get bitter, they cling to guns or religion or antipathy to people who aren't like them or anti-immigrant sentiment or antitrade sentiment as a way to explain their frustrations." Barack Obama

═══

There are a handful of political topics that I have avoided writing about like the plague. Some of the problems facing humanity strike me as genuinely intractable. Among these outwardly unsolvable issues is the incessant crisis of gun violence in the United States. Part of the dilemma is purely cultural; guns are as much a part of the American identity as baseball and jazz. The ownership of firearms has been woven into the fabric of our society, and, so too, has the horrifying consequences of mass shootings. More to the point, I would like to present myself as a neutral actor in this dialog. I am not a gun owner, and have long dithered on the preverbal gun-rights fence. It's fair to say I don't have much of a dog in this fight, insofar as I haven't completely decided which side is I believe most right, even at this very moment. Politically – yes – I am quite far to the left, and while this diaspora is most commonly associated with gun ownership restrictions and regulation, I have my problems with its firearms manifesto. I am torn (as I think most of the nation is, as well) on the problem of gun ownership, and in my view, this is largely because firearm regulation attempts to deal with two different aspects of gun ownership: the philosophical mechanisms of owning deadly weapons, and the *impact* of guns as a hazard to public safety. These are two different concepts, and each have their own nuances.

I find Republicans and Democrats both share an amusing mental tick when faced with opposition to some of their keystone beliefs. Ask a typical Democrat why abortion shouldn't be outlawed, and they'll say women will get abortions no matter what laws are enacted, but assault rifles should be banned. Ask a Republican why assault rifles shouldn't be banned, and they'll say that criminals will get them no matter what laws are put in place, but we should ban abortion. There's more to these arguments than what I've provided here, sure, but it should be sufficient to illustrate my point; the notion of personal autonomy and liberty can vary wildly from one American to the next, and I am of the mind that one's position on all issues should be reasonably consistent.

Said another way, if I tell Republicans not to have abortions or gay marriages if they don't like them (as I often do), I should carry that philosophical position into firearms as well. The trouble, here, is that many blind squirrels in the gun-rights communities have found some worthwhile nuts. It is important to seriously consider the ramifications of all concessions made to a powerful government. They are right to worry. It is a dangerous concept, indeed, to allow the federal government to dictate what citizens can, or cannot, purchase for their own use. The arguments from the left, specifically when they relate to the restriction of technical aspects of firearms are often patently foolish and quickly subverted by the gun manufacturing industry the instant they are enacted. My background in technology likely informs my disdain for this as well; enthusiasts will always sidestep product restrictions, when it comes to jailbreaking mobile phones or modifying firearms, and it has always struck me as a waste of time to attempt to legislate against such passionate and knowledgeable communities.

This, of course, is part of the reason I have stayed away from the gun issue entirely. There is nuance, subtlety, and complexity drilled into every inch of the problem, and taking a harsh stance in either direction seems fraught with ideological danger. The philosophical side of the debate is far more open-ended in my view, and it asks much deeper questions than many realize. The issue of gun violence as it relates to public health, however, is far more absolute. Americans are being routinely killed by firearms at an alarming rate:

> "Some 13,286 people were killed in the US by firearms in 2015, according to the Gun Violence Archive, and 26,819 people were injured [those figures exclude suicide]. Those figures are likely to rise

by several hundred, once incidents in the final week of the year are counted...The number of gun murders per capita in the US in 2012 - the most recent year for comparable statistics - was nearly 30 times that in the UK, at 2.9 per 100,000 compared with just 0.1. Of all the murders in the US in 2012, 60% were by firearm compared with 31% in Canada, 18.2% in Australia, and just 10% in the UK... So many people die annually from gunfire in the US that the death toll between 1968 and 2011 eclipses all wars ever fought by the country. According to research by Politifact, there were about 1.4 million firearm deaths in that period, compared with 1.2 million US deaths in every conflict from the War of Independence to Iraq." [1]

Regardless of where one lands on the philosophical issue of gun ownership, the mathematical impact of the widespread proliferation of firearms in the United States is undeniably significant. It is a serious problem by *any* appraisal. It represents a major threat to public safety. This simply cannot be disputed, especially when these figures are contrasted with rates of gun violence for developed nations with similar populations. Beyond these figures, the acquisition of firearms and ammunition is terrifyingly easy:

"I phoned Steve (Mostyn) a few nights before Christmas. "Steve, we have to do something about this epidemic of gun violence in this country," I said. "Gabby and I want to start an organization to try and get some reasonable legislation passed." After a long pause, Steve spoke. "Lemme tell you," he said in his Texas drawl, "I own thirty-five guns. You know I like to shoot. Last week I went to a local gun store near my house and bought three thousand rounds of ammunition." Half were for his 9mm pistols; half were .45 caliber. He told me how the store clerk helped him load the boxes in his truck before turning to Steve and asking, "Are you going to start a war or something?" Steve responded, "Of course no," and gave him a puzzled look. "So," I asked, "Why did you buy all the ammunition?" "Because it was on sale and I could," he said. The same month, Steve told me, he sold an old rusted Jet Ski trailer for $200. The buyer showed up, hooked the trailer to his truck, and drove away. A few days later, the man asked Mostyn to meet him at a local DMV so they could fill out some paperwork necessary to transfer ownership of the trailer. "So I had to go downtown and take the time to fill out a bunch of forms about an old trailer," he said. "You know how much paperwork I had to do to buy three thousand rounds of ammo? Nothing." He paid in cash and didn't even leave his name. "And we wonder why the murder rate is twenty times what it is in other countries," he said." [2]

Not many gun-rights advocates will take issue with this reality, anyway. It is not as if they could reasonably claim that an event like Columbine or Sandy Hook doesn't represent a serious problem, or that the tools used in such massacres were difficult for the murderers to obtain. Before continuing any further in this dialog, it is worth noting that mass-shootings are predominantly a male problem:

> "Of the 111 gun massacres that comprise my data set, only one – one! – was perpetrated exclusively by a woman. That was former postal worker Jennifer San Marco's 2006 shooting spree in Goleta, California, which left seven people dead." [3]

The phrase 'toxic masculinity' suddenly springs to mind at this juncture, and it comes as little surprise that the most rabid members of the pro-gun community are often white men. The crux of the disagreement between these two positions is how best to solve it: to the left, it is corrected by reducing gun ownership, and to the right, it is corrected by increasing gun ownership. On this point, the NRA has made it clear that the only thing that can 'stop' a 'bad guy' with a gun is, conveniently enough for their friends in the firearms manufacturing business, a 'good' guy with a gun. It should come as no surprise that this is flatly untrue:

> "Nearly 90 percent of the interventions commonly cited by gun-rights advocates as evidence that armed civilians bring shooting sprees to a halt are false positives. Only four of their examples are actually successful defensive gun uses...if one assumes that there have been at least 300 *attempted* mass shootings in the United States per year over the past quarter century – a rather conservative assumption given that there have been, on average, nearly 350 *actual* mass shootings per year in the past three years 0 then the rate of a private citizen employing a firearm to stop a potential or mass shooting is at most one in 1,875, or 0.05 percent. And in all probability, given that there have been only been four such interventions in recent history, the odds of an armed citizen successfully stopping a mass shooting are likely lower." [4]

I suppose – with a 0.05 percent chance – civilian gun owners who fancy themselves as a Dirty-Harry-in-waiting, ought to ask themselves just how lucky they feel. The odds are simply not in their favor. In fact, Columbine, arguably the most infamous American mass-shooting, could have been stopped by a security guard who had an opportunity to fire upon the active shooters and missed. The NRA's ideal scenario was fully established. Good guy with a gun meets bad guys with a gun, and the bloodbath isn't stopped. Forget, momentarily, about the laughable feasibility of this suggestion.

Civilians carrying firearms are dangerous and deadly (especially when it comes to active shooter events) in ways many people do not understand:

> "The most obvious – and tragic – illustration is the shootout that erupted between motorcycle clubs at a Waco, Texas, restaurant in 2015. With over one hundred bikers carrying weapons, an exchange of gunfire between rival gangs left nine people dead and another eighteen injured. The feud, caught on video surveillance cameras, was nothing short of an exercise in complete and utter pandemonium. People, unaware of where bullets were coming from, returned fire wildly. Even the presence of law enforcement just feet away – stationed outside the restaurant as a precaution – did absolutely nothing to deter the outbreak of violence. There are several other examples as well, including the 2012 murder of a man at a Jackson, Tennessee, nightclub, which resulted in his friends firing back in self-defense, leaving eighteen people wounded from the exchange of rounds; and the 2015 mass shooting that left four people wounded after a fight involving roughly one hundred people outside a bar in Elkhart, Indiana, escalated from words to weapons. In Waco, Jackson, and Elkhart, people were shot as a result of being caught in the cross fire between those seeking to kill foes and those seeking to defend themselves. And it's not just armed civilians. Police officers also accidentally shoot innocent bystanders. Case in point: the NYPD officers who tried to arrest a man following a gun attack at the Empire State Building in 2012. When two policemen confronted the perpetrator on the street as he was fleeing, the man drew his weapon. The officers fired a combined sixteen rounds, striking and killing the man – along with nine pedestrians who were in the vicinity." [5]

Multiplying the quantity of firearms in deadly situations does not seem to help, and often, so-called 'defensive' gun usage ends up killing and injuring more innocent people. My spouse is a teacher, and during her active shooting training, the police instructed her to flip over a trash can and place the firearm (if it is recovered from the active shooter) underneath it and sit on top of the bin while waiting for law enforcement to arrive. This contingency plan was created to prevent or avoid mistaking a victim for the shooter, which is another largely unconsidered side-effect of the 'good guys' with guns mantra. This nightmare nearly came to fruition during the attack that maimed Congresswoman Gabrielle Giffords:

> "Ken Veeder, the Vietnam vet, knew the pop-pop-pop was the sound of gunfire, not firecrackers. He saw Loughner shooting and started running toward him. He saw Mary Reed cover her daughter and

get shot in the back, Veeder took a bullet to the leg. As Loughner went down and his gun fell to the ground, Veeder grabbed it. "Give me the magazine," he told Maisch. "I'm going to shoot the son of a bitch." Maisch refused and urged Veeder to calm down. Joe Zamudio, had been buying cigarettes in the Walgreens next to the Safeway when he heard the shots. He was legally carrying a concealed weapon and had a handgun in his pocket. Zamudio, twenty-four, grabbed the handle of his pistol but kept it in his pocket. He rushed out, prepared to draw and fire. He saw Loughner pinned down and a man holding the Glock. "Put the gun down," Zamudio said. He grabbed Veeder's wrist and sat on Loughner. Veeder dropped the Glock. Zamudio later said in an interview: "I almost killed that guy" – meaning Veeder, who had grabbed Loughner's gun. Amid the chaos of the moment, the shooting was nearly capped off with a terrible accident where the "good guy with a gun," with the best of intentions, could have killed an innocent bystander." [6]

I'll appeal to bipartisanship at this juncture; no matter what your opinion on gun rights might be, the foolishness of the NRA's line of 'gun guy' reasoning is obvious. We are not speaking about the ideology of gun ownership, or legislation, but simply speaking in terms of a public health crisis. The solution proposed by the NRA does not make basic sense. In fact, it actively makes the problem *worse* in many cases. This isn't to say it is impossible for a civilian to save a great number of lives in cutting down an assailant before law enforcement can arrive. Should I ever find myself in a situation where such a person had saved my own life in such a fashion, of course, I would be extremely grateful. The odds of this happening (0.05 percent, by the estimate I referenced earlier) are incredibly slim. The active shooter that threatens your life is nearly as likely to be struck by lightning or a meteorite than he is by well-intentioned civilian rounds. Beyond mass shootings, the ownership of a weapon that has an instant potential for death is problematic in and of itself. "ND's" (negligent discharges) are yet another serious threat associated with firearms. The Centers for Disease Control reported in 2011 that 591 people were killed accidentally from a negligent discharge of a gun. Be it from operator error or mechanical malfunction, people are being killed every year as a result of negligent or accidental discharges. Of course – there are millions of firearms in the United States that are operated safely and responsibly by their owners – and mentioning this statistic is not intended to imply otherwise. This is simply another deadly threat unique to gun ownership in a long list of deadly threats. In the interest of comprehensively discussing all of the impacts to public health and safety, all aspects of gun ownership must be considered. Indisputably, possessing firearms, in many contexts and situations, threatens life more than it protects. Take, for instance, the shooting death of gospel singer Raymond Myles in 1998:

"New Orleans police said that Myles kept the handgun in the well between the Navigator's front seats so he could grab it if he felt threatened. But the gun was also an eye-catcher, its gleaming steel finish reflecting every streetlight. Morial learned that Myles' weapon ended Myles' life quickly: "Dead in thirty seconds," said coroner Frank Minyards. And it had offered no protection at all against his executioner. The killer had been so close when he pumped bullets into the singer that he left powder burns on Myles' chest. Myles' death was not unique. A high percentage of handgun victims are shot with their own guns. Policemen, truckers, and liquor store owners are particularly vulnerable." [7]

Or, take the case of the mass-shooting at a Navy base in Maryland:

"As often happens in rampages, the gunman exploited the element of surprise. Sneaking up on Ridgell, Alexis ambushed him. Despite being armed, Ridgell never had time to react. He fell to a shotgun blast almost instantly. At this point, nothing stood in the way between Alexis and the exit. He could have easily dropped his weapon and walked out of Building 197 as just another employee fleeing the violence. Instead, he chose to stay and seek more victims. However, Alexis must have sensed he was running out of ammunition because he bent down and took Ridgell's Berretta 9mm semiautomatic handgun before returning back into the building. He quickly ran into Ridgell's fellow security guard and the Navy MP. Alexis shot at them with his shotgun but missed. The security guard returned fire, but he too missed, as Alexis ducked into a corridor. As he was fleeing, Alexis encountered the other ad hoc active-shooter team. He opened fire on the three men, who exchanged rounds with Alexis, but no one was hit…While wandering around the first floor, Alexis had entered a stairwell and opened the exit door. Spotting Proctor and Jirus alongside the building's exterior, Alexis raised his shotgun and pulled the trigger. It didn't discharge. The rampage should have ended right there when Alexis's shotgun was rendered inoperable. But Alexis had Ridgell's sidearm, which he aimed at the two men and fired. As Proctor and Jirus were talking, two shots rang out. Jirus looked over and saw Proctor laying on the ground. The sight of the utilities foreman mortally wounded by a gunshot to the head sent Jirus into a mad sprint for his life. Meanwhile, behind him, Alexis nonchalantly shut the door and resumed his hunt for more people to kill inside Building 197. In the cruelest twist of fate, Proctor was killed with a firearm that was meant to protect him." [8]

Not only can the firearm you purchase be used against you, but in a roundabout way, can also be used against others. Under the right circumstances, a firearm can make you unsafe, and it can also make everyone around you unsafe. Again, none of this is mentioned in the interest of vilifying gun owners or firearm ownership; we are merely appraising the full weight of the threat to public health and safety that guns pose. Another primary motivation for gun owners is the notion of home defense; whereby firearms are stored in the home in the interest of killing an intruder. To be clear – home invasions and robberies are unspeakable acts of cruelty – and they occur more frequently than one might expect. The Department of Justice reports that approximately 3.7 million household burglaries take place every year (between 2003 to 2007) and a member of the household was present for 28 percent of the crimes. In 7 percent of all household burglaries, there was a violent confrontation of some kind with the intruder. It is certainly not unreasonable to want to have some form of defense in the event of a robbery or home invasion (or any other criminal interaction that requires defensive violence), but just how useful are firearms in a defensive capacity?

"A new paper from the Violence Policy Center states that "for the five-year period 2007 through 2011, the total number of self-protective behaviors involving a firearm by victims of attempted or completed violent crimes or property crimes totaled only 338,700." That comes to an annual average of 67,740 — not nothing, but nowhere near the N.R.A.'s 2 million or 2.5 million. Readers can judge for themselves whether the V.P.C. or the N.R.A. is likely to have better numbers. The V.P.C. used data from the National Crime Victimization Survey, conducted by the Bureau of Justice Statistics. The N.R.A.'s estimate is the result of a telephone survey conducted by a Florida State University criminologist. The V.P.C. also found that in 2010 "there were only 230 justifiable homicides involving a private citizen using a firearm" reported to the F.B.I.'s Uniform Crime Reporting Program. Compare that with the number of criminal gun homicides in the same year: 8,275. (That's not counting gun suicides or unintentional shootings.) Or compare it with the number of Americans killed by guns since Newtown: 3,458. As the V.P.C. paper states, "guns are rarely used to kill criminals or stop crimes." [9]

The number proposed by the NRA is absurd, to put it lightly. They arrived at the figure of two million, as the author points out in the paragraph above by way of a *telephone survey* whereas the VPC compiled data from the Bureau of Justice. It is quite clear which set of data is best. For the sake of stopping seventy-thousand crimes a year, we have chosen to watch thousands of Americans die a year on account of guns. This bargain doesn't seem like a rational one in the slightest. This, to me, is the most puzzling piece of the entire gun debate. I believe, sincerely, that gun owners are normal people like anyone else, and have every right to pursue their hobbies and interests as they see fit, and millions of them, as mentioned earlier, are responsible gun users. I think gun advocates, like any other normal American, are horrified and outraged at the never-ending parade of active shooter events. To put it bluntly, the pro-guns-rights position strikes me as a cynical one. *We know easy access to firearms causes mass-shootings, and that's a price we're willing to pay to keep our guns.* This is a bargain as simple as any other in my view; trading the epidemic of gun violence for the benefits of non-interference from the government. You are welcome to reach your own conclusion as to whether or not this bargain is a wholesome one, but I find it revolting. The world we live in now, as a result of the runaway power of the American gun lobbies, is a frightening one. The specter of gun violence hangs over all of us at all times. At a shopping mall, at a school, in a church, or even in your cubicle at work. We are confined to this prison of our own making, in which we can be brutally and savagely murdered in an instant.

> "When I was a child, we participated in civil-defense exercises out of fear that the Soviet Union would launch a nuclear strike. Are you old enough to remember "duck and cover" drills? That was the phrase drilled into students' minds during the height of the Cold War, the mantra for saving people from the biggest threat of that day and age. Today, the instruction is "run, hide, fight." It's the "duck and cover" of the current era – aimed to protect us from the biggest danger we now face: mass shootings. The most realistic violent threat to the American people no longer comes out of the sky on the tip of a missile. It now comes out of the barrel of a gun." [10]

In the beginning of this chapter, I separated the issue of gun rights into two separate categories; the philosophy of governmental oversight of firearm ownership, and the reality of gun violence as a pressing threat to public safety and health. How can the United States start to clean up this mess? Louis Klarevas holds up the United Kingdom as a roadmap:

> "The British experience with mass shootings can be seen in two different ways. On the one hand, despite the implementation of strict gun-safety measures following the Hungerford and Dunblane massacres, the nation has not been rampage-free. On the other hand, the island of approximately sixty-three million residents has come

pretty close to zeroing out high-fatalities mass shootings, suffering only one gun massacre since 1996. By comparison, the United States, which is roughly five times the population of Great Britain, has experienced *fifty-four times* the number of gun massacres over the same twenty-year time period. Given such a stark contrast, it's hard to escape the conclusion that gun control contributes tremendously to a reduction in rampage violence." 11 (Emphasis mine)

If one is *sincerely* looking for a solution to the epidemic of gun deaths, Britain's 'zeroing out' of the mass-shooting problem simply cannot be ignored. I tire, too, of the snide, sneering response that comparisons to the gun laws of other nations usually inspires from the pro-gun crowd. *It's not fair to compare our population to smaller nations.* Well – if they find the math troubling, this is not my problem – and furthermore, the arithmetic is *appalling* no matter how you look at it. It's often at this point that gun rights activists like to claim that laws never stopped gunfire, and restricting access to firearms is a policy that will grease the treads of tyrannical governments and make the population less safe. The argument, as it is often presented, lambasts gun control attempts on account of two basic points of contention. First, that criminals who are willing to break the law will not be impeded by gun control measures. Second, that even if guns were removed from the equation, mass episodes of murder will not be stopped. To the first point: gun control isn't intended to stop all illegal activity associated with the acquisition or use of guns, it is merely intended to *reduce* them. If such regulation is judged on the basis of its potential subversion, the point is missed entirely. The measure isn't intended to be perfect, but to be an improvement.

This is one of the most common failures in reasoning I encounter from the pro-gun crowd; it often fundamentally misunderstands the purpose of controlling guns. Yes, if thirty-round magazines were outlawed in favor of ten-round magazines, someone who was motivated enough could manufacture their own magazines, or carry three separate legal magazines and achieve the same impact. The *point* of such a restriction is not to make any circumvention of the law impossible, but to simply reduce as much potential damage as possible. This line of straw-man reasoning is incredibly popular within the more extreme pro-gun communities. It shows, too, the interests of the parties on both sides of the argument; one wants to preserve the status quo in a self-interested manner, and the other wants to stop the bloodshed.

The second point is equally fatuous; no one sincerely believes episodes of mass violence against 'soft' targets will ever fully stop. It is an attack on an ideological position that no one on the planet holds. Especially when considering the more recent terrorist attacks against European nations (like

Germany and France) who already have stringent gun control measures in place. Soft targets are just that – soft – and securing them from all potential threats is literally impossible. A motivated attacker will use a lorry, or a rented car, or a knife, or an ax, or any available tool at their disposal to accomplish a massacre. This is not being argued. The point is fully conceded. Again, as is the case on so many other occasions, the pro-gun community misses the forest for the trees; *reduction* is the only goal. Efforts to curb gun-related injuries and deaths are often unfairly painted as immature and short-sighted, largely on the backs of straw-man fallacies like this. The biting anxiety of the right-wing gun owner ("They're coming to take away my guns!") is an absolute fantasy. Removing guns from American society, in no small part, thanks to the rabid efforts of the NRA, is virtually impossible.

> "There are enough guns in the United States that if you gave one to every adult, you would run out of adults before you ran out of guns. Nearly two-thirds of U.S. homicides involve a gun, a far great fraction than in other industrialized countries. Our homicide rate is also much higher than in those countries. It would therefore seem likely that our homicide rate is so high in part because guns are so easily accessible. Research indeed shows this to be true. But guns are not the whole story. In Switzerland, every adult male is issued an assault rifle for militia duty and is allowed to keep the gun at home. On a per capita basis, Switzerland has more firearms than just about any other country, and yet it is one of the safest places in the world. In other words, guns do not cause crime. That said, the established U.S methods of keeping guns away from the people who *do* cause crime are, at best, feeble. And since a gun – unlike a bag of cocaine or a car or a pair of pant – lasts pretty much forever, even turning off the spigot of new guns still leaves an ocean of available ones." [12]

First, the presence of guns does not cause crime (although, unfettered accessibility to them certainly makes crime easier), so eradicating guns is simply not in the interests of liberals anyway. Second, even if such an endeavor was made undertaken, literally, it *would have no chance* of succeeding. Take buyback programs – a popular element of gun control in many countries – for example:

> "Another staple of 1990s crime fighting – and of the evening news – was the gun buyback. You remember the image: a menacing, glistening heap of firearms surrounded by the mayor, the police chief, the neighborhood activists. It made for a nice photo op, but that's about as meaningful as a gun buyback gets. The guns that are turned in

tend to be heirlooms or junk. The payoff to the gun seller – usually $50 or $100, but in one California buyback, three free hours of psychotherapy – isn't an adequate incentive for anyone who actually plans to use his gun. And the number of surrendered guns is no match for even the number of new guns simultaneously coming to market. Given the number of handguns in the United States and the number of homicides each year, the likelihood that a particular gun was used to kill someone that year is 1 in 10,000. The typical gun buyback program yields fewer than 1,000 guns – which translated into an expectation of less than one-tenth of one homicide per buyback. Not enough, that is, to make even a sliver of impact on the fall of crime." [13]

Taking away guns on a massive scale isn't feasible, and the limited scale of buyback programs does not appear to have any connection with a reduction in gun violence or crime. The reason special interest groups like the NRA repeatedly aggravate these fears in gun owners is because their anger is an asset to them. Invoking this boogeyman further galvanizes their supporters against any gun control legislation, or, indeed, many other types of regulation, too.

"The extremism of the American gun lobby always comes as a shock to the rest of the democratic world, which sees the regulation of guns as no less normal than the regulation of cars or consumer products that are far less lethal. The radicalization of the NRA is of a piece with the radicalization of the rest of the right, and the gun issue had provided a way for the opponents of regulations of all kinds – environmental, financial, workplace safety, consumer protection – to create a mass libertarian base ready to go on the attack at the mere hint of government action. Working-class and middle-class gun owners around the nation might not be ready to rally on behalf of Wall Street or a polluting business, but they could not countenance interference with their firearms. No wonder the weapons industry is the least-regulated enterprise in the country." [14]

Another troubling keystone issue for the anti-gun-control crowd is the perceived political pressure that they believe mass firearm ownership exerts on those in power. *The tree of liberty must be refreshed with the blood of patriots*, they ominously remind us, and the implication they make is a menacing one. If Americans 'gave up' their guns, a new Hitler would rise to power (they are always quite keen to bloviate about how dictators always take away gun rights before campaigns of genocide, as if a citizens with rifles could have meaningfully resisted the Wehrmacht in the 1940's) and the backbone of representative government would collapse just as soon as the threat of a military insurgency is removed.

In the first place, American lawmakers, Congressmen, Senators, and all other public servants and representatives are among the most well-protected people in all of human history. Washington D.C. (a municipality with strict gun laws) is one of the most hardened targets on the face of the earth. Your representatives don't live with the aching worry of an armed revolt of angry citizens; and you wouldn't either if you had the most sophisticated military as your own personal bodyguard. Secondly, superpowers, when occupying territory militarily, struggle the most with I.E.D's, roadside explosives, and other insurgent-based tactics that do not rely on a fully-stocked armory.

I'm sorry, but if we are to make the argument that holding meaningful military might over our political leaders is necessary to preserve freedom, I insist that we extend that argument to all other types of hardware too; that means the citizens will need nuclear weapons, a navy, an air force, artillery units, armored personnel carriers, tanks, *ad infinitum*, until the full might of the American military industrial complex is reasonably matched. After all, this is the ideological *reason* Americans need AR-15's with high-capacity magazines. We *need* to be able to defend ourselves from a military force that spends nearly a half-a-trillion dollars annually on itself. This is the *ideological reason* that those children in Sandy Hook were obliterated by tools reserved for the fiercest combat zones. This is the reason forensic investigators in Aurora, Colorado, were digging *bone fragments* out of the walls of a movie theater after innocent people were slashed to bits by yet another mass-shooting. In the interest of this goal – namely, the preparation for a conflict that will never come – we are to passively accept the scourge of mass-murders as the cost of doing business. This is lunacy, and anyone who wants to live in a world where our *fucking toddlers* are not safe from gunfire is delusional.

The first step in getting a handle on this issue is simple: treat firearms like vehicles. Make a database of their serial numbers, register them to their owners, and insurance premiums should be collected from the citizens who use them. Guns, like automobiles, have an inherent lethality, and the mature choice is to plan ahead for this contingency. No ability to own guns would be infringed; we would merely be casting a wider safety net to assist all of the victims of future shootings. Let's face it, there will be more mass violence, and the repercussions of these bloodbaths are expensive. The NRA and the die-hards won't like this, sure, but they have already had decades upon decades of unchecked firearm ownership. We know where it leads, and the mess it creates is expensive.

The Moscow Contagion

‡‡‡

Chapter 9

"IT IS FUNDAMENTALLY FLAWED TO BELIEVE YOU CAN ACHIEVE THE ENDS OF MORAL POLICY WITH THE MEANS OF MORAL COMPROMISE. YOU CANNOT GO NORTH NO MATTER HOW SMALL THE STEPS YOU TAKE SOUTH." –Gary Kasparov

===

"HAVE THEY FOUND HIM GUILTY? I DON'T THINK THEY'VE FOUND HIM GUILTY. IF HE DID IT, FINE BUT I DON'T KNOW THAT HE DID IT. YOU KNOW, PEOPLE ARE SAYING THEY THINK IT WAS HIM. BUT IN ALL FAIRNESS TO PUTIN – AND I'M NOT SAYING THIS BECAUSE HE SAYS 'TRUMP IS BRILLIANT AND LEADING EVERYBODY' – THE FACT IS THAT HE HASN'T BEEN CONVICTED OF ANYTHING. SOME PEOPLE SAY HE ABSOLUTELY DIDN'T DO IT. –Donald Trump, when asked if Vladimir Putin ordered the execution of Alexander Litvinenko.

===

"MY KGB INSTRUCTORS SPECIFICALLY MADE A POINT. NEVER BORDER WITH LEFTISTS. FORGET ABOUT THESE POLITICAL PROSTITUTES. AIM HIGHER. TRY TO GET INTO WIDE CIRCULATION, ESTABLISHED CONSERVATIVE MEDIA. THE RICH. FLITHY RICH MOVIE MAKERS. INTELLECTUALS. SO-CALLED ACADEMIC CIRCLES. CYNICAL EGOCENTRIC PEOPLE WHO CAN LOOK INTO YOUR EYES WITH AN ANGELIC EXPRESSION AND TELL YOU A LIE." –Yuri Bezmenov, former KGB agent, on recruitment policies.

===

In September, 2015, I wrote an article that appeared on my website entitled "How Russia is Ruining Everything." The article wasn't particularly amazing, but it has become a growing source of pride for me as a budding writer. It proves, too, that my criticism of Mr. Putin's pernicious little mafia state cannot be attributed to partisanship alone. I, like many others on the left, have been heavily critical of the Kremlin long before it became a popular political football in the Beltway. The list of offenses and outrages perpetrated by the Russian oligarchy are too lengthy and too heinous to catalog in full. To say it more simply; liberty, freedom, and justice do not exist for most of the people who live in the Russian Federation. This was, not too long ago, almost universally accepted as a bi-partisan political truth in the United States. Whatever the motivation, good or bad, the Russians were not often a point of contention in American politics. The Kremlin represented an affront to basic civility; it murdered journalists, it murdered political opponents, and before anyone forgets, funded and armed vassal states that killed scores of American troops in places like Vietnam and Korea. Fast-forward to 2016, and America's Red Fever broke suddenly and without warning. Why? Because the Republican nominee for the Presidency was being dogged by accusations that he was in cahoots with Mr. Putin's regime. The suspicion was certainly not unfounded; the GOP, on the eve of the Republican National Convention, had dropped "lethal" support for the Ukrainian army from its policy platform at the direction Paul Manafort (more on him later.) As the Ukrainians bravely resisted a Russian invasion of its Donbass and Donetsk regions, the Republicans, with notable Kremlin hawks like Senator McCain and Senator Graham in tow, inexplicably yanked their support:

"Senators Lindsey Graham and John McCain were some of the loudest voices opposed to Russia's aggressive dominance of territories. All cooperation, military, and civilian, under the NRC was suspended in April 2014 following the Russia-Ukraine conflict. NATO's stance: "The Allies continue to call on Russia to reverse its recognition of the Georgian regions of Abkhazia and South Ossetia as independent states." At the Wales Summit in September 2014, NATO leaders condemned Russia's aggression in the Ukraine, demanding that the nation comply with international law and end its "illegal" annexation of Crimea. Russia effectively ignored President Barack Obama's warnings, invaded Crimea, and annexed it within thirty days under armed occupation." [1]

I find this cowardice endlessly infuriating; McCain and Graham, clearly, understand how toxic the Russians truly are on the global stage, but both men caved to the pressure placed upon them by the Republican Party and not just chose to support Mr. Trump, but would also later vote for the confirmation of Rex Tillerson. Calling them both spineless simply doesn't do it justice; these are both tenured and experienced politicians who should absolutely know better. If they can't spot obvious interference by a foreign power, *who* among us could?

Trump would go on to win the Presidency, but would be continually pestered by investigations by the Department of Justice and the Federal Bureau of Investigation over his connections with the Kremlin. His denials, and the denials of his inner-circle were bad lies told poorly. Michael Flynn was fired early in the administration for his connections with Russian and Turkish intelligence. Paul Manafort, Trump's former campaign manager, was found to have been on a 'secret payroll' that belonged to the former Ukrainian dictator and Putin-backed-thug Viktor Yanukovych, and Carter Page, a former advisor to the Trump campaign *recused himself* from a federal probe into Russian interference in the 2016 U.S. election because he had, by his own admission, failed to tell the truth about his repeated contacts with Russian officials. Trump's newly-appointed Attorney General, Jeff Sessions, would go on to later recuse himself as well. The evidence was certainly beginning to mount. Then came the calls for equivalencies. Bill O'Reilly, former cable TV pundit for Fox, cornered Mr. Trump on the Russian problem by calling Mr. Putin a "killer" during an interview. President Trump's reply? "We've got a lot of killers here, too."

I have *never* been more outraged in all of my life. The President, with one clunky sentence fragment, had somehow managed to insult his own nation while simultaneously condoning the lengthy list of Mr. Putin's crimes over his years in power. The United States is certainly not without her shortcomings, and I am far from a doughy-eyed nationalist. The ugliness of the history of this country is not lost on me. America is a blighted beauty in many ways. She kicked open the doors to German concentration camps, but she also created Guantanamo Bay and was responsible for the Tuskegee Experiments. I, like the vast majority of educated Americans, do not operate from a haughty moral platform and gaze down at the rest of the world. I won't have it said, however, that the United States is ethically equivalent Putin's mafia state. The sitting U.S. President has not yet murdered the leader of his opposition party; Boris Nemtsov paid with his life for bravely standing up to Putin. The United States has not yet committed an act of nuclear terrorism; Alexander Litvinenko was brutally and cowardly murdered on Putin's orders with polonium. America hasn't yet legalized domestic violence, nor has it made its free press illegal, and on, and on, and on. The suggestion that the United States and the Russian Federation are morally equal is repulsive, and more often than not, betrays an embarrassing level of ignorance to the depth of Russian cruelty. Alexei Navalny – the charismatic leader of the political opposition party - is now blind in one eye after an acid attack by the Kremlin's thugs. The barbarity is truly staggering, and many on the right were willing to overlook it when it became politically expedient. Forget about whether or not the candidate you support is currently in the White House; surely *everyone* can agree that murdering journalists is bad, right? It is insulting to have to reach to such low-hanging fruit to convince conservatives that Russia is a global pariah, and has been for so many years.

Without Russian interference, brutal despot Bashar Al-Assad is easily ousted from power by a popular revolt from his own people. Without Russian interference, thousands of Ukrainians wouldn't be dead. Without this Russian government, the Russian people wouldn't be smothered under layer after miserable layer of theft and corruption. Russian power is not inconsequential, and without exaggeration, nearly every global problem either finds its origin from, or is aggravated by, the Kremlin. The Moscow contagion extends far beyond the 2016 U.S. Presidential election. Putin's fingerprints are smudged across the face of global politics at nearly every turn; Brexit and the French election chiefly among them. Marine La Pen - a vile and contemptable toad - had the gall to welcome Mr. Putin's violent annexation of Crimea (placing him firmly in the dubious company of other European land-grabbers like Slobodan Milosevich and Adolf Hitler.) She is nothing more than paid shill for the Kremlin, and her own political party was shameless enough to petition the French parliament for the right to accept campaign donations from Russian banks. As a result, she parrots Putin's philosophies of 'Euroscepticism' by promising to offer the French people a referendum on their membership in the European Union (credit to our French brethren for failing to fall for her race-baiting shtick in their own Presidential election.) Putin and his thugs want to weaken Western infrastructure like NATO - an organization literally constructed to contain Russian military aggression and expansionism - and the European Union because they threaten Putin's regional power. The Russian global political footprint, on the whole, is rotten and poisonous throughout:

"Out of a thesaurus of possible nominations, one would have to select George Bush's remarks about Vladimir Putin as the stupidest utterance of his entire presidency. Impressed beyond words by the fact that Putin was wearing a crucifix that had belonged to his mother and was thus a man of faith, our chief executive then burbled like a schoolgirl and said that he had looked into the man's eyes and knew he was the one to trust. (I have not checked, but surely someone can discover how many times Putin has worn that crucifix since. It could be a sort of emblem of the fatuity of the "faith-based.") Since then, Putin has been noticeable for his efforts to protect Saddam Hussein, Kim Jong-il, the Iranian mullahs, and the Sudanese racist cleansers from any concerted action by the United Nations and has instructed his troops in Chechnya to behave in a manner that would cause a storm of international outrage if emulated by coalition forces in Iraq. In response, Chechen insurgents have committed atrocities, such as the seizure of the Moscow theater or the Beslan school hostage-taking, which nobody would be so crass as to blame on the lack of vigilance of the Russian security services." [2]

These, of course, are just some of the Russian crimes of the past. The

Russian crimes of the present are just as bad, and all of them are orchestrated for the singular purpose of expanding the Kremlin's power. It is for this foul purpose that Syrian children are butchered by Assad's merciless barrel bombs. It is for this purpose that Ukrainian civilians catch shrapnel from Putin's army as it skips over sovereign borders with impunity. It is for this perverse goal that the email accounts of John Podesta and Emmanuel Macron were breeched by Russian intelligence. The list of their victims goes on and on, and the singular aim of these efforts is to strengthen and enrich Mr. Putin. It makes me sick to hear apathetic conservatives, solely interested in defending Trump at all costs, callously dismissing these outrages as liberal fantasies intended to reignite a new Cold War. The bodies of Putin's victims cry out to us from the grave. Are you listening? Indeed, the death toll is another list too long to fully catalog in these pages, but to speak about Russia without speaking of its martyrs is impossible. We should start with Anna Politkovskaya; a gifted journalist and author who was shot to death in cold blood. The killers were brazen enough to even leave the murder weapon at the scene:

"Politkovskaya's murder marked a distinct turning point. Her assassin made no attempt to disguise his crime as a theft or an accident: he not only shot her in broad daylight, he left her body in the elevator alongside the gun he used to kill her – standard practice for Moscow's arrogant hit men. Nor could her murder be easily attributed to distant provincial authorities or to the criminal mafia. Local businessmen had no motivation to kill her, but officials of the army, the police, and even the Kremlin did. Whereas local thieves might have tried to cover their tracks, Politkovskaya's assassin, like so many Russian assassins, did not seem to fear the law." [3]

Perhaps Putin's most infamous target is Alexander Litvinenko; his murder was so heinous it has been the topic of numerous books on its own. Alexander was poisoned by Russian intelligence agents with polonium-laced tea in the heart of London.

"Alexander Litvinenko was a KGB agent who broke the loyalty code by fleeing to the UK. Even worse, he violated the law of omertà by going to the press and even publishing books about the dirty deeds of Putin and his foot soldiers. Instead of being taken fishing in the old-fashioned *Godfather* style, in November 2006 he was killed in London in the first recorded case of nuclear terrorism. The Kremlin refused to hand over the main suspect in the murder and eventually Britain shelved the case, only to reopen it in 2014 when Putin's invasion of Ukraine finally persuaded the British that engagement with his regime was no longer a possibility." [4]

Litvinenko's killers left a trail of radioactivity wherever they went: in the airplane in which they arrived, in the hotel in which they stayed, even security camera footage corroborates the radiological evidence unearthed in the investigation after his death. The murderers, of course, were active members of Russian intelligence, and after the deed was done, Putin quickly rushed them home and refused any requests for their extradition. A U.K. court would later try them, *in absentia*, and also confirmed the obvious: the order for Mr. Litvinenko's cruel execution could have only come from Mr. Putin. I wouldn't kill an animal in the same agonizing and torturous method the Kremlin used to ice Alexander Litvinenko; (Chernobyl firefighters, in the throes of a radiation overdose death, purportedly described the sensation as "death by pins and needles.") There is no limit to Mr. Putin's savagery, barbarism, and violence. Boris Nemtsov, like countless other honorable and brave Russians who oppose Putin, also paid with his life:

"Boris Nemtsov, my longtime friend and colleague in the Russian opposition, was murdered in cold blood in the middle of Moscow on February, 27, 2015. Four bullets in the back ended his life in sight of the Kremlin, where he once worked as Boris Yeltsin's deputy prime minister. Photos from the scene showed a cleaning crew scrubbing his blood off the pavement within hours of the murder, so it is not difficult to imagine the quality of the investigation that followed. Putin actually started, and ended, the inquiry whole Boris's body was still warm by calling the murder a "provocation," the term of art for suggesting his enemies are murdering one another in order to bring shame upon his innocent brow. He then brazenly sent a message of condolence to Nemtsov's mother, who often warned her fearless son that his actions could get him killed in Putin's Russia. Hours after Boris's death, reports said that police were raiding his home and confiscating papers and computers. Putin's enemies are often victims and his victims are always suspects. Boris was a passionate critic of Putin's war in Ukraine and was about to finish a report on the presence of Russian soldiers in Donbass, a matter the Kremlin has spared no effort to cover up. But "Did Putin give the order?" rings as hollow today as it did when journalist Anna Politkovskaya was gunned down in 2006 or when MH17 was shot down over Eastern Ukraine last year. As long as Putin is in office we'll never know who gave the order, but there is no doubt that he is directly responsible for creating the conditions in which these outrages occur with terrible frequency."
[5]

This heart-wrenching account, written by his close friend, Gary Kasparov, tells us all we need to know about Mr. Putin's blood-thirsty behavior. He kills who he wants, when he wants, and world leaders everywhere either shrug with indifference, or offer lukewarm statements about how "troubled" they are by the recurring mess Putin creates. The scope of the Kremlin's reach extends far beyond their own internal affairs; the bodies of 283 innocent civilians aboard MH17 speak to the veracity of this claim:

> "So who is to blame? This is not a simple question even if you know the answer. That is, of course, the person who pushed the button that launched the missile is to blame; that is the easy part. Shall we just arrest him and try him for murder? Responsibility is a greater concept than that. You have the leader who gave the order to push the button. Then the person who provided the missiles to the separatists. Then there are the officials who opened the border to allow military weaponry to cross into Ukraine and the ministers and generals in Moscow who gave those orders. Then we come to the desk where all power resides in Russia today, the desk of the man those ministers and generals obey very carefully: the desk of Russian President Vladimir Putin. Blaming Putin for these deaths is as correct and as pointless as blaming the man who pressed the button that launched the missile. Everyone has known for months that Russia arms and supports the separatists in Ukraine. Everyone has known for years that a mouse does not squeak in the Kremlin without first getting Putin's permission. We also know very well what Putin is, a revanchist KGB thug trying to build a poor man's USSR to replace the loss of the original he mourns so much. But blaming Putin for invading Ukraine — for annexing Crimea, for giving advanced surface-to-air missiles to separatists — is like blaming the proverbial scorpion for stinging the frog. It is expected. It is his nature. Instead of worrying about how to change the scorpion's nature or, even worse, how best to appease it, we must focus on how the civilized world can contain the dangerous creature before more innocents die." [6]

It is for this reason that I personally became so incredulous when American conservatives started to openly defend the Kremlin when Mr. Trump came under fire for his ties to Moscow. I cannot – no matter if my preferred political candidate wins or loses – artlessly shove the bodies of Nemtsov, Litvinenko, Politkovskaya, and the 283 innocent victims of MH17 under the rug as if nothing happened. Putin is a reprehensible thug, and like any other thin-skinned despot, he murders anyone he pleases, steals from his own impoverished people to fund his opulent lifestyle, and spends his time propping up vassal states across the globe that carry out his wishes. This point, too, would provide ample ammunition to condemn Mr. Putin's mafia-state alone, so for the moment, let us move past the egregious roster of murdered men and women whose only mistake was irritating a dictator, and delve into the implications of Moscow's foreign policy. The scope and scale of the damage inflicted upon the world by Putin is far greater than the body count of his enemies. What sort of world is the Kremlin seeking to build? What kind of international reputation does Russia seek to maintain? Is claiming – as I have, echoing the thoughts of Russian exiles everywhere – that Russia is perhaps the most dangerous regime in the world baseless hyperbole?

> "Putin's Russia is clearly the biggest and most dangerous threat facing the world today, but it is not the only one. Terrorist groups like Al-Qaeda and the Islamic State are (despite the latter's name) stateless and without the vast resources and weapons of mass destruction Putin has at his fingertips. The attacks of 9/11 and others like it, however, taught us that you don't have to have a national flag or even an army to inflict terrible damage on the most powerful country in the world. What's more, state sponsors of terror are benefiting as democratic terrorist targets fail to organize an aggressive defense. The murderous regimes of Iran, North Korea, and Syria have enjoyed considerable time at the bargaining table with the world's great powers while making no significant concessions." [7]

It is not inappropriate to lay a staggering amount of responsibility for much of what ails the entire world at the foot of the Kremlin. Putin's regime is repugnant for its foreign policy in addition to the growing laundry list of political opponents it murders with impunity. I was floored to hear open praise of Mr. Putin on my personal social media feeds after the Kremlin announced they would operate jointly with the Syrian regime against ISIS. The subtext underneath this dopey dictator worship was obvious – Putin kills the terrorists and that's what Obama should be doing – but such commentary ignores, entirely, the nature of Russian policy throughout history: they create the problem, and then sell the solution.

> "Putin's foreign policy doctrine was essentially a broader version of the domestic strategy and it showed the opportunistic way he would operate for the next fifteen years. Both could neatly be summed up as "Rouge State Management, Ltd." Wherever there were trouble spots on the world stage or "threats" to Russia's domestic tranquility, the new president was there with a lever. He was everywhere! Worried about the North Korea nuclear program? The Russian president had already established personal relations with Kim Jong-Il and was ready

to play a broker role on the Korean Peninsula. Saddam Hussein, Muammar Gaddafi, or Bashar al-Assad – Putin was ready to generously offer his assistance with all of these illustrious leaders…Despite Russia's demonstrable weaknesses, Putin would often poke a finger wherever he could, especially in weak spots and in old wounds. He regularly made threats and promises no one was sure he could keep, even if he wanted to. Russia still had its seat on the UN Security Council and often found an ally in China when looking to thwart American initiatives. I believe it was Andrew Ryvkin at *The Guardian* who cleverly referred to this technique of Putin's as a "photobombing" foreign policy." [8]

Interjections of this sort are not always unwelcome; it is not the act of Mr. Putin intervening that draws my scorn, *but for whom he chooses to intervene.* Russia creates the crisis by funneling money and arms to North Korea, or by propping up other dictators like Assad in Syria, and when these issues boil over and create global problems that threaten millions of people, Putin waddles back into the fray and pretends he can play the peacemaker. His snotty little children have wrecked the inside of our store, and instead of rebuking and restraining them, he slithers his hand across our shoulders and tells us that he might be able to negotiate with these stunted pariahs for the right price.

Let's pivot from foreign blunders to domestic ones. What is life like for a typical Russian citizen living under the rule of Vladimir Putin? The answer is simple: for those who are (and can remain) friends of Putin, life could scarcely be better, and for nearly everyone else, everyday survival can be a pressing challenge. Average Russian citizens bear the brunt of the endemic corruption, and are crushed underneath a bribery system that only serves to line the pockets of the financial elites:

> "Transparency International estimates the annual cost of bribery to Russia at $300 billion, roughly equal to the entire gross domestic product of Denmark, or thirty-seven times higher than the $8 billion Russia expended in 2007 on "national priority projects" in health, education, and agriculture." [9]

Of course, the societal impacts of such wide-spread grift are not confined to the financial sector. The economic woes of the Russian economy – rotted and corroded from the inside out by systemic and state-sponsored corruption, theft, and bribery – have created a society in which horrifying abuses go unpunished and those in power have virtually no accountability for their mistakes and practically nothing is sacred.

"In Irkutsk, in the depths of Siberia, an old man was found frozen to the floor of his apartment. He was past eighty, an ordinary retiree, one of the people the emergency services refuse to help because they are just too old. Their response to a telephone call is straightforward and unreflecting "Well, what do you expect? Of course he's feeling ill. It's his age." This elderly citizen lived alone, a veteran of the Second World War, who freed the world from Nazism, with medals and a state pension. He was one of those to whom President Putin sends greetings on May 9, Victory Day, wishing him happiness and good health. Our old men, our veterans unspoiled by too much attention by the state, weep over these form letters with their facsimile signature. Anyway, in January 2003, he died of hypothermia. He stuck to the floor where he fell. His name was Ivanov, the most common Russian surname. There are hundreds of thousands of Ivanovs in Russia. Ivanov froze to the floor because his flat was unheated. It should have been heated, of course, like all the apartments in the block where he lived; like all of the blocks or flats in Irkutsk, in the third year of Putin's stewardship. Why did this happen? The explanation is simple. Throughout Russia, the heating pipes wore out because they had been in service since Soviet times, and those times have been gone for more than a decade, and thank God for that. For a long time the pipes leaked and leaked, and Communal Services, whose responsibility they are, did nothing about the situation. Communal Services is a centralized, state-run monopoly. Every month we pay a substantial sum for the agency's nonexistent technical support, but it virtually ignores us, goes on not doing its job, and periodically demands a rate increase." [10]

This story, and millions upon millions of others like it, serve to illustrate the cruelty of Putin's regime. Once the virus of corruption infects the body of a government, the quality of life for everyone except the privileged begins to slowly deteriorate. The public subsidizes agencies at great expense that simply do nothing for the people while the true purpose of these government monoliths – which exist to funnel cash from the public coffers to the private bank accounts of Russian oligarchs – works with machine-like efficiency. In a nation with an unobstructed press and a moderately powerful judicial system, a citizen maligned in this fashion by the state could have some method of legal recourse. Their grievances could be redressed. While far from perfect (or completely free from its own political corruption or bribery) the United States still occasionally gives the little guy a chance. In America, if you pay for a service to heat your apartment and it fails to do so, there are a swarm of regulatory bodies that can (and often do) hold those entities to account on your behalf. In short, and with no exaggeration, *if you enjoy living in a society that has some semblance of respect for the rule of law*, you have a lifestyle many Russians can only dream about. The Kremlin has only one obligation; to enrich Putin and his friends. This directive is all-encompassing, and it is unafraid to tarnish anything in the pursuit of this gluttonous goal. Their purportedly revered veterans are left to freeze to death in their own homes. Russian soldiers, even when killed honorably on the field of battle, are often unable to escape the indignities of state-run corruption in this life *or the next:*

"Pavel Levurda died in Ushkaloy, where the fighting was at its fiercest — a desperate partisan war in highland forests, on narrow paths. But where was Pavel's body? The family never received a coffin containing Nina Levurda's son for burial. His remains, she discovered, had been lost by the state he had tried with such desperate loyalty to serve. Nina Levurda then took on the tasks of military prosecutor and investigating officer…Pavel Levurda had been deserted on the battlefield and then forgotten. Nobody cared that his body was lying there, or that he had a family awaiting his return. What happened after his death is typical of the army, a disgraceful episode that stands for an ethos in which a human is nothing, in which no one watches over the troops, and there is no sense of responsibility towards the families…Back home, Pavel's mother was in a dreadful state. The only communication she had had was Pavel's letter, which she had received on February 7. The Ministry of Defense's "hotline" wasn't much help: talking to the duty officers there was like talking to a computer. "Lieutenant Pavel Petrovich Levurda is not on the list of the dead or missing," was the invariable reply she received. Nina went back to the "fully updated" hotline over the course of several months: even after she had located Pavel's body through her own efforts, even after official notification of his death, she continued to hear the same information…Seeing the state the family was in, Abramochkin strongly advised Nina Levurda to go to the main military mortuary in Rostov-on-Don as soon as she could…"We arrived in Rostov on August 20," Nina said. "I went straight to the laboratory. There was no security at the entrance. I walked in and went into the first autopsy room I found. I saw a severed head on a stand next to an examination table. More precisely, it was a skull. I knew immediately that it was Pavel's head, even though there were other skulls nearby." Is there any way to assess this mother's distress or compensate her for it? Of course not. Nina was given sedatives after the encounter with her son's skull, which she had correctly identified." [11]

No restitution, indeed, could ever come close to rectifying this unspeakably horrific treatment of an honorable soldier and his family. And make no mistake, every *ounce* of blame for this disgrace belongs squarely on the shoulders of Mr. Putin, who created the conditions for these kinds of egregious outrages. This is the result of his political corruption, and the army – equal parts corrupt and incompetent - followed the mold created for nearly every other aspect of Russian life and government itself. Nothing works, nothing is sacred, and those in power have absolutely no incentive to act with even a moderate amount of human decency. When theft and bribery become state-sponsored, the services offered by that state will eventually hollow out over time. There wasn't money for an investigation to ascertain where Pavel's body was, or to properly update the Defense Ministry's hotline, or to staff security at the military's primary mortuary to prevent bereaved family members from being horribly traumatized by seeing their loved ones flayed open on a table – because the budget for that organization was pilfered by Putin. It is *of the upmost importance* that the world starts to correlate these two truths together. They are not coincidences. They are connected, and one indisputably causes the other. Beyond ethics and basic human decency, an economy that is regularly pillaged by elites and is entirely propped up by a downward spiral of bribes ultimately drags *everyone* down with it in the end:

> "While Putin uses the revenues from oil and gas to fund large capital projects, from the multiple state residences to the Sochi Olympics, or allows his cronies to take it abroad, the population must contribute significantly to the budget through a combination of income taxes, high value-added taxes, and high duties on imported consumer goods. But the population also contributes a "tax" by paying bribes. Instead of cracking down on corruption, the state uses bribes both to feed the venality of the elites and as a way to supplement the insufficient salaries of low-paid workers. Instead of paying them from state coffers, the state allows low-level civil servants to supplement their meager incomes with petty bribes. This constitutes an additional tax on the population and a drag on the economy's overall efficiency. Over the long term this "corruption effect," equivalent to $2,000 per Russian and *equal* to the size of the Russian budget, can only slow economic growth and increase popular resentments, including among civil servants who feel degraded by the system." [12]

It is also imperative to note that these economic bear traps do not just ensnare the civil service sector. Nearly every enterprise that operates in Russia must pay-to-play. There is little separation between business and government, (which, by the way, what a surprise it is to see American free-market-Republican-capitalists suddenly in love with a man like Putin who nationalizes everything!) and the compounding costs of Mr. Putin's gluttony can occasionally drive divestment:

> "The demands of this tribute system have meant that the cost of doing business in Russia has escalated to such an extent that Russian and foreign businesses alike wonder whether they can even turn a profit. The global Swedish furniture chain Ikea threatened to call it quits after years of trying to run a clean business in Russia. When the head of Ikea Russia, Lennart Dahlgren, left the company in 2006, he revealed that they had been subjected to years of legal traps that they sought to solve by meeting personally with Putin. But a high-ranking official told them that meeting with Putin would cost $5 million to $10 million. Stating that he didn't know whether they were speaking seriously or joking, Dahlgren told reporters: "I sensed that it would be better not to get into that discussion any deeper.""

Mr. Putin never jokes about money, and he extorts anyone and anything he can in order to keep his opulent lifestyle funded. Can you imagine having the audacity to demand that a high-ranking executive of a successful multinational must *pay you $5 to $10 million for a single meeting?* If there was a punchline buried somewhere in Putin's goons telling Mr. Dahlgren to cough up if he wants to meet the boss, I must admit I am having some difficulty locating it. Skewering Vladimir Putin for his obvious and unmistakable theft is certainly not difficult, and the metric tons of evidence to support the sordid actions of his mafia state are impossible to overlook. But a far more compelling point to make, I think, is that all of this self-enrichment is flatly counterproductive and self-defeating. It stymies economic growth. It creates unbearable amounts of overhead. It fuels domestic resentment for the government. It drives international business into markets where the government doesn't expect a share so large that it destroys any hope of profitability. Again, it is not the Democratic Party in the U.S. that is calling for closer relations with this international pariah, it is the Republicans. Ann Coulter even Tweeted that the United States *should form a military alliance* with the Russians to "protect it from Western Europe." Make no mistake – when American conservatives shrug at the atrocities of Mr. Putin – they are pushing *us* down a slope that leads to an America that would be every bit as corrupt and dysfunctional as Putin's Russia.

On Hacking, Wikileaks, and Possible Trump-Putin Collusion

There is an inherent disadvantage (or, perhaps, foolishness) in attempting to meaningfully comment on a story as fast-moving as the Russian interference into the American Presidential election of 2016. Indeed, the investigation is still on-going, and new developments surface at break-neck speed. At the time of this writing, Mr. Trump has been in office for a little under six months, and there's a lot of time left on the proverbial clock. As a precautionary measure, I should preface this section by claiming that a full accounting of the events that took place before the ballots were counted will eventually come to light in time, and I understand, completely, that new information will surface. That being said, there are many conclusions which will age remarkably well, and are quite safe to put into print, in my view. The hack was *unquestionably* perpetrated by Russian Intelligence:

"The DNC's information technology team first alerted party officials that there was a potential security problem in late March, but the DNC didn't bring in outside help until May. This is when CrowdStrike's incident response team was brought in. CrowdStrike identified two separate ongoing breaches, as detailed in a June 15, 2016 blog post by CrowdStrike CTO Dmitri Alperovitch. The findings were based both on malware samples found and a monitoring of the breach while it was in progress.

One of those attacks, based on the malware and command and control traffic, was attributed to Fancy Bear. The malware deployed by Fancy Bear was a combination of an agent disguised as a Windows driver file (named twain_64.dll) in combination with a network tunneling tool that allowed remote control connections. The other breach, which may have been the breach hinted at by the FBI, was a long-running intrusion by a group previously identified as APT29, also known as The Dukes or Cozy Bear. Cozy Bear ran SeaDaddy (also known as SeaDuke, a backdoor developed in Python and compiled as a Windows executable) as well as a one-line Windows PowerShell command that exploited Microsoft's Windows Management Instrumentation (WMI) system. The exploit allowed attackers to persist in WMI's database and execute based on a schedule. Researchers at Fidelis who were given access to malware samples from the hack confirmed that attribution." [14]

Cozy Bear and Fancy Bear are, simply, Russian military hacking units who are staffed with Russian intelligence agents. These threats are so familiar to the American security services because they are, as the acronym indicates, *advanced persistent threats*. The intrusion attempts are sophisticated (almost as if they are state-sponsored!) and incessant. They were designed with political goals in mind, and the order authorizing this campaign could only have come from one person within the Kremlin.

"CrowdStrike assessed that COZY BEAR had breached the system in 2015 and had been engaged in gathering data for a year. They then found that a second group, FANCY BEAR had breached the server in April of 2016. They managed to penetrate through spear-phishing, the technique of sending a false email to a victim who would subsequently click on a link in the email, connecting them to a hacker's server...Several cyber security firms have examined the related metadata to the APT28 FANCY BEAR infections. They have nearly unanimously found that several combinations of factors tie this group to a large group of similar infections since 2007. In particular, the Internet Protocol or IP address like 176.31.112.10, used for its command-and-control server (C2), shows up repeatedly in other cyberwarfare campaigns. This IP was linked to the breaches at the German Bundestag, the DNC, and the DCCC." [15]

It is quite foolish, even at this early stage in the investigation, to suggest that Russian intelligence had no involvement in the attack, when the metadata of the attack itself leads straight back to the Kremlin. Furthermore, the sophistication of the attack points clearly to an experienced and well-funded state actor:

"Another indicator of professional intelligence agency involvement was the way they performed OpSec or Operational Security. OpSec was the methodology the operators used to evade detection and cover their tracks. CrowdStrike was impressed and called it "superb." They noted that they demonstrated a "live off the land" approach to evading security. In fact, just one year before the DNC hack was revealed, the firm found COZY BEAR responsible for hacks of the White House, the State Department, and the U.S. Joint Chiefs of Staff. "We have identified no collaboration between the two actors, or even an awareness of one by the other," Dmitri Alperovitch wrote in a blog post. "Instead, we observed the two Russian espionage groups compromise the same systems and engage separately in the theft of identical credentials." Alperovitch wrote this is "not an uncommon scenario" in Russia, where the primary domestic and foreign intelligence agencies – the FSB and SVR, respectively – have a competitive and even adversarial relationship. The hackers frequently cleared out the logs that would reveal their activities or reset the timestamp of files so that it appeared that they were never opened or tampered with." [16]

There was clearly a high level of sophisticated tradecraft; logs were erased to avoid detection, timestamps were modified to conceal prior access. The hit was, in every way, professional and precise. Speculation about buyer's remorse from the Russians, when Mr. Trump's polling numbers looked anemic, started to percolate in the last days of the election; occasionally this line of reasoning is held up as evidence that disputes Russia's involvement. Surely they couldn't have expected the Republicans to actually win, so why would the Kremlin take such a massive risk? The point of the hacking was not *just* to win an election, it was also designed to *weaken* an adversarial candidate before their administration could even begin. Don't take my word for it – this is also the view of the former Director of the CIA, John Brennan:

> "Brennan said Russia was motivated to back Donald Trump in the presidential election because of a "traditional animus" between Democratic nominee Hillary Clinton and Russian President Vladimir Putin. He told committee members there had not been a good relationship between Putin and the Clintons over the years. What's more, Brennan said Putin blamed Hillary Clinton's actions as secretary of state during the Obama administration for domestic disturbances inside Russia. He said Putin was concerned Clinton would be more "rigid" on issues such as human rights if elected president. But Brennan told the committee he believed that Russia anticipated that Clinton would be the likely winner of the presidential race, and that Russia tried to "damage and bloody" her before Election Day. Had she won, Brennan said, Russia would have continued to attempt to "denigrate her and hurt her" during her presidency. If Russia had collected more information about Clinton that they did not use against her during the campaign, Brennan said they were likely "husbanding it for another day." [17]

Mr. Putin stood to lose quite a lot from another four years of Obama-styled-economic-sanctions under Mrs. Clinton, and anything that would limit her power or political capital was worth the effort to obtain. The hacking wasn't a zero-sum game; the Kremlin was improving its position by weakening Mrs. Clinton at any degree at all. It was President Obama's economic sanctions, after the Russian invasion of Ukraine, that nearly *halved* the value of the Ruble, after all. Putin had every reason to oppose another four years of his inner circle being sanctioned and having their assets frozen.

We've established the origin of the attack as Russian. We've established that Russia certainly had the *means* to carry out the attack, and the *motivation* to do so as well. I think it should also be mentioned that, at this impasse, Russia's actions are not entirely salacious or uncommon. Nearly every intelligence agency utilizes some amount of their offensive cyberwarfare capabilities. While, strictly speaking, these actions are illegal under international law, it is a rule that nearly everyone breaks anyway. Russia isn't a pariah *just* because they authorized an attack on a Presidential candidate they didn't like, and it would be disingenuous to imply that the United States and other nations don't partake in activities such as these when it suits their interests, too. But the consensus amongst the international intelligence community seems to be that Russia has become increasingly more brazen and aggressive in their digital espionage campaigns. That said, the Russian government couldn't release the purloined emails in their own name. The DNC data, once stolen, needed a distribution network that was outside of the ambit of the American judicial system, and according to the former Director of the CIA, John Brennan, the Russians found it in WikiLeaks:

> "Under questioning from Rep. Ileana Ros-Lehtinen, R-Fla., Brennan said the Russians have been trying to disrupt Western elections since the 1960s, and that they've quickly adapted to the times. Brennan pointed to the ease with which Russia was able to hack Democratic operatives' emails, which were then published on WikiLeaks. "The cyber-environment now really provides so much more opportunity for troublemaking and the Russians take advantage of it," he said. Brennan said the use of spear phishing, and "whatever else so that they can then gain access to people's emails, computer systems networks," is something that the Russians are adept at. He said Russia used WikiLeaks as a "cut-out," or go-between, and that protests by WikiLeaks that it is not working with Russia and Russia's claims it is not working with WikiLeaks are "disingenuous." [18]

The cabal of far-right, anti-immigrant, and pro-corruption parties are tightly intertwined, and indisputably so. Whether connections like these are criminal in nature (I, of course, strongly suspect that this is the case) will be for the authorities to determine, but the threads that connect La Pen, Farage, Trump, and Putin are becoming more difficult to deny by the minute:

> "Nigel Farage, a British MEP and former leader of the Brexit campaign, is a "person of interest" in the US investigation into possible collusion between Russia and Donald Trump's presidential campaign, The Guardian newspaper has reported. Citing unidentified sources, The

Guardian reported on Thursday that Farage had not been accused of wrongdoing and was not a suspect or target of the US investigation. But it said the former leader of the United Kingdom Independence Party (UKIP) had "raised the interest" of FBI investigators because of his relationships with individuals connected to both the Trump campaign and WikiLeaks founder Julian Assange. A source told The Guardian newspaper: "One of the things the intelligence investigators have been looking at is points of contact and persons involved. "If you triangulate Russia, WikiLeaks, Assange and Trump associates the person who comes up with the most hits is Nigel Farage. "He's right in the middle of these relationships. He turns up over and over again. There's a lot of attention being paid to him." Contacted by Al Jazeera by phone, Farage said he was not making any comment yet. Still, he dismissed the idea that he could be a "person of interest" as "ridiculous", saying: "I am laughing so much I've not been able to finish the article in The Guardian yet." [19]

It seems boring, even predictable, that Trump would so closely emulate the Presidency of Richard Nixon (a person for whom Trump's good friend, Roger Stone, worked tirelessly) by reaching out to any like-minded oligarchs in defiance of international law, in much the same way that Nixon undermined President Johnson's negotiations with the Vietnamese before he was elected. The degree and legality of Trump's relationships with the Kremlin, and indeed, Farage's alleged relationship with Assange and Putin, too, are at least somewhat up in the air. What is not, however, is that all of the aforementioned parties share the same goals, and loathe the same enemies. I anticipate, as more facts begin to surface, that it will not be long before we will not be asking *if* they colluded, but when did it start, and how long did it last? I had written before the election, of course, that I suspected Russian money was behind the Brexit campaign. This isn't much of a leap of faith; UKIP is a vicious anti-immigrant party, and France's own nasty anti-immigration party, the National Front, led by La Pen, was literally taking campaign donations from Russian banks in Rubles.

"In April 2015, Russian hackers took over the transmission of a French television station, pretended to be ISIS, and then broadcast material designed to terrorize France. Russia impersonated a "cybercaliphate" so that the French would fear terror more than they already did. The aim was presumably to drive voters to the Far-Right National Front, a party financially supported by Russia. After 130 people were killed and 368 injured in the terrorist attack on Paris of November 2015, the founder of a think-tank close to the Kremlin rejoiced that terrorism would drive both Europe toward fascism and

Russia. Both fake and real Islamic terrorism in western Europe, in other words, were thought to be in the Russian interest." [20]

What a surprise it was, then, to hear La Pen gleefully praise Mr. Putin's violent annexation of Crimea to the French press. The connection was not a difficult one to make. Any European political party that blathers about immigration quotas and leaving NATO or the EU are almost certainly in league with the Russians who want desperately to weaken both institutions. Again, don't take just my word for it:

> "Every six years Russia creates a strategy document to assess and guide its strategic policy. At the end of 2015 they submitted the National Security Strategy of the Russian Federation until 2020. This document is multidimensional in that it reflects not only the risks Russia faces in defense, foreign affairs, and geopolitical challenges but also internal security, cultural, and economic risks. The first major takeaway was that above all, Russia views the United States and NATO as a threat to their global position." [21]

Straight from the horse's mouth: NATO is their primary problem, and Russia intentionally directed its resources towards causes that would weaken and undermine it. If Russia was cutting checks to La Pen for this purpose, which has been proven, it stands to reason Russia might be supporting other causes under the same banner, too. It is one thing to connect the Russians to the DNC hacking campaign, and quite another to connect Trump to the Kremlin. While ironclad evidence exists for the former, the latter has yet to be fleshed out in full. Yes, Mr. Trump did encourage the Russians from the campaign trail to illegally steal Mrs. Clinton's data; while this was in boorishly poor taste, it seems a stretch to describe that action as criminal. Yes, Roger Stone, in a speech that was filmed (and later found its way into a *Netflix* documentary about Mr. Stone) boasted of having a direct line of contact with Julian Assange. (A charge Mr. Stone would even deny in an interview filmed for the *same* documentary). WikiLeaks, with its attacks on Emmanuel Macron, Hillary Clinton, and basically anyone else who opposes pro-Russian politicians, have solidified their position, however big or small it might be, in the Russian intelligence ecosystem.

While fascinating, these connections, in my view, have not developed into anything overwhelmingly substantial (at least from the perspective of impeaching President Trump.) Even if incontrovertible evidence was unearthed that linked the Trump campaign to Putin, we could probably presume someone in Mr. Trump's orbit would be sacrificed to protect the President. Generally speaking, I believe if Trump had an arrangement, he would have been basically intelligent enough to insulate himself from the day-to-day operations of that connection. I think Mr. Trump would have kept himself at a plausibly deniable distance. But if something truly damaging ever manages to shake loose, I personally suspect it will originate from Donald Trump's relationship with Paul Manafort.

"Manafort was a close paid advisor to Trump. On August 14, 2016, The *New York Times* published a story "Secret Ledger in Ukraine lists cash for Donald Trump's campaign chief," which detailed Manafort's relationships with Viktor Yanukovych, the deposed president of the Ukraine and close Putin loyalist. Before his abrupt departure and exile in Russia, Yanukovych was a master manipulator of Ukrainian politics. He hired Manafort to help with some of that manipulation. When he escaped a popular uprising against him it was a severe blow to Russia, as the people had been agitating to get closer to the European Union and NATO. Manafort's dilemma following the disclosure of the ledgers, numbering around four hundred pages, was that he claimed to have never worked for either the Russian or Ukrainian governments. The hand-written ledgers reflect large projects including the sales of a Ukrainian cable company under the Pericles banner. They show cash payments for Manafort over a period ranging from 2007 to 2012. The article also claims that Manafort never registered his work as a "foreign agent" as required with the U.S. Department of Justice. According to investigators, Manafort's name appears twenty-two times. He was allegedly paid $12.7 million in cash or untraceable investments over a span of five years." [22]

Again, without dispute, we can see that not only has Manafort – Trump's close advisor and former campaign manager – worked extremely close with the Kremlin in the past, but he has also lied about doing so when asked. The connection from Manafort to Putin is not at all tenuous, and it stands to reason that the rest of Trump's close confidants are not so far removed from Mr. Putin as well.

"Once Trump took on the Presidential campaign, he also managed to acquire the most controversial of all the Putin-associated characters: Paul Manafort. Before becoming Trump's campaign manager, Manafort was known as the leader of the "Torturer's lobby" while working for the law firm of Black, Manafort, Stone and Kelly. They represented some of the worst dictators in the world, including Mobutu Sese Seko of Zaire, the Filipino President Ferdinand Marcos, and the brutal Angolan warlord Jonas Savimbi. Manafort has also been an advisor to the Trump kingdom since the mid-1980s." [23]

Once Manafort took control of the Trump presidential campaign, it was, in my own personal view, an obvious and undeniable message from the Trump campaign to the Russians. They were signaling – at the very least – that a Trump White House was willing to play ball with Moscow in ways Mrs. Clinton would not, and was even willing to use some of the same tools Putin had previously used in Ukraine. It was, in fact, the sudden change in the GOP's language towards Ukraine itself that I found so alarming:

> "Throughout the campaign, Trump has been dismissive of calls for supporting the Ukraine government as it fights an ongoing Russian-led intervention. Trump's campaign chairman, Paul Manafort, worked as a lobbyist for the Russian-backed former Ukrainian president Viktor Yanukovych for more than a decade. Still, Republican delegates at last week's national security committee platform meeting in Cleveland were surprised when the Trump campaign orchestrated a set of events to make sure that the GOP would not pledge to give Ukraine the weapons it has been asking for from the United States...On the sideline, Denman tried to persuade the Trump staffers not to change the language, but failed. "I was troubled when they put aside my amendment and then watered it down," Denman told me. "I said, 'What is your problem with a country that wants to remain free?' It seems like a simple thing." Finally, Trump staffers wrote an amendment to Denman's amendment that stripped out the platform's call for "providing lethal defensive weapons" and replaced it with softer language calling for "appropriate assistance." That amendment was voted on and passed." [24]

Even if we discard the hacking scandal in its entirety, Russian influence upon Trump and the Republican Party is impossible to ignore. It was under Mr. Manafort's leadership that these changes occurred, and the Republican National Committee watched, either with indifference or impotence, as a foreign power started to aggressively mold and shape its policy. This, of course, should not have *ever* been a partisan issue; a nation as corrupt and evil as Russia should not be able to influence the American political landscape with such sweeping power. Republicans and Democrats alike should be able to agree on such a basic premise. It is deeply troubling that Mr. Trump has yet to publically criticize Mr. Putin; in this way, Jeb Bush's energy level warranted a blistering rebuke, but the murder and theft Mr. Putin perpetrates on a daily basis simply does not. This fact is frightening, alarming, even, but it is not surprising. Trump trumpets praise for vile and contemptable despots like Recep Tayyip Erdogan, Rodrigo Duterte, and Abdel Fattah el-Sisi, just to name a few. The reason he is enamored with these thugs is clear; Trump admires them and aspires to their level of unchecked power, and it does not come as a shock that a man who slanders immigrants from Mexico as "rapists" will share in the dictators' disdain for human rights. The admiration is a two-way street; and this is especially true when it comes to Putin, and has been for some time:

> "In August 2005 Vladimir Putin received a visit at his Sochi residence from his new friend Silvio Berlusconi. After the Russian president introduced the Italian prime minister to his pets, Kino the Labrador retriever and Vadik the pony, the two leaders spoke at length about Italian business in Russia before turning to Russia's support for Italy's aspiration to become a permanent member of the UN Security Council. Since this was unlikely, they agreed that Russia would at least try to stop Germany from acquiring such status. Putin liked to chat with Berlusconi ever since he had become disillusioned with Bush. The Italian prime minister was now his role model. Berlusconi had used his business empire to win elections and then used politics to further enrich his business. That made Berlusconi a natural ally of Putin's." [25]

Trump's rise to power is not new, and the same attraction that drew Putin to Berlusconi is precisely the same appeal that brings together Trump and Putin. The expansion and exportation of Putin-styled governance should be one of the primary concerns of the civilized world. This is not, as so many on the right in the U.S. claimed, a liberal attempt to kick start a third world war. This is, without exaggeration, the conflict between totalitarianism and democracy. And in this battle, sides must be picked, for these two systems are mutually exclusive. Democracy cannot exist if those in power can murder, without consequence, the leaders of the political parties that oppose them. Totalitarianism cannot exist with a free press that creates transparency. What's more, if you take seriously, as I do, the charge from Dr. Martin Luther King that injustice anywhere is a threat to justice everywhere, then Russian fascism must be actively opposed.

This, too, is a prickly point of contention, even within politically liberal circles in the U.S. One of my favorite authors – Christopher Hitchens – drew the ire of democrats everywhere by supporting the wars in Iraq and Afghanistan with a similar philosophy. In his view, democracy should be exported. I find myself, especially as I get older, increasingly more sympathetic to this mindset. The United States should take to heart the words of the classical liberal, President Kennedy, when he said America was a foe to anyone who opposed liberty, and was a friend to anyone in search of it, but after two decades of war in the Middle East, the enthusiasm for "world policing" began to fade. Couple this steady decline with the ethical outrages perpetuated by Americans throughout this era (Abu Gharaib, Guantanamo Bay, and Obama's extrajudicial drone strikes, just to name a few) and moral equivalences became far easier to strike. The context of Russia's meteoric rise is intriguing, as it is only a few short years removed from global embarrassment, and was eager to shake its reputation for ineptitude.

> "The unpleasant feeling of international isolation continued to worsen. Another nadir was the Munich Security Conference in February 2015. Twice the hall burst into laughter during the speech of Russian foreign minister Sergey Lavrov. Russian foreign policy was not greeted with shouting or booing but chortling. Lavrov barely kept his cool, finishing his speech with the words, "You can laugh if you want. Laughter makes the world go round." The first ripple came when Lavrov stated that the accession of Crimea had happened in accordance with the founding principle of the UN Charter – "the right of nations to self-determination." The UN Charter is famous for being contradictory and containing two mutually exclusive principles: "the right of nations to self-determination" and the "inviolability of frontiers." Crimea's "self-determination" was blatantly at variance with the second principle of the UN Charter. Ukraine was against it, and even Russia had repeatedly recognized the inviolability of its neighbor's borders; Putin had signed a treaty to that effect in 2003. The smirks became guffaws when Lavrov claimed that West Germany had annexed East Germany in 1989, since there had been no referendum in the latter. When Russian Duma Speaker Sergey Naryshkin had made the point in Moscow, no one had laughed. But over in the West it was greeted with howls of derision." [26]

Russia's newly-found aggression finds its origin in a position of weakness. What did the Kremlin have to lose in the first place? It was already a laughing stock, was openly mocked on the global stage, and much like Trump, was tired of "losing" and sought to make itself great. Trump's nationalism is just retrograde isolationism, and it became more attractive as Americans lost their moral backbones, weary of perpetual war in the Middle East, patience for the "war on terror" growing thin, and over time, the United States started to become insular. This newly-discovered timorousness should not be mistaken for intellectual maturity or humility. It is moral *cowardice* that takes the form of spineless and shapeless partisanship that opposes anything opposed to ones' own party, regardless of content. A perfect example of this morally bankrupt ideology was the sudden rise of Putin's popularity among Republicans. The *Washington Post* published Vladimir Putin's approval ratings in the United States, post-election, in

February of 2017:

> "In new Gallup polling, more than 3 in 10 Republicans have a favorable view of Putin — almost three times the percentage who said the same in 2015. Twice as many independents have a favorable opinion of Putin as did two years ago. Those numbers have helped bump Putin's overall approval numbers to their highest mark in five years." [27]

It seems quite unlikely that this unexpected uptick in domestic support for a violent dictator is unrelated to the praise heaped upon him by Mr. Trump. No, we should all be able to recognize the zombie-like groaning of lobotomized Republicans, cheering anything the party tells them to cheer, yelling at anything the party tells them to yell at, and faithfully averting their eyes when the party tells them to look the other way. Trump and Putin, both, inspire similar types of blind loyalty and even rose to power with the same type of crude pandering:

> "The apartment buildings that terrorized Russia in September convinced even those who thought Russia should have let Chechnya go its own way in 1991 that the Chechens deserved everything they got. Laying siege to a hospital, bombing the families of soldiers: these were inhuman acts, so the gloves were off. The public cheered Putin as their new gladiator and enjoyed the rough, even profane language he occasionally used when talking about what he would do to those who would threaten Russia. "We will find the terrorists anywhere," he once said, "and if we find them in their shithouses, we'll wipe them out in their shithouses." [28]

I cannot *stand* the right-wing's constant insistence that they are chained to *values* and can still lecture the rest of the world about *mortality*. Don't waste my time. They worship war and finance above everything else, and nothing secures their affections quite like vulgarity and boastfulness. Don't pretend – American political do-gooders – that your *family values* are as important as protecting a reptile like Mr. Trump, or, crucially, that those beliefs, if properly read and practiced, would ever *allow* for such grotesque murderers like Putin to be condoned in the pursuit of it, swallowed obediently by the herd as the cost of doing business. For me, the peak of this insipid hive-mindedness reached its crescendo immediately after Trump won the election. Gleeful Republican Christians flocked to social media to gloat – *finally we have a Christian in the White House*, they exclaimed – and the "moral majority," decidedly less silent now, was grinning from ear-to-ear as the very antithesis of their Savior ascended into power.

Jesus Christ healed the disabled; Donald Trump mocked them. Jesus Christ called his followers to a life of poverty; Donald Trump boasts of his wealth and opulence. Jesus Christ abhorred violence, refused to lead an armed rebellion against their occupiers, and healed the Centurion's ear after Peter hacked it off with his sword; Donald Trump wants to defeat ISIS by killing their families. Jesus Christ told his followers that the meek shall inherit the earth; Donald Trump boasted about the size of his penis during a political debate. Jesus Christ told his followers to give unto Caesar what is Caesar's; Donald Trump avoided paying income tax for eighteen years. Jesus Christ flipped over the tables of the money-changers in the temple when they practiced business unfairly; Donald Trump stiffed small-business owners during the course of his multiple bankruptcies. Jesus Christ told his followers that if you look lustfully at a woman that you have committed adultery in your heart; Donald Trump grabs women *by the pussy*.

I won't sit idly by while brain-dead Republicans pretend this man represents even the tiniest bit of their values and morality, and neither should anyone else. Don't worry – the Evangelical retort to this line of reasoning didn't take long to surface – *God selects pottery for noble and ignoble purposes,* they stammered, *and Trump is the vulgar instrument God has chosen.* Mr. Trump was suddenly being compared to King David of the Old Testament; a flawed vessel through which God would implement his Divine plan. There is no rock-bottom too low for them to sink. No depth too far for them to dive. No grisly means unjustified by their divine ends. But yes, *of course,* when I see the Republican political manifesto being implemented in the United States (the reduction of taxation on the incomes of billionaires, the destruction of entitlement programs that feed the poor, the obliteration of a universal healthcare system that gave impoverished people access to medical treatment, and the erection of a wall on the Southern border with Mexico to keep out starving refugees) my mind *immediately* shifts to the life of Jesus Christ, who fed the poor, healed the sick, and who, as a child, was displaced from his own home by King Herod and was forced to seek asylum in another country as a result. *This cannot be believed by a thinking person.* It is this kind of willful ignorance that keeps men like Donald Trump and Vladimir Putin in power.

My Life as a Christian

‡‡

CHAPTER 10

"AND DO YOU THINK THAT UNTO SUCH AS YOU
A MAGGOT-MINDED, STARVED, FANATIC CREW
GOD GAVE A SECRET, AND DENIED IT ME –
WELL, WELL, WHAT MATTERS IT? BELIEVE THAT TOO."
-OMAR KHAYYAM

There are a couple of issues that prevent me from effectively writing a salient and dependable memoir about my time in the Christian church. The first (and perhaps most irritating) is that my memory is not above reproach. Twenty years of ice hockey, as I like to joke, was probably responsible for decimating what little remains of my memory. I'm often forced to reach out to my wife, my friends, and other family members to confirm some of the more hazy memories about my religious past. I think it's only fair to preface my recollections with a disclaimer that I'm human, and liable to forget or exaggerate events on occasion.

Secondly, my story isn't some biting expose of the American church. I can't show anyone where the bodies are buried. I wasn't unfairly maligned by anyone, and I genuinely harbor no bitterness or malice towards any of my old religious cohorts. Many are still close friends that I cherish, but my life in the American church is largely typical. Others have more compelling and dramatic tales of ecclesiastical drama and suspense. Mine borders on the monotonous; I went to college to become a Christian preacher and lost my faith towards the tail-end of an undergraduate program. While I did, occasionally, sprinkle some of my relevant experiences into previous chapters, I feel this period of my life so powerfully colors the perspective I present in this book that it would be disingenuous to exclude it.

Admittedly, I was a bit of a black sheep in Bible college. I was especially out of place in the classes specific to preaching. An avid fan of death metal then (and still am, today), I remember fetching quizzical looks from the straight-laced, khaki-and-polo crowd when I waltzed into a pastoral ministries class with an Acacia Strain sweatshirt that was decorated with a bloodied, decapitated head. As I recall, it became a conversation piece for the remainder of the semester. I can't quite decide if this was a cry for attention in the typical teenage fashion, or if I was simply disinterested in impressing any of my colleagues. A little column A, little column B, no doubt. I should say, of course, that I was never bullied by these ministers-in-training. I was something of a novelty to them, but generally speaking, a Bible college is a place where the non-Christian world gets locked out. I may have been a little off kilter, but Jesus was my Lord and Savior just as he was to them. As far as I knew, few of my classmates had any malice towards me, but even as I studied the Bible with every intention of becoming a preacher, my disdain for my classmates and peers grew and grew. They seemed to blur together as time passed; I was drowning in wave after wave of khaki shorts with Wal-Mart polo shirts. They were truly homogeneous in nearly everything; political opinions, appearance, and even musical taste. You would be hard-pressed to find exceptions to the rule. I was one of them, and spent a lot of time looking for a running partner. There's an inherent foolishness and immaturity laden in my life choices during this era of my life, unquestionably, but the Christian world was making my skin crawl at every turn.

In any event, I loved what I did, and I believed in my "calling" and chose to trust it implicitly. I took the job seriously. In what *I believe* was my only official Sunday morning sermon, (there may have been more but I cannot remember) I followed the playbook handed down to me. We were trained as preachers, to spend half of your forty-hour work week crafting the message. You should be dedicated to studying the Scripture you are teaching, and ensuring that your exegesis was accurate. Twenty hours were spent. I was challenged, by my Greek professor, that the Lord has higher expectations for those of us who are called into the ministry, and we should always go the extra mile and translate, personally, the Scriptures we used in sermons. My sermon was covering the book of Daniel in the Old Testament. This is linguistically unique in the Bible, as it is the only book that has a portion of it written in Aramaic. So – I did just that – and translated every passage I used personally. Then there were the hours upon hours spent in prayer, combing over your every stray emotion, attending to your 'spiritual' health as you prepared. I finally delivered the sermon, and for all I can remember, it seemed like a modest success. After the service, however, I was haunted with an inexplicable guilt. Cashing the check from the church made me feel ill; I pictured elderly women scraping together pennies and felt terrible. The parts of the sermon I really enjoyed appeared to fall on deaf ears. An academic message often doesn't get you far; hellfire, brimstone, charisma, or anything basically accessible often does.

This was a test the Lord had given me, though, and it was on me to pass it with flying colors. I was determined to persevere. I enjoyed public speaking, and possessed some amount of natural skill in this arena. Later in life, I'd go on to officiate weddings of friends and family members, and I did have some level of charisma, however small, and used it for odd jobs here and there. I preached in a congregation only once, but the usual bits-and-bobs and odd jobs sprang up; leading Bible studies, helping a local Methodist congregation with a Sunday School program for kids, playing guitar and leading worship here and there, and so on and so on. These are the usual kinds of piecemeal jobs that Bible college kids scape together for a few bucks, and I was no exception. But living, studying, and working in Lincoln was awful. Central Illinois has a whole lot of nothing. The winters were long and bitingly cold; the summers were humid and muggy. The isolation led to boredom, and church life had a way of spicing up the doldrums. The environment a church creates is compelling, and often, quite difficult to describe. Over the years, I've found that certain types of people are attracted to the kind of permissive atmosphere that a typical congregation builds.

I was chatting with an old-coworker some years ago, when suddenly, in a pivot that would make any Human Resources expert cringe, he artlessly shifted the conversation to his church life. He described a friend of his who used to be a "real low life" until he came to his church (this is a theme that reoccurs endlessly in Evangelical circles.) Upon his very first visit, this friend shook the preacher's hand after the service had ended, and asked the minister if he truly "loved everyone unconditionally." The preacher nodded and confirmed that he did. The low-life friend then extracted a knife from his pocket and sliced the preacher across his palm and repeated the question. "Do you still love me *now?*" The co-worker paused, briefly, in hopes that I would exclaim some shock and alarm, I think. "You know Christ is real when a guy like that does a complete 180, am I right?"

As strange as it might sound, these kinds of stories aren't uncommon (although I suspect this particular one is flatly untrue or highly exaggerated). The kinds of high-strung personalities that would either be moved by an idiotic story like this - or worse - would be unstable enough to perpetrate it on their own, often find a nice social home within the walls of a church. There is an inexplicable sort of magnet that draws personalities like these into the religious orbit. The church is always in need of volunteers, and can always find some busy work for people who have too much pent up energy and whose calendars are usually empty. The bargain struck with this social contract is somewhat symbiotic, however, as the easy access to social outlets and a sense of community are worth their weight in gold to people in search of a place to belong. I don't say any of this, for whatever it's worth, with a sneer. I often miss the community the church provides, and while the concerns about church life are too serious too ignore, there is certainly something to be said for the millions of American congregations who treat people well, and offer an unconditional acceptance to people who may not get it with their friends, families, or co-workers. Atheists who leave the church are usually branded as embittered quitters who may not have ever had faith to begin with, but in my case, neither statement could be any further from the truth. From birth, I believed in the Bible and steadfastly believed that I had a personal relationship with Jesus. Not only did I enjoy my time at church, but as a homeschooler with stunningly few social events on my calendar, I needed church. My family needed the church. It fed us through food banks when my parents ran into financial trouble. It occasionally ate the costs and fees associated with all of the summer camps and missions trips my parents couldn't afford. I'd take a polygraph to this effect; I don't hate the church. I rather liked it, actually. But the church wasn't - and isn't - a gentle-hearted oasis from all life's problems.

My largely-problem free experience might just be atypical. Children are often very much in danger at church, and abuses of all sorts are frequently perpetrated within its walls. Perhaps the most at-risk dynamic (and, in my opinion, far and away the *creepiest*) are the "youth" ministries aimed at teenagers. Adolescence is a trying time for anyone. Hormones are raging, social pressures on teens and pre-teens are immense, and through this hurricane of emotions, in steps the goateed youth minister. He's usually in the 25-35 year old range, and up-and-coming ministers use these positions to build experience for a job down the road as a senior pastor. The effects, on both the minister and the laity, are enormously dangerous. To start with, there's an undeniable and suffocating sexual tension between the almost-exclusively male youth pastor and the teenage girls. It is no surprise, that as a result, many youth pastors exploit their position of power over these girls and parlay that respect into an abusive sexual relationship. I saw at least one youth pastor being fired for this very reason. A 25 year old man seems alluring to girls at that age, and the open-ended access parents often grant the youth minister to can fuel these types of abuses.

Ministers fresh out of Bible college are recruited for youth ministry for a handful of reasons: senior pastors often have trouble relating to the kids, or simply lack the patience to effectively teach or entertain the teens. Certainly there are plenty of youth ministers who either start in youth ministry at an older age, or who enjoy or excel at working with teenagers and never transition out of that role. In my own experience, however, I find those ministers to be few and far between. And, to be clear, I am not implying all youth ministers are rapists waiting to pounce. My point is quite basic: the concept of ministering to teenagers, as typical American congregations usually do, is inherently susceptible to abuse. When your high-schooler signs up for a sports team, you would be alarmed to hear that the coach was advising your teenager on their sexual lives. You wouldn't allow the coach to host an all-night "lock in" but these events are common at churches; and many parents don't think twice. What could go wrong? It's a *church*. Beyond this, I am very much of the opinion that children of any age shouldn't be subjected to religious teaching at all, outside of a proper history or anthropology classroom that is flatly disinterested and teaches simple facts about all religions equally. At Greenville college, I scoffed when a left-leaning professor mentioned during a lesson on the Emerging Church that he did not want his toddler taught about the crucifixion in Sunday School. I was a sneering, fundamentalist little shit in those days, and I rolled my eyes at what I perceived was intellectual weakness. I couldn't have been more wrong; explaining to a toddler (as some Sunday School curriculum does) that we know Jesus had the nails driven into his wrists so they could support his full body weight is grotesque, morbid, violent, and runs a serious risk of traumatizing a young child for no reason. To my shame, I complained about this 'liberal' professor later in the semester to the administration, and to the infinite credit of the administration, they listened to me completely, even though I was utterly and completely blinded by my fundamentalism. The complaint that is so often made by fundamentalist Christians is that the world refuses to hear them out – well, in my experience, the opposite was *always* true. I was listened to, fairly, and I was in the wrong, and wasn't discriminated against in the slightest.

Speaking of cursing, there's something of an odd and disjointed relationship that the Christian world has with "cuss" words. There's an illuminating delineation in the Christian community between believers that curse, drink or smoke and those who don't. I, at the time, did all three with great enthusiasm. Evangelicals who partook in these activities – myself included – usually justified it with a passage from the Epistles. *Everything is permissible for me* unless it causes my brother to sin. Less ambiguous, and more legally binding, of course, were the "lifestyle statements" both universities required students to sign. It outlawed drug use, alcohol and tobacco consumption, as well as sexual intercourse outside of marriage. Breeching this contract, however sinful, was done by virtually everyone to some degree, and often with great zeal. I was very much of the opinion that cursing was morally acceptable; Jesus himself used an Aramaic curse word – *"raca,"* meaning "empty-head" – and I saw language of nearly any kind as largely morally indifferent. If one can use it to get an important message through, why not? Jesus certainly appeared to push the preverbal envelope, and so did the prophets of the Old Testament, so why should the rules be any different for us? Jesus, too, seemed quite found of wine in the Gospels, and no matter how fundamental I got in my religious philosophies, I am not sure I ever believed God would send someone to hell for draining a pack of Marlboros. Let's call these popular Christian aversions what they really are; *cultural partitions.* Wherein Christians cordon off certain activities as a way of elevating themselves over their friends, neighbors, and family members. But likeminded people have a way of finding each other, and one such person was a roommate I lived with for many years. He was a terrific match.

Our tastes in music weren't identical (I was a scene kid, and he enjoyed Megadeth), but where they didn't match, they were generally compatible. At first, we would sneak furtively off campus to drink and smoke; the concealment of a nearby grain silo gave us a reasonable amount of cover to light up. As the years progressed, we became more brazen and sophisticated in our collective efforts. Towels got jammed under doorframes, windows got cracked, and smoke detectors got disabled in order to facilitate in-room smoking. Alcohol, once confined to forty ounce cans of cheap beer that were consumed quickly as they couldn't be kept in dorm room mini-fridges, quickly escalated to handles of smuggled liquor, trafficked into the alcohol-free, Bible college campus in spare backpacks. I'm sure I was anything but subtle – those habits have a certain way of betraying their presence to the senses of those around you – but I was slowly becoming disillusioned and cared less and less. I should make it clear that the tobacco and alcohol didn't fuel my atheism; these were poor efforts at self-medication for my undiagnosed ADHD and the crippling spiritual doubts that crept into my sober mind. Drink or no drink, smoke or no smoke; my days as a Christian were certainly numbered. Christians, by the way, *love* to blame "sinful" things like drugs, booze, or even secular music and entertainment for apostasy. (If *anything* has the power to make people renounce Jesus, surely, it is the unforgivably bad phenomenon of Christian rock music.)

But in those days, I didn't have the self-awareness, maturity, or coping mechanisms to manage my adult life. I was (and still am now) a terrible student, and I lacked the impulse control to finish homework, or to arrive at class on time, and like millions of other college students, quickly found myself being routinely defeated by the basic responsibilities of an adult life. Bills went unpaid. My GPA fell through the floor and I swiftly ended up on academic probation. I would usually flat-out fail at least one class a semester. I can't say, for sure, just how many classes I failed in total, but the number is unquestionably and embarrassingly large. I'm not sure I can say I was depressed at this time in my life – I've never had a suicidal thought in my life, and never lost interest in things I enjoyed – but I was struggling professionally, I was struggling as a student, and my relationships with friends and my family were strained at best. I wasn't taking care of myself, and I think it started to show.

The academic probation came with a weekly counseling session with an academic advisor. During one such meeting, I wondered openly to the counselor if perhaps I wasn't struggling with some form of ADHD. She bristled at the suggestion, and told me I didn't display any of the symptoms she had come to recognize over her many years of counseling students. Her denial seemed disingenuous to me, so I made an appointment with a medical doctor a few days later and emerged with a prescription for Strattera. During my entire tenure at Lincoln, I would abuse nicotine and caffeine in obnoxious quantities; a pack or half-a-pack of cigarettes a day coupled with a litany of coffee, soda, and energy drinks. I believe I was self-medicating; coming up with the caffeine, and calming myself down with the smokes. I quit smoking (and never meaningfully relapsed) not long after my doctor switched me from Strattera to Adderall. I believe these two events were correlated, and medically treating my mental issue alleviated my desire to self-medicate with anything else. Had I started a course of medical treatment for these issues before I left for college, at the very least, I think I might have had a chance to tie off a degree before I defected.

The ADHD medication came far too late to help with my fledgling academic career, however. The financial aid simply ran out as I approached my forth year at Lincoln Christian, and I moved into a dirt-cheap apartment off-campus a few months later. I had been wrestling with my faith during these days; they were tumultuous, and I took to writing to help soothe some of the pain. I've been publishing my work online since the days of Angelfire and Geocities (don't ask how old I am) and I used this medium, primarily, to agitate stuffy believers. I wrote about how I would build a "smoking room" in my church so I could "speak to people in their natural element." I also started to outline how I would run my own congregation; skipping a traditional service altogether on Sunday morning to volunteer, or holding membership drives for the homeless to join our church, and the haughty comments these kinds of provocations caught were endlessly entertaining. I first learned how to needle Evangelicals in these exchanges. The pleasure I got out of their outrage, of course, was quickly becoming too difficult for me to ignore. Suddenly, I was discovering that *I* didn't believe some of these things. That realization was frightening, and was far from inconsequential. The list of Christian doctrines I flatly rejected grew and grew until there wasn't anything of value left.

I knew, for sure, that I no longer believed in God by 2007. This was horrifically bad timing, as my wedding had been scheduled for the summer of 2008. My wife and I debated whether or not we should tell my family, and how we could plan a wedding without any religious ceremonies. You might be wondering why I didn't decide to simply fake it, and usually this question originates from people who were not born into the type of religion I was born into. There is no way to fake a Christian wedding – the preacher needs to be called, the hymns and songs need to be selected, and the Scripture readings need to be decided in advance. Bible colleges themselves, to put it crudely, are often little more than marriage mills, and Melissa and I had endured far too many Christian weddings. Some of our friends and families would hire worship bands to play a mini-worship-song set for the ceremony. They were *cringe-worthy*. The Christian wedding is just that; and there was no way, apart from a brief jaunt to the courthouse, to avoid all of the noise. We wanted nothing to do with all this, and wanted something simple, direct, and untarnished by religion. This became impossible to do without raising some alarm bells with those around us. My fiancé rejected the idea of telling my family about my apostasy completely out of hand. It seemed needlessly controversial, almost attention-grabbing, and as religiously conservative as they were, we both worried my family would refuse to attend if they found out. The thought of even having a single prayer in our wedding became unbearable for both of us. In hindsight, it was easy to see why; religion was causing, not curing, all of this wedding anxiety. We didn't want to have a reading from the Bible. It didn't have anything to do with our relationship. We had spent the last seven years of our life being hammered to death with the Bible. We were tired of being judged, tired of the constant gossip, and sick to death of the Christian lifestyle. We wanted a clean break. I should mention here that the family minister – Larry Fry – did us a tremendous act of kindness by complying with our unconventional wishes. We had some uncomfortable conversations with him about why we didn't want prayer or Scripture in our wedding, and he had his reservations, but performed the ceremony nonetheless. I feel the man deserves credit for this, and provided grace and flexibility to a young couple during a tense period in our lives. We didn't want religion in our wedding, and more and more, I now find myself officiating weddings for other couples for the same reasons.

But I complied with Melissa's wishes, and held off on the news of my atheism until after the wedding. A few months after we were married, I wrote a lengthy post on social media, going public with my disbelief. I couldn't stand being dishonest. I *had* to tell the truth. I wrote that post because I *had* to write it. I couldn't mislead my friends and my family any longer. It was tearing me up inside. I felt bad then – and still feel bad now – for obliterating the hopes of my parents, who longed to have their first-born son as a minister. My preacher dreams (and no doubt, those of my parents) were misguided; not because I secretly disbelieved in the Gospel all along, but because I didn't have something that all good ministers seem to have in spades: natural charisma. Sure, I enjoy public speaking, and talking in front of people doesn't give me nightmares, but pastors have a mystique. They can work a room. They remember people's names, they laugh just a little bit louder than everyone else, and they have a personality that can draw in people instinctively. I didn't have that in the slightest; I was bookish, coarse, and had an innate ability to rub people the wrong way. I was the opposite of whatever *that* ministerial personality was, I think. And while I don't know if I ever envied that type of relatability, I am of the belief that I knew inwardly it was lacking, and it was the sort of thing that couldn't be learned, at least by me.

Another bone of contention, between my values and those of the Christians that I increasingly found myself with, was *who* I wanted to minister to. I can recall some impassioned arguments with my dad; he once accused me of using my Christian bands as an excuse to waste time with my friends (I don't resent him for saying so – he was more right than wrong - in retrospect). But while that charge was at least half-true, there were occasional flirtations with open Evangelism during my teenage and college years. I can recall sharing a stage with a secular band, and I asked if they wanted to pray with us before the concert began. They politely and quite maturely declined; but acts like this represented our conversion attempts. Were they a bit weak-willed? I think so, but there was also an enormous philosophical (and notably generational) difference between our versions of Christianity. Older Christians saw value in, say, leaving a Gospel tract underneath someone's windshield wiper. Younger Christians rejected this "drive-by-Evangelism" as cold and impersonal, and only saw true results through a relationship-based model. If they come to know us, Jesus will come up, we thought, and the conversations that follow will be far more productive.

What I resented, hated, even, were the Gospel tracts themselves. Even as a Bible college student, I would destroy them on sight. They were nasty little bits of awful literature; usually drawn in a comic-book style that depicted homosexuals, or other sinners, being burned in hell. American readers, no doubt, have likely seen the popular style of Gospel tracts I'm referring to, and even as an aspiring minister, they sent me into a rage. This was the judgementalism – I thought – that kept people away from God in the first place. They were opening up wounds that I believed I would have to close later. My discomfort with the message of a "Biblical" hell, too, was growing with every hour spent reading the Scripture. The New Testament uses a couple of Greek words to describe a place of punishment; *gehenna* and *ades,* predominantly, and building the kind of hell most Christians believe in devoutly is somewhat difficult to support linguistically with these words.

In the first place, *ades* has connections to Greco-Roman mythology, which any real Christian would disavow as a form of pagan, polytheistic influence. Equally troubling, too, is that *ades* appears in the Septuagint (the Greek translation of the Hebrew text of the Old Testament) as a stand-in for the world Hebrew word *sheol,* which as even Wikipedia notes, was used interchangeably for the word "grave" or "death" which everyone experiences irrespective of behavior. *Gehenna* isn't much better; it is a geographical reference to a trash dump (some scholars believe that Jesus' line about "the gnashing of teeth" refers to the face we make when we encounter something foul-smelling, like a landfill). The connections made with these words are intriguing. Some interpret the act of burning trash in *gehenna* as evidence that Jesus was making clear that sinners were in for an eternal fire, as an ancient-landfill no doubt never stopped burning trash. This claim, in my view, is an *enormous* stretch, and I think it infers far too much into Jesus' words. I think Jesus knew a good visual metaphor when he saw one, especially when it came to his Parables (camels into the eye of a needle, faith as small as a mustard seed, lamps under a bushel, *et al.*) and communicated them strikingly well. Further, the Jesus who would condemn people to unending and unspeakable torture seemed wholly incompatible with the Jesus who saved the adulteress from stoning, or the Jesus who immediately healed the Centurions' ear. Combine this with the undeniable fact of Jesus' Judaism (which did not have the concept of an afterlife *until* they encountered the Greeks) and the case for a literal hell becomes even shakier. I did not see any value in attempting to scare people up to heaven; surely an all-knowing God wouldn't be fooled by a coerced conversion, right?

The ideology of heaven was even worse. Conjuring images of hellfire and brimstone to use as a crude scarecrow was one thing, but heaven was used shamelessly as a divine fishing lure. It was grotesque, sickening, and inhumane. I have seen pastors, with a casket behind them, promise the bereaved family that they will soon enjoy an eternity with their recently-deceased loved one. I was incensed when, at the funeral of a close friend, the minister exclaimed that if "he had the choice to come back to earth, he would choose to stay at home with the Lord." The friend in question was a young man, killed by a drunk driver that was going the wrong way down an interstate. My friend was a young father, in his twenties, and left behind two young children. He wouldn't come back, even for a *second*, to say goodbye to his kids? This was a vulgar insult, and one I will never be able to forget or forgive. The promises extend beyond bad lies told to soothe grieving people at funerals; I have watched youth ministers, in an attempt to land new converts, promise that "in heaven, you can do anything you could never do on earth. Always wanted to learn guitar? In heaven, you'll be the best guitar player ever."

It wasn't just the abuses of the afterlife that stung me, though. In truth, I found the concept of heaven as something entirely unattractive. *We'll be praising the Lord forever, singing for years and years, perfectly content, one with our Savior.* I resonated with Christopher Hitchens' perspective, when he wrote that this entire concept was Orwellian; under the constant gaze of the divine, and somehow, with my empathy for the rest of humanity barbequing in the basement totally removed. I couldn't reconcile this with the commands issued in Scripture – to love your enemies, to pray for those who persecute you – with the sudden wave of calloused apathy that strikes all of us upon our entrance into heaven. Theologians will grumble at this line of reasoning. *The sinners already had their chance*, they'll tell us, *and Jesus was the mercy they rejected.* The message isn't about forgiveness. It's not even, really, a message, so much as it is a threat: love me because of what I might do to you otherwise.

It was these factors, among many others, that led me to abandon some of the traditional tenets of Christian doctrine as I started to bend politically to the left. I dropped the "Christian" title and updated my religious affiliation on my Facebook page to "Yahweyist" for reasons I can't really explain, other than to say the Christian lifestyle had worn me down, and I was tired of wearing the label. I was sick of associating myself with the hatred directed towards homosexuals. I adopted two positions which are oddly controversial in Evangelical circles: annihilationism (the belief God simply destroys unrepentant souls rather than torturing them forever) and Theistic Evolution (an acceptance of the science behind evolution with the caveat that this was the method an infinite and incomprehensibly powerful God used to create the cosmos.)

The other Evangelical thorn in my side was Christianity's treatment of women. Make no mistake; women are second-class citizens in much of the Christian world, and I became more acutely aware of this reality the deeper I went. I was aware of what some women and girls go through in the walls of the church, but before I left the faith, I considered their struggles to be normal burdens unique to their gender. The obsession with their modesty and appearance did not seem out of place; Eve first tempted Adam to bite the apple, and their role as vehicles for male influence did not appear to be out of the ordinary. I will admit to some light-eye-rolling when I encountered obvious sexism in the Bible; Ester righteously fucking her way to the top of the harem to spare her people, Delilah being blamed for Samson's hilarious stupidity, or the patronizing way in which the Epistles treated female believers (cover your heads, and if those tiny little brains of yours have questions about the sermon, ask your *husbands* after the service.) But these coarse edges, along with so many others found in the Old Testament, particularly, could be explained away with the concession that the Bible wasn't *completely* perfect. The logic went something like this: mankind couldn't write a perfect book, even with the divine inspiration of the Holy Spirit, so the Bible bore many of the shortcomings that sinful humans have everywhere. Did God really command the Israelites to massacre the Amalekites, or did the power-hungry and sinful *human* leadership of that tribe just do it, and then claim God told them to do it after the fact? Did Noah really stuff two of *every* animal into a boat, or did the human authors exaggerate somewhere down the line? The famous quip, often attributed to Mark Twain rang true for me; the best cure for my Christianity was reading the Bible.

But I threw the blatant sexism into this exegetical boat, and believed that Scriptures that were written during an era in which women had basically no rights were destined to be sexist, so a responsible Christian explains around them or cuts them out. The Bible being anti-woman was one thing, but the unforgivable sexism, to me, was the kind that was found within the walls of the modern church. Women, in most typical American congregations, are not allowed to be pastors. In fact, to my knowledge, the very first accepted female applicant to the Lincoln Christian College pastoral ministries program was a contemporary of mine and a good friend of my wife. Feminist progress in Christian circles, apart from some liberal denominations, is quite slow-going. Men are the pastors and women are, nine times out of ten, chained to subservient roles underneath them. The experiences of the women in my family informed my viewpoint powerfully; their choices in dress were closely monitored for their modesty, not just by my father, but by males in positions of authority at the church. My sisters – all fiercely and vibrantly independent – clashed often with the men in charge. My youngest sister, Lydia, was physically assaulted by a church elder during a "Bible Bowl" event. The family pressed charges, and the elder, when asked by the judge why he "decided it was a good idea" to hit a young woman, replied that she "had lipped off" to him. The elder cracked a clipboard in half over the top of Lydia's head and put her in the hospital with a concussion.

Acts of physical violence aside, church drama often originates from the very narrow and patronizing roles men usually set aside for women in the congregation. Without much deviation, women got to help out with programs, or collection plates, or got to work as organists, secretaries, or could be tasked with handling childcare or Sunday school. Women could only teach Bible studies if they only taught other women (taking quite literally, Paul's edict in the Epistles that does not "permit women to teach men.") and these restrictions did not sit well with the women in my family. The story of their experiences in Christianity are theirs to tell, however, and I have no desire to steal a platform from them. I believe a progressive feminine voice could fix much of what is wrong with American Christianity as it exists now, in any case.

Christians, rather annoyingly, love to talk about their scars; they relish any opportunities to chitter about that one time they had doubts about whether or not God was real, or that one time they got really intoxicated or debauched. I think Christians believe this makes them *cool* to outsiders. It doesn't, but they boast about this kind of pseudo-inquisitiveness because they believe it bolsters the legitimacy of their faith. Well, let me be the first to corroborate this claim! Faithful believers love to talk to *me* in secret about their doubts. Since leaving Christianity, I have been the recipient of several breathy phone calls (one from an employed minister) that pointedly asked me why I left the faith, and after some awkward pauses, why they were thinking of leaving it, too.

Oscar Wilde said it best; you can't reason someone out of something they weren't reasoned into in the first place. These people didn't get into Christianity because it was the most logical choice. They're Christians for the same reasons anyone else is – because their parents passed the faith down, or because they came to the Lord during a trying time in their life, or because they encountered some emotional hardship or loss – and with almost every conversion story, there's a converter. When people think about leaving religion, often, they try to escape it in the same way they found it; by latching on to a charismatic person who made the same choice. In these conversations, I never advised anyone to leave their faith. Why? Because I understand that the motivation that drove them to call me is almost certainly informed by sorrow that is totally unrelated to religion. One near-defection was spurred by a breakup with a long-term girlfriend. What kind of person would I be if I pounced on their grief in order to bag a new recruit for my own belief system? Additionally, I am also of the mind that these types of calls aren't genuine and usually don't originate from a place of sincerity.

I took a programming class a couple years ago, and a student asked the portly professor a meandering question about loops. "You will answer that particular question," the professor muttered, "with the principles you have learned in a previous section." I recoiled at this terse answer initially, but over time learned to appreciate its wisdom. The professor *could* give the answer, but in so doing, would undermine the value in learning to attain it. The thing about free inquiry, is, simply, that *you* have you ask and answer the big questions yourself. If my old classmates and acquaintances can't look at the Old Testament and at least find *a couple of troubling passages,* then what's the point? The journey *is* the destination. And, in retrospect, I think their desire to reach out to me about atheism was perhaps motivated by something they didn't want to share; maybe they were upset by my apostasy, but too timorous to openly confront me so they pretended to have doubts too, just to open the conversation. Maybe they called out of pure curiosity and ended up exaggerating the length of their own spiritual consternation in a bid to empathize. In any case, I had then, and have now, no desire to proselytize. The encounters that have truly wounded me are the conversations with people who contact me privately to explain that they no longer believe, but for one reason or the other, are forced to keep it a secret. I can remember, quite vividly, how painful it was to conceal my lack of faith, and how lonely it made me feel. I wouldn't wish it upon anyone; and there is something intangibly degenerative about living a lie for any significant length of time. I'm not sure I know precisely *what* it is, but I know what it feels *like*. I'm ashamed to admit that at some point, I thought about faking it, too. There's something unsightly, dehumanizing, even, in outwardly supporting something you have inwardly abandoned. Everyone has a reason for religious doubt, and for me, much of it originated from church trips to Mexico.

The mission trips (two separate, one-week long excursions into Juarez and Tijuana) were formative experiences for me personally. For the first time, I came into direct contact with crippling poverty. The image that most stuck with me was a panoramic picture (taken with a disposable Kodak camera, yes, such things existed back then) taken from the rooftop of a corrugated sheet shanty. The slums were visible for miles and miles in every direction. Families of six were living together in homes the size of an American toolshed with no floors or plumbing. I was devastated by what I saw. Arguably, this was the first time I came into contact with the world as it really was; filled with suffering, pain, and poverty.

A brief lesson on corruption arose during one of these trips, too. While our church group was building houses, someone had broken into our van and swiped some purses and various other belongings from the interior of the vehicle. The Mexican police soon arrived in their hunter-green pickups, and after a short discussion through an interpreter, we were curtly told not to pursue it any further. The theft was likely carried out by a member of the cartel, and for our safety, the authorities explained, it was best to "leave it alone." I am struck, now, both by the recklessness and naiveté of our collective response to this petty theft. The perpetrator left a literal trail of anything valueless in the purse, like documents and cosmetics, and all of us followed it down the road and into an open field. Curious gringos have caught bullets in Juarez and Tijuana for doing far less. It was needlessly dangerous, and while all of us soberly accepted the risk of the missions trip, I get the sense that everyone failed to realize how serious a threat it really was at the time. I certainly didn't. The answer, for what it's worth, if you had asked any of us at the time about our concern for our own personal safety, would have been an immediate explanation about how God was in control. We were, in our own words, F.R.O.G, or *fully reliant on God.* The act of building the houses, if you could call them that, was flatly pointless, too. The houses were constructed largely out of chicken wire and stucco, and while they were indisputably a significant improvement over most of the other domiciles in the slum, a ticket out of poverty it definitely wasn't. It was explained to us that the Mexican government was so corrupt, that they refused to allow these impoverished people an opportunity to buy the land that they live on, and were required to pay rent on the land itself, which often kept them in poverty and made home improvements or construction financially impossible. These political realities behind the poverty, of course, didn't preclude the Christians in our group from passing judgment against these desperately poor people. During the construction of one new home, the father of the recipient family briefly emerged from the existing dwelling, and despite the language barrier, insisted on helping us shovel the sand needed for the stucco. At first, we all cooed; impressed by the pride and work ethic. After an hour or so, he began to show signs of fatigue, and returned to the house shortly thereafter. This produced a series of under-the-breath scoffs amongst the missionaries. One of the adults broke the silence. "That's really the root problem here, isn't it? They just don't want to work, do they?"

The church-group snootiness, as millions of former and current church-goers can often attest, can be suffocating, and these missions trips were no exception. As we drove past a Tecate (a Mexican beer manufacturer) billboard, we asked our Spanish translator what the text in the advertisement meant in English. *"EL SABOR DE TU MUSICA"*, she replied, "the flavor of your music." Heads disapprovingly shook, tongues clicked and collectively tutted. Beyond the danger, naiveté, and judgmental attitudes, the memories of these trips have bothered me because they were more like vacations than humanitarianism. Sure, there were eight hour (maybe longer) days of strenuous manual labor, but at most, it was three to four days of time spent in the slums. The remainder was spent sightseeing in San Diego, strolling up and down Mission Beach, or spent shopping and watching movies in El Paso. It was a lazy half-measure, akin to modern clicktivism; *missionary-tourism*, as I like to call it.

I shouldn't pretend to be entirely jaded about the whole experience. The missions trips made me aware of poverty and human suffering on a visceral level, and it helped shape my empathy for both conditions. And while two nicer-than-normal shacks in a slum won't change the bigger picture, certainly the improvement of those families' living standards, however slight, was not inconsequential to them and no doubt mattered a great deal. That said, Christian missionary work does not get a free pass. It is often counterproductive, and it usually creates more turmoil than it solves. This comes as no surprise, because the goals of true philanthropy and humanitarian work are naturally at odds with the goals of international evangelism. Talk to a Christian missionary today, and they will pretend these goals are perfectly congruent; Christ calls them to help the poor, and by doing humanitarian work, they answer the call and as if by total accident, if some of their targets decide to come to Jesus as a result, it's a win-win. This almost never happens in practice, and Christian organizations often dangle any tangible assistance to their impoverished audience with despicable strings attached. Want a free meal? Come to our church service first. Other organizations attempt to help people in need for its own sake; often, the same thing cannot be said of missionary organizations. Ulterior motives abound, and it's no surprise that a religious community that stores up treasures in heaven would be unwilling to improve life on Earth without trying to shoehorn their religion into humanitarian work first. It is a hateful thing to look at a problem like malnutrition, or displacement from homelands on account of famine or war, and to *first* ask those suffering for religious commitments before providing assistance.

Naiveté, pseudopateralism, and straight, unfiltered imperialism can become defining characteristics of Christian humanitarian work. Donating money to corrupt governments often harms the impoverished people more, injecting new religious pressures into a new society often creates new fault lines and divisions into communities, and missionaries have a nasty habit of coming home in body-bags. If you're troubled by the image of a family grieving over the loss of a post-college-twenty-something, don't worry; the Christians regard these human sacrifices as the required cost of doing business. The Lord calls them to the darkest, most dangerous corners of the globe, and if they catch a bullet in the line of duty, don't get upset with the Almighty; the Lord was just calling them home for good. I hope that line of reasoning sickens everyone, Christian or not. Often, the Christians indulge in the same disgusting martyr-worship that you would commonly find in an organization like Hamas.

In my view, the problem of dualism rears its head here again. To the Christians, the problems of the world have a single source; sin, Satan, and moral deficiencies. To the humanist, practical problems have practical causes, and in general, they require practical solutions. Religious intellectuals might call this "materialism" or "reductionism" but I find no discomfort in either title. My discomfort, to put it bluntly, was when my former ideology implied that the sins of the impoverished caused their own suffering, or that their station in life was created by their own moral shortcomings. This strikes me as calloused, heartless, and it seems totally devoid of basic human empathy and compassion. And it's not as if I'm claiming all missionaries do counterproductive work, or that all religious organizations don't genuinely help people in need for its own sake, but there's a fundamental difference between the goals of secular and religious charity. Christian missionaries who pretend otherwise are being flatly disingenuous; they might tell the secular world that they are just trying to help people, but in the decidedly non-mixed company of their Bible studies and prayer groups, this is not their stated goal. They are going into the world to *baptize* all men. They are, upon the orders of Christ, to become fishers of men. They are to make converts. They are to encourage defection from other religions. Their goals are a universe removed from the goals of a secular non-profit organization who just tries to help people for its own sake. I find the latter infinitely more noble than the former, and so should you.

As I began to grow older, unlike most of my Christian contemporaries, I was increasingly seeing religion as the problem, rather than the solution. My disgust with organized religion came to its apex during Joseph Ratzinger's reign as Pontiff. Rather than depart from John Paul the Second's ignominious condom ban, he held on to it steadfastly as the body count in Africa rose and rose from the epidemic of HIV and AIDS. The Vatican, too busy with the cover up of their systematic rape of children, found enough time to shrug with heartless indifference as easily preventable diseases claimed the lives of thousands of their devoted parishioners, who cling to their every syllable. There are no words, in any language, strong enough to condemn such an evil organization. And it is precisely this organization that millions of people will ardently rise to defend when these facts are said plainly; a church with centuries of blood on its hands, a cabal of jackals who hide pedophiles from prosecution while secretly slipping hush money to the victims of these unspeakable crimes. I am told by members of this church that it is a force for good in this world because it does charitable things. I am told by apologists of this church that the newest Pope does not share the prejudices of his predecessors (if this is true, show me where Pope Francis has approved the use of condoms for millions of his African adherents.) No, at nearly every turn, this religion, and nearly all others like it, openly harms people and has the gall to pass around a collection plate afterwards. It is a force of division rather than unity, and has been since the beginning of human history.

Whatever my present disagreements with religious charity, missionary work, and evangelism, I didn't have them when I was in Mexico, and those experiences didn't leave me feeling disillusioned. I had a good time, generally, and enjoyed the time I spent with friends. Rightly or wrongly, I left feeling I had done something important, and that it was something to be proud of doing. I didn't entertain any notions of entering the missionary field (some of my acquaintances did afterwards) mostly because I was wrapped up in my own world, playing music and playing hockey. I had hoped either one would give me the opportunity to do it professionally, but my musical and athletic skill fell well short of a professional level of proficiency. Towards the beginning of my college years, music had started to push hockey out of the picture. I was, I think, reasonably talented at hockey, but once I got a taste of serious development leagues, it became clear that I was far out of my depth (the last gasp was a walk-on tryout for a CHL training camp in which I got body-checked so hard that I flew four or five feet in the air).

In some way, I suppose you could classify my musical resume as marginally professional. I was something of a paid amateur; we cashed checks for concerts we played, and rolled the money over into studio time and other needed equipment. The finished recordings, for both bands, went largely unfinished or were mostly unlistenable when completed. There were bright spots, sure, and the two albums I helped created were an achievement, but I stumbled frequently as a vocalist and in my first album, it showed. Spending my first year at the epicenter of Christian music – Greenville College – exposed me to artists far more skilled and it became clear that I couldn't compete. But the friendships I forged while playing music were far more rewarding than the casual connections I would make playing sports, and truthfully, I never had the social skills required to truly excel in a locker room environment. While I was moderately talented at hockey, and was skilled enough to play at higher and higher levels as I aged, I was largely non-verbal around most teammates through my teenage years. I was hopelessly awkward, and it made me an easy target for some light abuse. I don't actually resent it - none of the ribbing was ever really nasty or physically violent - and it taught me how to respond to things under pressure, but it wasn't fun, to say the least. And towards the end of my amateur hockey career, I did start to loosen up and enjoy myself more, but part of me really wishes I hadn't been homeschooled. I might have enjoyed hockey much more if the social anxiety wasn't so intense. Homeschooling, too, was another formidable influence upon my character development. My parents were (and still are today) very committed Evangelical Christians. They decided to homeschool their children for a whole litany of reasons, but the predominant motivation was religious. That meant curriculum from Bob Jones University Press (my mother loved to bake 'breakaway bread' which was a recipe that provided an edible model to the pseudoscientific creationism theory of the origin of the universe.) It also meant that our social lives, as children, were heavily hamstringed from the start. I don't believe this choice was negligent; I should make that clear from the beginning. My mother was a qualified educator, and had a undergraduate teaching degree from Illinois State, which is far more than most Christians who homeschool often have, but it was not exactly a healthy learning environment. There was little formality to our daily routine, and the quality of our education undoubtedly suffered as a result. Our family was huge - six children, two boys, four girls - and the work required to educate all of us must have been daunting. We didn't all exclusively homeschool; I can remember some of my sisters taking some public school courses at one time or another, but predominantly, schooling happened at home.

There weren't many boundaries, and this was both a blessing and a curse (but mostly, a curse.) Once I got into a formal educational setting, I struggled to adapt with routine and discipline, but the topics I spent time learning appealed to my own interests, and I could dive deeply into subjects I loved, like history, without restraint. Maybe it can be argued that this is an indiscernible case of nature versus nature, and that I would have developed these traits with our without a homeschooling background. But the answer makes little difference to me; I would never advocate for homeschooling in the slightest. I believe it powerfully stunts the development of social skills, elevates unqualified people into educational roles that they are not trained to hold, and the religious impulses that motivate many homeschooling parents often ends up poisoning the curriculum. Furthermore, I believe the roles of the parent and teacher should not permanently blur as they usually do in homeschooling; a good parent doesn't always share the interests of a good teacher, and vice versa.

This isn't to generalize all homeschooling, however. Many parents do an excellent job as educators, and do their children no disservice as both parents and teachers. I think we should be able to fully admit that the incredibly unique skill set required to wear both of these hats simultaneously is *uncommon*, and that the best option for a proper education is to utilize public or private schools who employ professionals. And, of course, I love my family very much, and I don't resent them for making the choice to homeschool, but like all of the experiences here, it colored my worldview. I think it must be said (my parents lovingly excluded) that there is an undeniable amount of arrogance to a parent who believes they can be everything to their child; they'll teach them everything they need to know about history, literature, and arithmetic. Really? There's no gap in their own knowledge of these subjects? They can confidently hand down lessons from all of these vastly different fields without issue? I find this mindset to be unbearably arrogant and presumptive; and it comes, again, as no surprise that in many cases, homeschooling is just used as another instrument to inject religion into a child's mind. Talk with any Christian homeschooling parent, and they will often speak in anxious tones about drugs, violence, and sexual promiscuity in our craven and morally bankrupt public schools.

Well, I get quite offended when public schools are baselessly impugned in this fashion. Through my wife (a public school teacher in St. Louis for six years) I have had the opportunity to meet these men and women who devote themselves tirelessly the educational needs of the communities they serve. I have never, ever, been able to conceal my admiration of their work, and the impact they make on the lives of these children are not inconsequential. Conservatives don't like public schools because they teach actual science, and occasionally they teach children how not to catch sexually transmitted diseases. This makes them recoil in horror, and usually, they rush to throw the entire baby out with the evolutionary bathwater. I have seen the totality of the weight our public teachers bear; I watched my wife wake up for work at 5AM, and watched her return home at 8PM. I watched her spill bitter and angry tears over unspeakable horrors endured by young children in abusive or negligent homes. I watched her spend hour after countless hour crafting lesson plans during her own time in the nights and weekends. She, and millions of public school teachers like her, make these enormous sacrifices for the benefit of the children of strangers, for the betterment of the collective future of our society. I can think of only a few vocations that are as noble and selfless. And for this work, they are given insulting low compensation, and greeted with sneers and jeers from religious zealots who stamp their feet and pout and moan because they aren't allowed to force their ancient beliefs down the throats of everyone's children. This ideology is immature and truly menacing; and caught in the crossfire of the Christian-Culture-Warriors are the dedicated, professional, and selfless public school teachers who do so much more than most people realize.

This disdain for education, by the way, is a hallmark of Republican delusion. My go-to line, when chatting with a room full of teachers, is to jokingly explain that Fox News told me that teachers only work until 1PM. This is based off of an interview by some faceless talking head who claimed his mother was a teacher, and that she worked a glorified half-day and was in the grocery store by 3PM. Of all the vocational enemies to make on the face of the earth, these conservative buffoons go after the school teacher? Not the payday lender, not the CEO that makes an average yearly salary in a few hours, but the professional educator? What could possibly motivate someone to think like this?

I can't (comprehensively, anyway) answer that question, but I can say with some authority that conservative religious circles like the one I grew up in loathe and despise public schools, and see them as a direct threat to their Christian way of life. And, let us give them credit where they are due; a proper education is a grave threat, indeed, to Christianity itself. A proper education will teach you about the barbarity of the Crusades. A proper education will present all religions equally and without bias. A proper education will teach you about your body, and won't shame you for having normal sexual urges. A proper education will teach you about the actual origins of the universe, rather than pummel you over the head with an ancient set of sexist, racist, and violent documents that were written during the worst eras of human history. They draw the lines of battle at these junctures for good reason; the world is far more beautiful, nuanced, and intricate than their Bible clumsily states.

Less fundamental Christians and conservatives often concede this point; they recognize the Bible can't be our guide to everything. It would be terrific if all Christians made their personal relationship with God actually personal, and stopped dragging it into the public square at any available opportunity. I believe this impulse is what drives religious zealots to slander educators; their war against sex education and evolution is yet another attempt to export their faith into the daily lives of people who don't adhere to it. I remember, too, growing up with this mindset as a zealous Christian.

Like any child, I parroted what my parents said. And the talking points were largely straightforward; there was archeological evidence for Noah's Ark (this is a hilarious obsession in the Evangelical world), and the fossils that those evolutionary scientists have found were faked. It seems so strange in retrospect - how could we say God didn't use evolution to create the universe if he was incomprehensibly powerful? - but we clung tightly to our narrow interpretations in the face of it all, and the resistance we encountered only served to galvanize us further.

The Path Forward

‡‡

CHAPTER 11

"THERE IS NO HUMAN PROBLEM WHICH COULD NOT BE SOLVED IF PEOPLE WOULD JUST DO AS I ADVISE." -Gore Vidal

═

The election of President Trump signaled the end of conventional American politics as we knew them, or, at best, represented a wild deviation from their typical expressions. Having gone to great length to identify and detail the neoconservative right, I should take some measures to ensure that I am prescribing some medication for the illness I have diagnosed. Before embarking on such an endeavor, I should preface these findings with a healthy disclaimer. I am convinced, sincerely, that the future failure of this ideology is assured in any event. The Berlin Wall crumbled at the hands of a divided and oppressed people, and Trump's supposedly impenetrable wall on the southern border is destined to meet the same fate in time. Political repression might win in a sprint, but the thirst for liberty always wins in a marathon.

I was moved, recently, by the images of civilians being liberated from ISIL, expertly captured by photojournalists in Iraq and Syria. The photographs were powerful, jaw-dropping, and spoke to our shared humanity. Hijabs were being torn off, men joked with reporters about shaving their beards, or how desperately they were looking forward to their first smoke – tobacco usage under Daesh was an offense punishable with an arbitrary number of lashes. My aim, of course, is not to equate the fundamentalism of the American right with the death-worshipping cult of ISIL, but to simply relay the basic fact that autonomy is universally more attractive than complying with orders from others. This appeal is a human one, and it transcends the bounds of religion and culture. For this reason, I am not uncomfortable in issuing reassurances – the fundamentalists will lose and humanity will triumph. The most worrisome variable in this discussion, however, is the cost. What sort of damage gets done when, as Christopher Hitchens liked to call them, "The parties of God" are able to call the shots?

I cannot give an accurate appraisal of what sort of damage might be done in the future, but I am confident that I can illuminate a reasonable path forward for a people in opposition to theocracy. Beyond this, especially in the wake of Mr. Trump, the Democratic Party in the United

States made some unfortunate errors during the election cycle. Many of these wounds were entirely self-inflicted, and stood witness to another uncomfortable truth for the DNC; they had become isolated from the concerns of Red-State voters, they had colluded against Senator Bernie Sanders unfairly during the primaries, and they had failed to meaningfully articulate their plans for governance in a way that average Americans could understand. As such, the Democrats were engaged, on many issues, on the basis on principle, where the Republicans had engaged upon pragmatism. Trump said whatever undecided voters wanted to hear, in the obvious interest of courting their support. Mrs. Clinton was risk-averse, and famously wanted to 'go high' when her opposition went 'low.' This approach casts doubt on the DNC's ability to prioritize items based on their importance, and a central theme of this chapter will be focused on how best to recalibrate that ability.

Collective Action

Younger generations (I am intentionally avoiding the tired phrase 'Millennial' here) are excellent protestors, but a thickening sense of cynicism has started to weave its way through their ranks. Pejoratives like "Clicktivism" or "Virtue Signalers" have cropped up as sassy reprimands to empty-headed protestors who march for a few hours and believe that they have changed the world. For those who are skeptical, they are right to wonder if collective assembly makes a tangible difference in our society, and I am quite right to assure them that it does.

In February of 2017, the Romanian government withdrew a previously issued anti-corruption decree. As written, the had edict decriminalized bribes or abuses of power that did not rise above the amount of 200,000 Lei (approximately $48,000 USD). All that was required to reverse this action was 500,000 Romanians willing to take to the streets. The pressure built by protests are very real indeed, and it is truly the most powerful weapon in our toolbox. Those Americans keyed in enough to read this book will likely not need any motivation to have their grievances redressed when necessary, (nor do I have any interest in holding myself up as a community organizer when I am clearly not on at all) so to sharpen my point in this regard, I want to define precisely how discretion ought to be used in this aspect of political resistance.

There is an allure to playing a "Call-and-Response" game with the talking points that capture attention within any given media cycle. Some of these are so noxious that they must meet a meaningful reply – Trump's boasts about sexually assaulting women are a perfect example – but responding to every issue as it arises is dangerous, and often counterproductive. The primary goal of a protest is to apply pressure to those in power – the secondary goal is to illicit new supporters from opposing ideologies. The greatest risk to recruitment is repetition, and if every blip on the Trump radar creates noise, as former Breitbart columnist Ben Shapiro recently wrote, the audience begins to go deaf, and those in power have a vested interest in making any dissent appear to be misguided or permanently displeased regardless of circumstance. Picking battles wisely, and fighting them with the highest amount of intensity when they occur, will determine the scope of future success. The power in a protest, simply, is that it is the final resort of a maligned people. When it is the first tool out of the bag, it is drained of its sovereignty and stripped of its power.

Economic Disruption

As technology eases the workload required to connect like-minded people with each other, the ability to shake cages will become easier. I have already seen efforts like these in their incubatory stages online – the "Women's March" that drew millions to the streets after Trump's inauguration announced some time later that a general strike entitled "A Day Without a Woman" was in the works. Imagine, then, how simple it will become to coordinate an economic sit-in with ten million people abstaining from purchasing activity for a day, for instance. The rattle and hum of a normal economy can be altered for political effect, and could be used to introduce a new pressure point to a demographic that is quite skilled at inoculating themselves from pressure.

In the same way that withholding collective resources can produce political results, so too can collective financing. "Crowdfunding" (or internet begging, as I like to call it) is another effective method for applying support in a rapid fashion. The break-neck speed of "signal-boosting" is often incomprehensible. Celebrity Twitter accounts can, in a single click, elevate the audience of any message as they see fit. Viral personalities or causes can often catch fire online and whip up funds within mere hours. In many ways, the internet (and, it should be mentioned, the future neutrality of it will be vital to the future success of continued human liberty) will become the Super PAC of the low and middle economic classes in the United States.

Voter Suppression

It is painfully clear that voter suppression primarily benefits the Republicans, rather than the Democrats. Both parties, it is safe to say, participate in this nasty business to some degree, but to speak generally, the

GOP does it the most and stands to gain the most from its practice. What the Democrats must do (especially if they are able to wrestle a majority in the Senate back in 2018) is to focus *exclusively* on what can defeat the Republicans in the next Presidential election. There are many issues the DNC can choose to weigh in on, and there are many worthy causes worth its political capital. In my view, the baked-in idealism of liberalism is naturally distraction-prone. Egalitarians, by definition, want a fair world for everyone, and real fairness is quite uncommon. The temptation is to speak up for everything, and while this is admirable or even righteous, *it does not win elections.* This urge should be completely resisted by Trump's political opposition. Everything else must come secondary to victory.

This means, necessarily, that important issues might get knocked down a peg or two. To use a rather crude metaphor; it is time for Sophie to make a choice. This Republican supermajority, in just a few short months, has rewritten the procedure for Supreme Court Justice nominations and used military force against another Middle Eastern nation – eight years of this administration could be inconceivably dangerous. The nation has spoken clearly to the Democratic party. It wants security and projections of strength. Trump delivered this and rode a wave of nationalist fervor to the White House. The DNC, to be blunt, has to learn how to play the same game as the Republicans. The time for haughty idealism is long gone, and the Democrats will need to abandon anything that doesn't directly correlate to winning back the White House. Let me state this plainly; the Republicans cannot win elections without suppressing Democratic voter turnout. There must be meaningful reform in voter registration laws in order for the Democrats to win back power.

For many years, I worked for a retail chain as a photo technician, and I spent a lot of time operating a mobile photo kiosk. Essentially, all it was, technically, was a couple of printers connected to a desktop computer. One of its most popular functions was the instant production of photos for passport applications. Is there any reason (especially if the Democrats meaningfully win back power over the next three years) that a 'mobile ID station' law couldn't be enacted? Let the Republicans insist on photo identification for voters if they like, but put a federal law in place that allows the production of those documents at the polling station itself. Another option in this same vein could also be tethered to mobile phone ownership; car insurance documents (at the time of this writing) are legally accessible through an application on a cellular phone. Identifying documents – a common Republican gatekeeper for low to middle-class voters – could also be delivered and authenticated through the now-ubiquitous cell phone almost all of us carry. Kenya currently has a massive adoption rate for mobile-phone-powered banking, and a large segment of their economy operates solely on phone-to-phone funds transfers. Downloading a driver's license, social security card, or birth certificate pales in comparison to the Kenyan's technical achievements. (And, before anyone interjects about information security, let us not forget the U.S. government lost, literally, millions of social security numbers in digital breeches over the years, so our analog-only program isn't keeping that data safe to begin with.) Whether by this method, or any combination of any others, the truth must be understood completely; the DNC has failed its own voters, and has not delivered a meaningful counterattack to the Republican war on voter registration.

Data Responsibility

In the era of "fake" news, the importance of caution is paramount. Both in the information we choose to intake, and the information we choose to disseminate to our own spheres of influence, however large or small. It is all too easy to relax one's own standards when a questionable article or news source pops up in our social media feeds. Especially when that snippet of information adheres neatly to a pre-conceived notion we held before reading it. Timothy Synder really says it best:

> "We do not see the minds that we hurt when we publish falsehoods, but that does not mean we do no harm. Think of driving a car. We may not see the other driver, but we know not to run into his car. We know that the damage will be mutual. We protect the other person without seeing him, dozens of times every day. Likewise, although we may not see the other person in front of his or her computer, we have our share of responsibility for what he or she is reading there. If we can avoid doing violence to the minds of unseen others on the internet, others will learn to do the same. And then perhaps our internet traffic will cease to look like one great, bloody, accident." [1]

Technology has served to demolish gates that previously denied entry to industries; people no longer need a recording studio to make an album, no longer need a local news station to record video for millions to see, and similarly, anyone can create, post, and share news-related content. The data we choose to share should be safe, well-sourced, and should always originate from reputable sources.

It is *far* too easy to let your own personal social media turn into a tightly-curated echo chamber. News stories that appear to rigidly support your existing point of view have a noxious charm; it is a siren song that offers your brain a tantalizing taste of affirmation. These urges must be resisted at all costs. Our consumption of news and the sources of our current affairs commentary should be scrutinized heavily and taken seriously. What we choose to share impacts our circle of influence, and it has consequences. Following the money, too, is an important guiding principle in this struggle; I personally enjoy Al-Jazeera's journalism, but I take it with a grain of salt the size of Jerusalem (they do terrific work, but are funded by the Qatari government and often do not cover Israel fairly, or, indeed, Qatar's own deadly World Cup project). This is the kind of engagement required to intake data properly, and while I personally have not perfected the practice, I aspire to improving my media diet every day, and I believe everyone else should as well.

Dirty Tricks

I was of two minds on the verge of 2016's Presidential Election. I reviled Mr. Trump's vindictive and toxic speech, and his rhetoric, often bordering at times on literal free-association and obvious psychological projection, seemed as if it would collapse under its own weight. If Mrs. Clinton partook in the same type of confrontation, it would be far beneath her station as a tenured and experienced diplomat. She ought to take the high road, I often thought, and was right to let the mudslinging stay mostly one-directional. On the other hand, I grew weary of Donald Trump perpetual attacks, and longed for Mrs. Clinton to deliver a true knock-out punch. The material for such a blow was certainly far from scarce. Mr. Trump was vulnerable from a plethora of different angles, and in the face of truly vicious and vulgar attacks, Mrs. Clinton (rightly or wrongly) upheld a modicum of dignity throughout. I cannot say whether this choice made a significant impact on the result of the election, but I think it is quite fair to say that some Democratic ammunition never really got fired. For starters, the Democratic party is, by nature, slightly more tethered to the observable truth than their Republican counterparts. The GOP courts the values-based voters in Alabama and Georgia, not the adjunct professors in New York or California. As such, the Republicans can twist and distort the truth with fewer consequences or accountability. To say this another way: when it was discovered that the Kremlin had started churning up fabricated news stories on the internet to influence the election, the United States could not response *exactly* in kind. Why? Because the Russians, by and large, control the output of their media. The freedom of the press put the Americans at a competitive disadvantage. It created an attack vector that simply did not exist within the walls of their enemy. In the same way, the Republicans have a longer leash with the truth than the Democrats.

"Motivated reasoning this helps to explain all manner of maddening, logically suspect maneuvers that people make when they're in the middle of arguments so as to avoid changing their minds. Consider once classic: goalpost shifting. This occurs when someone has made a clear and factually refutable claim, and staked a great deal on it – but once the claim meets its demise, the person demands some additional piece of evidence, or tweaks his or her views in some way so as to avoid having to give them up. That's what the Seekers did when their prophecy failed; that's what vaccine deniers do with each subsequent scientific discrediting of the idea that vaccines cause autism; that's what the hardcore Birthers did when President Obama released his long-form birth certificate; that's what the errant prophet Harold Camping did when his predicted rapture did not commence on May 21st, 2011, and the world did not end on October 21, 2011." [1]

Imagine how the cracks in the democratic voting base would widen if Mrs. Clinton started in on an imaginary story like Mr. Trump did with President Obama's birth certificate. Democrats would distance themselves from her in droves. The Republicans weld a tool that the Democrats either can't (or won't) use, so how, exactly, does this party go about finding unique Republican weaknesses? One such method was devised by a crafty group of gay-rights activists in a Texas election:

"With Christian Coalition of Texas totally dismantled, it also fell to Shackelford's Family Policy Council, called the Free Market Foundation, to distribute three million voter guides about Proposition 2. And just when he thought he had it all under control, Shackelford's fear about gay rights activists mobilizing against the amendment was realized. Just two weeks before Election Day, a group called No Nonsense in November began placing automated 'robocalls' to millions of Texas homes. The calls employed a novel tactic, alleging that the amendment was written so broadly that it threatened to undo heterosexual marriage. The call were taped by a Presbyterian minister, invoked the writings of two well-known Texas Republican figures as being against the proposition – even though both vigorously insisted they were not – and ended the salutation 'God Bless You,' allegedly giving the impression that the Republican and religious establishments opposed Proposition 2." [2]

It should be noted that this dirty trick did not completely work – the proposition still passed when it was all said and done – but look at just how far a little dirt under the proverbial fingernails can really go. I understand, and fully appreciate, the importance of a fair election and in a perfect world, I would love to see each and every political punch land well above the belt. This isn't the world that we currently live in, and being a squeaky-clean loser, when the opposition is so incompetent and greedy, isn't doing anyone any good.

Redistricting, Gerrymandering, Cracking and Packing

Much like scourge of political action committees, both political parties utilize a form of voter suppression known as gerrymandering. To put it simply, this is the act of manipulating subsets of voters for the electoral benefit of one party over another. Districts unfavorable to a parties' chances for success are 'cracked' and split up into irrelevance, pockets of support that are too anemic for meaningful impact on their own are 'packed' together. The boundaries for districts are written and rewritten, often in secret, and if it sounds like cheating, well, that's because it is. This disease, like many others in the American political diaspora, exist on account of the peculiarities of our electoral system. The instatement of a popular vote (a measure often brow-beaten by people on both sides of the aisle) would have no need to tally up districts in this fashion. The purpose of the electoral college, ostensibly, exists to prevent the rise of a dangerous populist. After this mechanism failed to prevent the election of a dangerous populist, many people, like myself, are now openly questioning the need for such a system in the first place. The business of politics in the United States is a filthy one, and this reality is not lost on average Americans. Congressional approval numbers are usually laughably low, and most Americans are acutely aware of how corrupt their representatives actually are. In this way, we can see that institutional trust has been eroded over decades of political races, and if districts can be divided up on a whim, well and truly outside of the view of the typical American voter, what is the point of voting at all?

The system is far from democratic and representative when jackals from both sides of the political aisle can rearrange votes like chips on a roulette table. I had this discussion on with a couple of fellow Democrats on a business trip in the great city of New Orleans. The younger Democrats (myself and a few others) made the argument I mentioned earlier – the electoral system was supposed to be a safeguard against nationalists rising to power and it failed – and were willing to rip up the electoral college in favor of a simple popular vote. The older (perhaps wiser) Democrats bristled at this suggestion. A popular vote is an unknown entity in the American political landscape, they insisted, and while Mr. Gore, Mr. Kerry, and Mrs. Clinton were edged out of the White House on account of the electoral system, it is impossible to say if it would benefit the nation as a whole if it was scrapped. This dialog is a compelling one; and I believe the electoral college, as an institution, perhaps does more harm than good.

Reverting to a popular vote would, however, get rid of the unsightly business of redistricting and, for better or worse, would reseat the nation's political processes back to a more basic version of democracy. The path to this destination (or, the path to meaningful reform of the districting system) is not a clear or simple one. For the foreseeable future, the Supreme Court has been returned to overwhelmingly conservative hands, and the adjustment of our electoral architecture would likely hinge upon their approval. The opposition, again, finds itself in the same ethical dilemma as before – reform the broken system or out-cheat your opponents – in order to remain relevant in the competition for power.

Professional Sports

At first glance, this pressure point may seem inconsequential. Figures in the entertainment industry are almost universally despised when they choose to speak up in regards to political issues. As an avid sports fan, I too would prefer it if the sports entertainment industry remained a politically demilitarized zone. That, in my view, is one of the most incredible things about sport to begin with; the game doesn't care where you're from, or what god you worship, or what political party you voted for. Part of its sheer entertainment value is derived from the purity of its Darwinian nature. Only the best of the very best succeed at the upper echelons of professional sports, and it is a joy to watch. That exhilaration is not exactly universal in conservative circles, but is quite well-spread, especially in the United States. One of the primary reasons I specifically mention athletes over other entertainers is that Republicans are infinitely more attached to sports than film or music, and they are quite disturbed when this arena does not adhere to their political beliefs.

When Colin Kaepernick, former quarterback of the San Francisco 49ers, began a silent, anthem-protest against racially-motivated police brutality, the controversy wasn't contained to just fans of the National Football League. It made international headlines, and started a powerful dialogue about what it was like to be black in the United States. As someone who often despises protest, ceremony, and attention-grabbing, I could not bring myself to be cynical of Mr. Kaepernick's actions. I wrote a piece in his defense when he was being crucified in the court of public opinion. His silent protest was not a fatuous gesture. It was not superfluous. It was a compelling and powerful statement that, unlike so many others, *actually landed in the minds of its target audience*. One of the most intriguing ideas that emanated from the Black Lives Matter group was the prospect of a racial strike from all professional sports. If Kaepernick taking a knee during the *Star Spangled Banner* stirred the pot, imagine what a unified black athlete labor strike could accomplish. What if, right before the NFL playoffs, all African-American athletes refused to play unless body cameras were federally mandated for all police officers? The power to disrupt a billion-dollar industry lies in their hands, and under the right context, could meaningfully enact needed change. Beyond their potential efficacy, professional sports are often some of the most egregious offenders of important public policy.

For example, the NFL's dangerous and self-interested refusal to acknowledge the long-term medical and neurological impacts of their industry reflects precisely the same vile greed that underlines the entirety of the oil and natural gas sectors that destroy the planet for their own personal gain. Labor disputes are often most acute within sports as well; collegiate sports are perhaps the most shameless in this respect. On ethical reasons alone, I have long refused to watch any NCAA-sanctioned sport. Collegiate athletes in the United States are often little more than slaves. They do not share in the prosperity that their own athletic performances generate (unable to even profit from the sale of the jersey that bears their own name, if you can believe it) and unlike professional sports, where the athlete is handsomely financially rewarded on account of the medical risk they assume for the sake of entertainment, the student-athlete is not just on the hook for medical expenses later in life, but often, is on the hook for those expenses immediately after they arise. Universities issue free scholarships to promising young athletes, which is terrific, until they get yanked away from the student on account of a career-ending injury. The quality of the education of a student-athlete is questionable at best. The quality of play (as is often the case, is only slightly below the highest tiers of professional sport itself) can only be maintained by operating on the same rigid schedule as professional athletes and professional organizations themselves. The students endure back-breaking schedules that plainly put education second. They are subjected to multiple practices a day, followed by hours in the gym, followed by individual coaching sessions, playbook memorization, and video analysis of their own play and the performances of their opposition. All of this is tethered to the same bruising academic calendar that burdens normal students. Who among us could bear this daily yoke and retain any knowledge at all? Many times, collegiate athletes are essentially pro athletes who are also expected to pretend that they are getting a college education. It is no surprise that academic programs across the nation are littered with ethical abuses at every impasse. Professors fabricating homework in order to make a star athlete meet academic requirements or coaches bribing prospective athletes are just par for the course. The system is replete with corruption because it is entirely predicated upon a corrupt concept: monetizing on free labor. It is disgusting and rotten to its very core, and those athletes deserve to be paid like the professionals that they truly are. Unified political action, boycotts, or protests that could hamstring the

NCAA would be incredibly transformative, and the fallout from such efforts could certainly cross-pollinate to other vital sectors of civil life. The Northwestern football team in Illinois made international waves when it attempted to unionize. The NCAA managed to strike down this measure, but the statement was no less powerful or important. A pressure point like this, with such widespread devotion amongst such a large and politically diverse audience simply cannot be ignored.

Universal Basic Income

Within the next two or three decades, we will likely see basic income programs expand within the United States, particularly within liberal metropolitan strongholds. As usual, European and Scandinavian nations have beaten the Americans to the punch, and several have already implemented a limited form of universal basic income. The concept, of course, is bound to be politically unpopular with millions of American citizens, but some of the early results show promise. In my own view, I see UBI as no different than any other entitlement program, and if the expenditure can be proven to prevent or reduce higher costs down the line, it seems entirely worth our time.

Keep in mind, this idea is not new; Dr. Martin Luther King Jr. himself argued for its virtues, and there is plenty of evidence to support the claim that economic stress is the catalyst that drives a host of other harmful and collectively expensive behaviors. I am no expert on automation or artificial intelligence, but United States will be hit with a widespread wave of economic displacement by robotics, AI, and automation within the next twenty years. Almost certainly, this will be the cause of the next economic recession, if we are lucky, and depression, if we are not, and our current politicians would be wise to plan ahead for the coming storm. Other trusted voices in tech have been calling for a small AI tax to be levied on the sale of job-replacing systems. I think this is a prudent measure; the government could stash the tax revenues from the sales into trusts or budgets that can be used for vocational training classes for millions of out of work Americans, or the proceeds could be processed as educational grants that could be exclusively paid out to American workers who lost their jobs on account of automation. Universal basic income is going to powerfully shape this discussion, too. It will take education to migrate labor from vulnerable industries like trucking, and the government could reduce the future strain on entitlement systems by making wise investments in educational grants or vocational training.

Getting Better at Dancing with the Devil

At the risk of stating the obvious, the future success of the Democratic party will hinge on how well it is able to operate as an opposition party. Mr. Trump's administration is unconventional, and the rational world will have to learn how to parry his attacks, and exploit his unique vulnerabilities. I was stunned by the election, as most Americans were, and like most Americans, I held my nose and voted for Mrs. Clinton in an unsuccessful bid to keep Mr. Trump out of power. The turning point, for me, personally, was to hear a belligerent Trump crudely imply that the only election result he would respect would be a result in his favor and no others. This bellicosity was a call to action for me, and is my personal alarm bell to my fellow citizens. Democracy only survives when we tend to it, and when we sacrifice for its sake alone. Mr. Trump is the epitome of ego, greed, and self-aggrandizement. He is a blight on the nation, and he is so uninformed that he himself does not fully understand how poorly he is performing.

In an article I wrote on the heels of the election, I lamented how sharply Mr. Trump has tarnished the once-respectable office of the Presidency of the United States. Once, it was synonymous with class, dignity, restraint, and diligence. Mr. Trump possesses none of these qualities. He blames his military leadership for the deaths of American serviceman who perished on his orders. He demonizes the American media for simply doing its job. He spews racist bile in order to secure the votes of American bigots. He boasts of loving the 'poorly educated' and has no qualms slandering billions of Muslims. Everything about his administration is repugnant, repulsive, vile, and detestable. In moments of great moral conflict, our ethical positions define us, and I shall not be silent on such a horrifying president. He is a bigot, he is a demagogue, and he is a self-interested hack who is only concerned with inflating his own ego and filling his own bank accounts. It is easy to be outraged, and even easier still when the outrages never stop, but the naked white nationalism of the Trump administration exposed a litany of American misconceptions.

First, the ethnocentric, white-male, conservative power base isn't new. As I argued throughout this book, it is an acceptable lens with which the whole of American history can be viewed. White liberals reveal the depth of their insolation from this fact when they speak about the unprecedented nature of Mr. Trump's unvarnished racism; in the Democratic metropolitan hotbeds, perhaps racism and overt sexism are far less frequent. In Missouri, Tennessee, Kentucky, and the rest of America's rural roots, the story is far different. Second, the Democratic party believed that declining religious attachment would diminish Republican support. This was not true, (at least, not true enough to make a meaningful difference) and some recent research appears to indicate that as conservative Americans leave religion, they become more accepting of homosexuality, but at the cost of becoming more nationalistic. Third, the intellectual left believed that shame could be weaponized against Mr. Trump after he was elected. This, too, was a costly miscalculation; President Trump's supporters are attracted, rather than repelled, by his self-aggrandizement, casual racism, angry over-simplifications, and vapid appeals to nationalism. In raising our voices to object, we merely acted as Mr. Trump's amplifier.

Equally foolish, too, was the rigid fact-checking campaign undertaken by the left-wing. To President Trump, words are superfluous. They have no meaning. He says anything that wants, without regard to the truth, and his target audience has no interest in any relationship with the truth at all. Even when it comes to what are, traditionally, sacred institutions to the conservatives, Trump has no need to restrain himself. The president even blamed his military commanders for the deaths of American servicemen acting under his orders and there was no serious objection from his base. Mr. Trump has no reason to tell the truth, in fact, because it does little to keep him in power. He projects an image of intelligence, strength, and experience while being bereft of all three in reality. It doesn't matter to the president, it doesn't matter to the people who support him, and attempting to unseat Mr. Trump from power using this method is tremendously foolish. Some chatter about whether or not Trump was to be taken literally started to spring up, too. His supporters and detractors alike began to make bizarre claims about how the world ought to parse the president's sporadic vocabulary. Mr. Trump reverses positions and policies at a breakneck speed.

Not ten years ago, this type of "flip flopping" would have sunk any other candidate, but against all odds, Mr. Trump found a way to change the way the game of politics are played, for better or worse. I scolded myself, post-election, for overlooking the warning signs. Mrs. Clinton was particularly weak with white male voters, and there was some defection (however small) from Senator Sanders' supporters to Trump. I believed that couldn't happen. These two candidates couldn't be any more different, and that was true, but Americans don't vote on policy: the vote with their hearts before anything else. I believed, too, that Mr. Trump would "gaffe" his way out of contention. Emotionally, it felt as if he was only one stray comment or insult away from destroying himself.

Perhaps this was true, but from the outset I should have cast this possibility aside. The speech with which he announced his campaign should have been enough for all of us to throw away our old conceptions of what a bad beat in the press looked like. Mr. Trump is a walking "gaffe" himself, and this is quizzically part of his charm and appeal to the Republican base. I overestimated the support Mrs. Clinton was going to receive from voting women. 52% of white women voted for Trump; this is a stunning figure I cannot bring myself to reconcile. Of those women, how many, one is forced to ponder, had *themselves* been sexually assaulted by a man? What manner of delusion is required to go cast a vote for the same type of sexual predator that attacked you personally? There was something far more sinister than religion or gender at play - this was a racial divide at heart, this was a result fueled by anger, rage, and anxiety - and the white discontent that was festering underneath the Obama administration was unavoidable. Supposing Mrs. Clinton had won, the House and the Senate would still have been firmly in Republican hands, and it would have only been a matter of time before the conservatives wrestled back the Oval Office. The country is indisputably divided now, and this division is fierce, raw, and contemptuous.

The petty and aggressive tone the Trump-led White House now takes with the press will only end in embarrassment and failure. So, too, will his sustained attack against countless wings of the media. Those enemies, once made, are contentious ones who hold long grudges. No good could come of it, and in my view, this is a significant miscalculation by Mr. Trump. In the first place, Mr. Trump's supporters have no relationship with the kinds of media he vilifies. They watch Fox News until the ticker is burned into the bottom of their screens. Generally speaking, they are not voracious readers of the *New York Times* or the *Washington Post*. It does him little good to instill a deeper hatred of media his base doesn't consume. Secondly, the American entrainment-centric media (specifically, cable news networks like CNN, MSNBC, and FOX) are in constant search of a narrative to push. Once an overarching theme is installed, content can be easily created underneath it. The ebb and flow of this policy will create peaks and valleys by its very nature; so Mr. Trump is making a future rod for his own back when he buddies up to Fox and Friends. They'll turn on him the second he becomes a liability to another Republican term in office (something that seems likely in the course of President Trump's first four years) and the same machine that brought him into this world, so to speak, could just as easily take him out. The blueprints are already in place. Spurned Evangelicals who never publically endorsed Trump could take the lead as usurpers (Evan McMillan and Gary Kasparov are notable Republican voices with moderates), and, of course, Mr. Pence is the GOP's safest security blanket. Incompetence never hides for very long, and the lack of political experience will expose Mr. Trump in time. Business magnates often find themselves quickly worn out by the grindingly slow pace of bureaucracy. This point, raised by many other analysts, turned out to be quite accurate. President Trump, in an uncharacteristic burst of self-awareness, admitted to the press that his 'previous' life was easier, and that he was 'learning' more about pressing global issues, like NATO and North Korea. In these orange hands rests the future of the United States. The truth is far stranger than fiction, indeed.

The resistance to Trump is often petty and often makes a lot of noise while accomplishing a whole lot of nothing. Much of the Democratic opposition is distasteful to me. Often, it's not only dour bitching, but it is actively counterproductive. Complaints about the amount of time Mr. Trump spends golfing, for instance, isn't a meaningful objection to any of his policies, and isn't likely to produce any results. It is an accusation that clearly doesn't needle the president, doesn't land with his base, and distracts from other, more important, issues. More to the point, when President Obama took vacation time during his time in office (to the chagrin of conservatives), liberals dutifully pointed out that vacation time wasn't a barometer of success (FDR came up with the monumentally significant Lend-Lease program while on vacation). If one is to take a position on this issue, it should be consistent, rather than being yet another vapid political football carried on a partisan basis alone. Once the opposition is reduced to a series of incessant moaning complaints, entirely predicated upon the frivolities of his personality, the battle has already been lost. This is the trap of Trump; his detractors get sucked into the cult of his bombastic personality rather than substance.

One of the many nails driven into the coffin of the DNC in 2016 was the sense that Mrs. Clinton did not adequately outline her own vision for her America. This is an improvement that must be urgently made to the party platform. Trump's vision – however blithering and stupid – was infinitely easier to understand. Anyone could comprehend the message. *The Mexican rapists needed to get out. The trade deals the U.S. made were bad.* Trump promised to fix them, and his voters understood the dilemmas he presented. This is not a criticism of Mrs. Clinton, nor is it a critique of her ability to stay on message, but a rebuke of the timorousness of her campaign. It was clear from the beginning that Trump was going to attempt to beat her by leaning on the lowest common denominator, and nothing significant was done to compete for those same voters. In response to this line of reasoning, Democrats will often claim that the 'zingers' were there, along with the simple two-word slogans that anyone could understand, and that the lowest common denominators just liked Trump better. I don't buy this, at least not to the extent that it was a deficiency the Democrats couldn't adequately address.

Mrs. Clinton should have attacked Mr. Trump in the same fashion he was attacking her. She should have used the *ad-hominems,* and she should have mocked him just as cruelly as he mocked her. It should have been eye-for-an-eye, rather than the somewhat-dignified, cautious, and level-headed talking points that emerged instead that revolved around Trump being "unqualified." Middle-America interpreted these as yet another example of liberal pretention. What was Hillary to Trump's base? Crooked! What did

Trump's base want to do to Hilary? Lock her up! The fewer syllables, the better. Go dumb or go home.

And while this point has been made by so many others, and with so much more eloquence, I have to insist on making it here. Republicans play dirty, they cheat, they lie, and they exaggerate to stay in power, and if Democrats want to win, they will need to do it, too. Yes, I am well aware, and fully agree in principle, that Mrs. Obama is right when she says the proper thing to do when your opponent goes low, is to go high. If it was up to me, I would restore our former civility to our electoral process in an instant. But you can't play a game of tennis if your opponent doesn't bring a racquet; and Trump wasn't interested in the truth, or facts, or civility, or decorum, so why was Mrs. Clinton? What purpose did taking the high-road serve? Donald Trump called Bill Clinton a rapist and insulted Mrs. Clinton's appearance; what, exactly, was wrong with counterattacking in the same way? Say what the rest of America was always thinking – *who's going to take this guy seriously with that nasty, cotton-candy toupee?*

Mention this to a committed Clintonite, and they will respond in dignified, paternalistic tones. *She couldn't stoop to his level, or else he'd win.* Well, she didn't, and he won anyway, so what was the point of it all? Losing with character is better than winning with some dirt under your fingernails? If American voters were stupid enough to be swayed by "Let's build a wall," they were stupid enough to be swayed by "Your hair looks stupid." Schoolyard jabs, especially defensive ones in reply, when instigated by a clown like Mr. Trump, aren't undignified. The real indignity will be powerlessly watching your loved ones being deported on President Trump's orders. The real indignity will come when our valuable institutions that act as a check on executive power are destroyed. The real indignity *has already come* in the successful theft of a *lifetime* Supreme Court appointment.

During the Presidential debates, I found myself leaning forward in my seat, hoping for some *intangible* thing to come out of Mrs. Clinton's mouth. I was inwardly pleading for her to strike back, to stop absorbing so many punches, to give the American people the bloodbath they clearly wanted. I wanted the bloodbath, too. I was eager for someone, anyone, to put Mr. Trump in his rightful place. It isn't difficult to speculate about the counterpunches Mrs. Clinton and her campaign staff left on the cutting room floor; the creepy retraction of a rape allegation Mr. Trump and his attorneys forced out of a memoir by one of his ex-wives, his strange, borderline-incestual comments about his own daughter, or the indignity of Trump being forced to do advertisements for Pizza Hut and McDonalds for a quick buck. These pressure-points, and countless others like them, went untouched. The mud was *always* there to sling, and it was *never* in short supply.

The Clinton campaign likely avoided taking the dialog further into the sewer for a litany of different reasons; the desire to appear 'Presidential,' or the impulse not to 'punch down' to a weakened opponent trailing mightily in the polls, or the need not to increase her already sky-high disapproval ratings, or perhaps they were suspicious that Mrs. Clinton wouldn't have been able to match Trump, blow-for-blow, if they let her escalate the rhetoric. These were certainly not unfounded fears, and considering Mrs. Clinton won the popular vote by several million votes, her strategy was far from untenable or foolish. With that concession made, however, the context of this election should have made her more willing to take risks, not less. It was a competition for votes in Ohio, Florida, and Pennsylvania; not California or New York. Bruise Trump, punch back, drag it into the sewer, and if it bristles your Democratic base of snooty Berkley liberals, so what? What were those voters going to do? Vote for Trump out of spite?

Trump's victory over other lukewarm suitors in the Republican primary should have been signal to the DNC; America wants a juvenile contest, America wants a petty, snark-filled brawl, and the either the tone of the campaign shifts to meet the desires of the electorate, or it fails because it doesn't. This disconnection speaks to the degree to which the ideological, establishment left, has been separated from the economic, classist left. With a phone in everyone's pocket, the winner was so clearly going to be decided on the best five-second-put-down. It was going to be decided on the playground, not the university. It was going to be a universe removed from sanity, academia, and rationality, because, let's face it; American voters who valued those three were almost universally voting for Mrs. Clinton anyway. The Democrats didn't meaningfully pander, didn't meaningfully compete for that battleground, and instead, elected to concede that territory to Trump who took it without contest.

ACKNOWLEDGEMENTS

To Melissa; thank you for your love and support. Without you, none of my achievements could have been possible. I love you.

To my friends and acquaintances; you deserve a medal for enduring my ramblings, and I cherish your companionship.

To my family; stay weird, do your own thing, and whatever happens, know I love you all very much.

ABOUT THE AUTHOR

Adam Steevens is an author who lives with his wife, Melissa, and his cat, Ranger, in St. Louis, Missouri. *The United States of Repression* is his second publication, and is his first non-fiction book. Adam published his first novel, *Six-Twenty*, in 2016, and both books are available for purchase on Amazon.

NOTES

Chapter 1:

1. Christopher Hitchens, *Arguably*, (Hatchette Book Group, 2011)
2. Gore Vidal, *Dreaming War*, Thunder's Mouth Press / Nation Books. (2002)
3. Paul Krugman, *The Conscience of a Liberal*, W.W. Norton Company. (2007)
4. George M. Fredrickson, *Racism: A Short History*, (Princeton University Press, 2002)
5. Chris Hedges, *American Fascists, Free Press*, (2006)
6. *Ibid, p12.*
7. Ian Haney Lopez, *Dog Whistle Politics*, (Oxford University Press, 2014)
8. Chris Hedges, *American Fascists, Free Press*, (2006)
9. Noam Chomsky, *Power Systems*, Metropolitan Books, (2013)
10. Michael P. Colaresi, *Democracy Declassified*, (Oxford Press, 2014)
11. Katha Pollitt, *Pro: Reclaiming Abortion Rights*, (Picador, 2014)
12. Chris Mooney, *The Republican Brain*, (John Wiley & Sons, 2012)
13. Elicka Peterson Sparks, *The Devil You Know*, (Prometheus Books, 2016)
14. Tim Wise, *Dear White America*, (City Lights Books, 2012)
15. Mark Ellingsen, *When did Jesus Become Republican?*, (2007, Rowman & Littlefield Publishers)
16. David Simon, *David Simon on Why He Created The Wire*, (Observer Ideas, *The Guardian*, 2014)
17. Tim Wise, *Dear White America*, (City Lights Books, 2012)
18. *Ibid, p65.*
19. Andrew Greeley & Michael Hout, *The Truth About Conservative Christians*, (University of Chicago Press, 2006)
20. James Baldwin, *Notes of a Native Son*, (Beacon Press, 1955)

21. Ian Haney Lopez, *Dog Whistle Politics,* (Oxford University Press, 2014)
22. Tim Wise, *Dear White America,* (City Lights Books, 2012)

Chapter 2:

1. Darryl Pickney, *Blackballed: The Black Vote and U.S. Democracy,* (NYRB, 2014)
2. George M. Fredrickson, *Racism: A Short History,* (Princeton University Press, 2002)
3. *Ibid, p136.*
4. Darryl Pickney, *Blackballed: The Black Vote and U.S. Democracy,* (NYRB, 2014)
5. Ian Hanley Lopez, *Dog Whistle Politics,* (Oxford University Press, 2014)
6. Tim Wise, *Dear White America,* (City Light Books, 2012)
7. Jamala Rogers, *Ferguson is America,* (Mira Digital, 2016)
8. James Baldwin, *Notes of a Native Son,* (Beacon Press, 1955)
9. Tim Wise, *Dear White America,* (City Light Books, 2012)
10. James Kilgore, *Understanding Mass Incarceration,* (The New Press, 2014)
11. Tim Wise, *Dear White America,* (City Light Books, 2012)
12. National Research Council of the National Academies. (2014). *The Growth of Incarceration in the United States.* Washington, D.C: The National Academies Press.
13. James Kilgore, *Understanding Mass Incarceration,* (The New Press, 2014)
14. Tim Wise, *Dear White America,* (City Light Books, 2012)
15. Martin Gilens, *Why Americans Hate Welfare,* (University of Chicago Press, 2009)
16. Chris Mooney, *The Republican War on Science,* (Basic Books, 2007)
17. Tim Wise, *Dear White America,* (City Lights Books, 2012)
18. Ian Hanley Lopez, *Dog Whistle Politics,* (Oxford University Press, 2014)
19. E.J. Dionne, *Where the Right Went Wrong,* (Simon & Schuster, 2016)

20. Peter Beinart, *Breaking Faith,* (The Atlantic, April 2017)
21. Steven Pinker, *The Blank Slate,* (Penguin Books, 2003)

Chapter 3:

1. Katha Pollitt, *Pro: Reclaiming Abortion Rights,* (Picador, 2014)
2. Christina Page, *How the Pro-Choice Movement Saved America,* (Basic Books, 2006)
3. Katha Pollitt, *Pro: Reclaiming Abortion Rights,* (Picador, 2014)
4. Christina Page, *How the Pro-Choice Movement Saved America,* (Basic Books, 2006)
5. Katha Pollitt, *Pro: Reclaiming Abortion Rights,* (Picador, 2014)
6. Christina Page, *How the Pro-Choice Movement Saved America,* (Basic Books, 2006)
7. Stephen Dubner, *Freakonomics,* (Harper Perennial, 2005)
8. *Ibid, p138.*
9. Leora Tanenbaum, *I am not a Slut,* (Harper Perennial, 2015)
10. Liz Hodgkinson, *Why Women Believe in God,* (Circle Books, 2012)
11. Rachel K. Jones, Susheela Singh, Lawrence B. Finer and Lori F. Frohwirth, *Repeat Abortion in the United States,* (The Guttmacher Institute, 2006)
12. Leora Tanenbaum, *I am not a Slut,* (Harper Perennial, 2015)
13. Michael Kimmel, *Angry White Men,* (Nation Books, 2013)
14. Marueen Dowd, *Are Men Necessary?* (Penguin Books, 2005)
15. Michael Kimmel, *Angry White Men,* (Nation Books, 2013)
16. *Ibid, p119.*
17. Marueen Dowd, *Are Men Necessary?* (Penguin Books, 2005)
18. David Clay Johnston, *Divided,* (The New York Press, 2014)
19. Marueen Dowd, *Are Men Necessary?* (Penguin Books, 2005)
20. Malaka Gharib *Why do Men Harass Women? New Study Sheds Light on Motivations,* (NPR, June 15th, 2017)
21. Adi Robertson, *The FBI has Released its Gamergate Investigation Records,* (The Verge, January 27th, 2017)
22. Vera Papisova, *Joe Biden Interview on Rape Culture and Campus Sexual Assault,* (Teen Vogue, April 14th, 2017)

Chapter 4:

1. Eve L. Ewing, *Why Authoritarians Attack the Arts*, (The New York Times, April 6, 2017)
2. Elicka Peterson Sparks, *The Devil You Know*, (Prometheus Books, 2016)
3. Mark Taylor Dahlhouse, *An Island in the Lake of Fire*, (International Books, 1996)
4. *Ibid, p157.*
5. *Ibid, p153.*
6. *Ibid, p144.*
7. Frank Thomas, *What's Wrong with Kansas?* (Owl Books, 2004)
8. *Ibid, p218.*
9. *Ibid, p225.*
10. Ian Hanley Lopez, *Dog Whistle Politics*, (Oxford University Press, 2014)
11. NPR, *Is St. Louis' School Transfer Program 'A Mess?'*, (Michel Martin, November 8th, 2013)

Chapter 5:

1. Elaine Pagels, *Adam, Eve, and the Serpent: Sex and Politics in Early Christianity*, (Vintage, 2011)
2. Katha Pollitt, *Pro: Reclaiming Abortion Rights*, (Picador, 2014)
3. *Ibid, p131.*
4. Chris Hedges, *American Fascists*, (Simon & Schuster, 2007)
5. Elicka Peterson Sparks, *The Devil You Know*, (Amherst Books, 2016)
6. Mark Taylor Dalhouse, *An Island in the Lake of Fire*, (Books International, Inc., 1996)
7. Chris Mooney, *The Republican Brain*, (Wiley, 2012)
8. Elicka Peterson Sparks, *The Devil You Know*, (Amherst Books, 2016)
9. Chris Hedges, *American Fascists*, (Simon & Schuster, 2007)
10. Mark Taylor Dalhouse, *An Island in the Lake of Fire*, (Books International, Inc., 1996)

Chapter 6:

1. Bertrand Russell, *Why I am not a Christian,* (Simon & Schuster, 1957)
2. Richard Lawrence Miller, *The Case for Legalizing Drugs,* (Praeger Books, 1991)
3. *Ibid, p31.*
4. *Ibid, p112.*
5. Emily Corwin, *Trespass, Jail, Repeat: How One Man Has Spent 575 Days in Jail,* (NPR, April 15th, 2017)
6. Andrea D. Lyon, *The Death Penalty,* (Rowman & Littlefield, 2015)
7. Stephen J. Dubner, *Freakonomics,* (Harper Perennial, 2005)
8. Andrea D. Lyon, *The Death Penalty,* (Rowman & Littlefield, 2015)
9. Patricia Sabga, *How Trump's Immigration Policies Could Hurt the Economy,* (Al-Jazeera, March 5th, 2017)
10. Sylvia Longmire, *Border Insecurity,* (St. Martin's Press, 2014)
11. Adam Goodman, *How the Deportation Numbers Mislead,* (Al-Jazeera, January 24th, 2014)
12. Louis DeSipio and Rodolfo O. de la Garza, *U.S. Immigration in the Twenty-First Century,* (Westview Press, 2015)
13. Paul Krugman, *The Conscience of a Liberal,* (W.W. Norton and Company, 2009)
14. Chris Mooney, *The Republican Brain,* (Wiley, 2012)
15. Sylvia Longmire, *Border Insecurity,* (St. Martin's Press, 2014)
16. *Ibid, p55.*

Chapter 7:

1. Christopher Hitchens, *Arguably,* (Twelve, 2002)
2. Paul Krugman, *The Conscience of a Liberal,* (W.W. Norton and Company, 2009)
3. Thomas Frank, *What's the Matter with Kansas?* (Henry Holt and Company, 2007)
4. Paul Krugman, *The Conscience of a Liberal,* (W.W.

Norton and Company, 2009)

5. *Ibid, p47.*
6. Noam Chomsky, *Power Systems,* (Metropolitan Books, 2013)
7. Tim Wise, *Dear White America,* (City Lights Books, 2012)
8. Katherine Q. Seelye and Jeff Zeleny, *On the Defensive, Obama Calls His Words Ill-Chosen,* (The New York Times, April 13th, 2008)
9. Domenico Montanaro, *Hillary Clinton's 'Basket of Deplorables,' in Full Context of This Ugly Campaign,* (NPR, September 10th, 2016)
10. Christopher Hitchens, *America the Banana Republic,* (Vanity Fair, October 2008)
11. Joseph Stiglitz, *Inequality is Not Inevitable,* (The New York Times, June 27th, 2014)
12. Christopher Hitchens, *America the Banana Republic,* (Vanity Fair, October 2008)
13. Gary Kasparov, *Winter is Coming,* (Public Affairs, 2016)
14. *Ibid, p226.*
15. Kevin Phillips, *American Theocracy,* (Penguin Books, 2006)
16. Peter Beinart, *Breaking Faith,* (The Atlantic, April 2017)

Chapter 8:

1. BBC, *Guns in the US: The Statistics Behind the Violence* (BBC, January 2016)
2. Gabby Giffords and Mark Kelly, *Enough,* (Simon & Schuster, 2014)
3. Louis Klarevas, *Rampage Nation,* (Prometheus Books, 2016)
4. *Ibid, p169.*
5. *Ibid, p175.*
6. Gabby Giffords and Mark Kelly, *Enough,* (Simon & Schuster, 2014)
7. Peter Harry Brown and Daniel G. Abel, *Outgunned: Up Against the NRA,* (The Free Press, 2003)
8. Louis Klarevas, *Rampage Nation,* (Prometheus

Books, 2016)

9. Juliet Lapidos, *Defensive Gun Use,* (The New York Times, April 15th, 2013)

10. Louis Klarevas, *Rampage Nation,* (Prometheus Books, 2016)

11. *Ibid, p245.*

12. Steven J. Dubner, *Freakonomics,* (Harper Perennial, 2005)

13. *Ibid, p133.*

14. E.J. Dionne, *Where the Right Went Wrong,* (Simon & Schuster, 2016)

Chapter 9:

1. Malcom Nance, *The Plot to Hack America,* (Skyhorse Publishing, 2016)

2. Christopher Hitchens, *Stop Blaming the Good Guys in Iraq,* (Slate, July 5th, 2006)

3. Anna Politkovskaya, *Putin's Russia,* (Metropolitan Books, 2004)

4. Gary Kasparov, *Winter is Coming,* (Public Affairs, 2016)

5. *Ibid, p257.*

6. Gary Kasparov, *The Price of Inaction in Ukraine,* (Time Magazine, July 18th, 2014)

7. Gary Kasparov, *Winter is Coming,* (Public Affairs, 2016)

8. *Ibid, p110.*

9. Karen Dawisha, *Putin's Kleptocracy,* (Simon & Schuster, 2015)

10. Anna Politkovskaya, *Putin's Russia,* (Metropolitan Books, 2004)

11. *Ibid, p23.*

12. Karen Dawisha, *Putin's Kleptocracy,* (Simon & Schuster, 2015)

13. *Ibid, p27.*

14. Sean Gallagher, *Did the Russians Hack the Election? A Look at the Established Facts,* (Arstechnica, December

12th, 2016)

15. Malcom Nance, *The Plot to Hack America,* (Skyhorse Publishing, 2016)

16. *Ibid, p127.*

17. Brian Naylor, *Former CIA Director Tells Lawmakers About 'Very Aggressive' Russian Election Meddling,* (NPR, May 23rd, 2017)

18. Brian Naylor, *Former CIA Director Tells Lawmakers About 'Very Aggressive' Russian Election Meddling,* (NPR, May 23rd, 2017)

19. Vincent Kessler, *Farage 'Person of Interest' in Trump-Russia Investigation,* (Reuters, June 1st, 2017)

20. Timothy Snyder, *On Tyranny,* (Tim Duggan Books, 2017)

21. Malcom Nance, *The Plot to Hack America,* (Skyhorse Publishing, 2016)

22. *Ibid, p51.*

23. *Ibid, p49.*

24. Josh Rogin, *Trump Campaign Guts Anti-Russia Stance on Ukraine,* (The Washington Post, July 18th, 2016)

25. Mikhail Zygar, *All the Kremlin's Men,* (2016, Pereus Books)

26. *Ibid, p333.*

27. Chris Cillizza, *Vladimir Putin's Popularity is Soaring Among Republicans,* (The Washington Post, February 21st, 2017)

28. Gary Kasparov, *Winter is Coming,* (Public Affairs, 2016)

Chapter 10: (N/A)

Chapter 11:

1. Timothy Snyder, *On Tyranny,* (Tim Duggan Books, 2017)

2. Tim Wise, *Dear White America,* (City Lights Books, 2012)

BIBLIOGRAPHY

Abel, P. H. (2003). *Outgunned: Up Against the NRA.* New York, New York: The Free Press.

Baldwin, J. (1955). *Notes of a Native Son.* Boston, MA: Beacon Press.

Beinart, P. (2017, April). Breaking Faith. *The Atlantic.*

Chomsky, N. (2013). *Power Systems.* New York, New York: Metropolitian Books.

Cillizza, C. (2017, February 21). Vladimir Putin's Popularity is Soaring Among Republicans. *The Washington Post.*

Colaresi, M. P. (2014). *Democracy Declassified.* New York, New York:

Oxford University Press.

Colby, T. (2012). *Some of My Best Friends Are Black.* New York, New York: The Penguin Group.

Corwin, E. (2017, April 15). Trespass, Jail, RepeatL How One Man Has Spent 575 Days in Jail. *NPR.*

Dalhouse, M. T. (1996). *An Island in the Lake of Fire.* Athens, Georgia: Books International Inc.

Dowd, M. (2005). *Are Men Necessary?* . New York, New York: Peguin Books.

Dubner, S. D. (2005). *Freakonomics.* New York, New York: Harper Perenial.

Engstrom, M. E. (2001). *Fair and Effective Representation? Debating Electoral Reform and Minority Rights.* Lanham, Maryland: Rowman & Littlefield Publishers.

Ewing, E. L. (2017, April 6). Why Authoritarians Attack the Arts. *The New York Times* .

Frank, T. (2004). *What's the Matter with Kansas?* New York, New York: Owl Books.

Fredrickson, G. M. (2002). *Racism: A Short History.* Princeton, NJ: Princeton University Press.

Gallagher, S. (2016, December). *Did the Russians Hack the Election?* Retrieved from Arstechnica: https://arstechnica.com/security/2016/12/the-public-evidence-behind-claims-russia-hacked-for-trump/

Garza, L. D. (2015). *US Immigration in the Twenty-First Century.* Bolder, Colorado: Westview Press.

Gharib, M. (2017, June 15). Why do Men Harass Women? New Study

Sheds Light on Motivations. *NPR* .

Giffords, M. K. (2014). *Enough.* New York, New York: Scribner (A division of Simon & Shuster, Inc) .

Gilgoff, D. (2007). *The Jesus Machine.* New York. New York: St. Martins Press.

Goodman, A. (2014, January 24). How the Deportation Numbers Mislead. *Al-Jazeera.*

Hedges, C. (2006). *American Fascists: The Christian Right and the War on America.* New York, New York: Free Press.

Hitchen, C. (2011). *Arguably.* New York, New York: Hachette Book Group.

Hitchens, C. (2006, July 5). Stop Blaming the Good Guys in Iraq. *Slate.*

Hitchens, C. (2008, October 8). America the Banana Republic. *Vanity Fair.*

Hodgkinson, L. (2012). *Why Women Believe in God.*

Hout, A. G. (2006). *The Truth About Conservative Christians.* Chicago, Illinois: University of Chicago Press.

Johnston, D. C. (2014). *Divided: The Perils of Our Growing Inequality.* New York, New York: The New Press.

Kasparov, G. (2014, July 18). The Price of Inaction in Ukraine. *Time.*

Katherine Q. Seelye and Jeff Zeleny. (2008, April 13). On the Defensive, Obama Calls His Words Ill-Chosen. *The New York Times.*

Kessler, V. (2017, June 1). Farage 'Person of Interest' in Trump-Russia Investigation. *Reuters* .

Kilgore, J. (2015). *Understanding Mass Incarceration: A Peoples Guide to the Key Civil Rights Struggle of Our Time.* New York, New York: The New Press.

Klarevas, L. (2016). *Rampage Nation.* Amherst, New York: Prometheus Books.

Krugman, P. (2007). *The Conscience of a Liberal .* New York, New York: W.W. Norton Company.

Lapidos, J. (2013, April 15). Defensive Gun Use. *The New York Times.*

Longmire, S. (2014). *Border Insecurity: Why Big Money, Fences, and Drones Aren't Making Us Safer.* New York, New York: Palgrave Macmillan.

Lyon, A. D. (2015). *The Death Penalty.* Lanham, Maryland: Rowman & Littlefield.

Miller, R. L. (1991). *The Case for Legalizing Drugs.* New York, New York: Praeger Publishers.

Montanaro, D. (2016, September 10). Hillary Clinton's 'Basket of Deplorables,' in Full Context of This Ugly Campaign. *NPR.*

Mooney, C. (2012). *The Republican Brain.* Hoboken, New Jersey: John Wiley & Sons.

Nance, M. (2016). *The Plot to Hack America.* New York, New York: Skyhorse Publishing.

National Research Council of the National Academies. (2014). *The Growth of Incarceration in the United States.* Washington, D.C: The National Academies Press.

Naylor, B. (2017, May 23). Former CIA Director Tells Lawmakers About 'Very Aggressive' Russian Election Meddling. *NPR .*

Page, C. (2006). *How The Pro-Choice Movement Saved America: Freedom, Politics, and the War on Sex.* Basic Books.

Pagels, E. (1989). *Adam, Eve, and the Serpent: Sex and Politics in Early Christianity.* New York, New York : Vintage.

Papisova, V. (2017, April 14). Joe Biden Interview on Rape Culture and Campus Sexual Assault. *Teen Vogue.*

Phillips, K. (2006). *American Theocracy.* New York, New York: Penguin Group.

Pickney, D. (2104). *Blackballed: The Black Vote and US Democracy.* New York, New York: NYRB.

Pinker, S. (2003). *The Blank State.* New York, New York: Penguin Books.

Pollitt, K. (2014). *Pro: Reclaiming Abortion Rights.* New York, New York: Picador.

Purdum, T. S. (2014). *An Idea Whose Time Has Come.* New York, New York : Henry Holt and Company.

Rachel K. Jones, Susheela Singh, Lawerence B. Finer, & Lori F. Frohwirth. (2006). *Repeat Abortion in the United States.* The Guttmacher Institute.

Robertson, A. (2017, January 27). The FBI has Released its Gamergate Investigation Records. *The Verge.*

Rogers, J. (2015). *Ferguson is America: Roots of Rebellion.* St. Louis, Missouri: Mira Digital Publishing.

Rogin, J. (2016, Jult 18). Trump Campaign Guts Anti-Russia Stance on Ukraine . *The Washington Post.*

Sabga, P. (2017, March 5). How Trump's Immigration Policies Could Hurt the Economy . *Al-Jazeera.*

Snow, J. (2014). *Mass Incareration on Trial.* New York, New York: The New Press.

Sparks, E. P. (2016). *The Devil You Know: The Surprising Link Between Conservative Christianity and Crime.* Amherst, New York: Prometheus Books.

Stiglitz, J. (2008, June 27). Inequality is Not Inevitable . *The New York Times.*

The British Broadcasting Company. (2016, January). Guns in the US: The Statistics Behind the Violence. *BBC.*

Vidal, G. (2002). *Dreaming War: Blood for Oil and the Cheney-Bush Junta.* New York, New York: Thunder's Mouth Press / Nation Books.

Weitzer, R. (2012). *Legalizing Prostitution.* New York, New York: New York University Press.

Wise, T. (2012). *Dear White America: A Letter to a New Minority.* San Francisco, California: City Lights Books.

Zygar, M. (2016). *All the Kremlin's Men.* New York, New York: Perseus Books.

www.ingramcontent.com/pod-product-compliance
Lightning Source LLC
Chambersburg PA
CBHW070838310526
45788CB00018B/2119